Praise for *The Money Man*

"*The Money Man* seized my attention from the opening page and never let go. The people, events and intrigues of Joseph Caplan's life are too amazing to be real but they are."
George Brown, Investment Analyst, Georgia

"I found it fascinating. It really is a rags to riches story. A real win."
Dr. Jane Derrig, Rheumatologist, Virginia

"Excellent! I couldn't put it down. The characters are fascinating. This story has so much intrigue."
Dr. Daniel Goldberg, Bible Professor, North Carolina

"Captivating, I could not put it down. It will appeal to a diverse audience. It is courageous and thought provoking. Deserves to be a best seller."
Joyce Moran, House Wife and Avid Reader, Virginia

"What an amazing journey Joseph has had! May our Lord Jesus use his moving testimony to transform many lives for His kingdom."
Derick Harbin, Pastor, Virginia

"This book will be loved and surely a best seller."
Rick Rogers, Attorney, Oklahoma

"It must have taken you to your knees to deal with all of this and it's remarkable that you live to tell the tale, quite remarkable."
Mary Samuel, Movie Connoisseur, Los Angeles

"I recently read Joseph Caplan's book which when I started could not put down. I thought it was extremely well written and a compelling story."
Martin Samuel, International Film and Celebrity Hair Stylist, Los Angeles

"A thread of gold…"
John Sherrill, Formerly Publisher Chosen Books, M

"Many men will identify with being torn between their dreams and their role of husband and father. A powerful story of endurance, redemption and faith. An intriguing, soul searching book and one to read again."
Gail Theriault, Owner Tae Kwon Do School, Virginia Beach, VA

"Captivating – could not put it down. Thought provoking. A story that needs to be shared."
Lisa Tarling, House Wife, London England

"A great book."
Gary Tereshita, Senior Editor, Nashville, TN

"Joseph is a real person. He made mistakes and admits them. I couldn't stop turning the pages – loved it."
Reed Williams, Hairdresser, Virginia

THE MONEY MAN

A True Life Story of One Man's Unbridled Ambition,
Downfall, and Redemption

THE
MONEY
MAN

A True Life Story of
One Man's Unbridled Ambition,
Downfall, and Redemption

JOSEPH CAPLAN

NEW YORK

LONDON • NASHVILLE • MELBOURNE • VANCOUVER

The Money Man

A True Life Story of One Man's Unbridled Ambition, Downfall, and Redemption

Published in New York, New York, by Morgan James Publishing. Morgan James is a trademark of Morgan James, LLC. www.MorganJamesPublishing.com

The Morgan James Speakers Group can bring authors to your live event. For more information or to book an event visit The Morgan James Speakers Group at www.TheMorganJamesSpeakersGroup.com.

ISBN 9781683507673 paperback
ISBN 9781683507680 eBook
Library of Congress Control Number: 2017914241

Cover Design by:
Megan Whitney
Creative Ninja Designs
megan@creativeninjadesigns.com

Interior Design by:
Paul Curtis

In an effort to support local communities, raise awareness and funds, Morgan James Publishing donates a percentage of all book sales for the life of each book to Habitat for Humanity Peninsula and Greater Williamsburg.

Get involved today! Visit
www.MorganJamesBuilds.com

Table of Contents

A Moment in Time
Can Change Everything

I kept glancing at the phone, willing it to ring at any moment. What I needed was that one important phone call.

Instead, the next five minutes would more likely bring the office clerk, who would, as usual, drop one more thick and mundane legal brief in front of me. As always, I would be taking a nearly impenetrable file home with me, and the evening would not be my own. Not that I minded that much. After all, following my stint in the military and my law training I'd had the great good fortune to be mentored as a Barrister here at a firm headed by the renowned Senior Crown Counsel, Sir Christmas Humphreys.

Even so, I stared out of the window, looking at cars and passersby on the street below, restless. It was late in the day, starting to get dark, and these people moving quickly through the lengthening shadows were likely headed home to flats along the Thames or by train to London suburbs to enjoy a relaxing evening, or so I imagined.

That would not be the case for me.

Evenings belonged to my career. There was rarely much time to prepare for court appearances, given the volume of cases the firm represented. Since I was the newest member a weight of files was handed to me, I suppose, to see how much I could really handle. And so I would study a case at night and the following morning rush to court, put on my wig and gown and defend someone. I'd already had a few minor successes, but I longed for a greater challenge – a case I could argue and prove my abilities. My aspiration was to become a great barrister and to serve many people in need of legal help, as had my personal hero, Sir Edward Marshall Hall, the great 19th—Century public defender in London, who had often defied social barriers by defending the working—class and the poor against the rich and mighty.

Where is that clerk? I thought, glancing at the door. I wanted to be on my way, before the trains filled up and I'd have to stand all the way to my station.

Home.

Hoping to follow in Sir Edward Marshall Hall's imposing footsteps had put me at odds with my own family. We were the working class he had defended, not the cream of society, who so often sought the services of Sir Christmas Humphreys.

My father had worked all his life in the rag trade, as did so many other Jews who had come to England to escape persecution on the Continent. I was his only child and he had wanted me to use my college education to help him in the business. All my dad's brothers, and all my mum's brothers, as well, were rag merchants. Which meant they bought old rags, sorted them into grades and sold them to cloth merchants for recycling. That's how they put bread on the table. It's also what their fathers and grandfathers did before them.

But I had wanted a different life. I was not interested in the unwritten law of tradition or in throwing my energies into just making a buck. My ambitions lay along a higher pathway. I was interested in affecting the law of the land. And so I defied the family. Somewhere in my youth I had read the story of Sir Edward Marshall, and was deeply moved and inspired. From that day on I'd envisioned myself in black robes and a white wig, arguing for justice in the courts of London. That's what I wanted, to be like this great man. That's who I wanted to be in my generation.

If only the phone would ring, with the one call that could change everything.

Outside the streetlights were starting to blink on. Where was that clerk?

The ringing phone startled me from my reverie. Eagerly I lifted the receiver, but instead of the client with the challenging case I was hoping for, Mum's voice came at me in a rush.

"Your father has had an attack — his heart. He's in the hospital. Oh Joseph, it's bad. Can you hurry?"

I sat upright in my chair. "Mum, slow down. What's happened? What hospital?"

Barely pausing for breath, my mother rapid-fired the details to me. Dad had been at work — where he always was — and had suffered chest pains and collapsed. He'd been rushed to the nearest hospital and was in intensive care.

"Can you hurry?" Mum repeated. "You're all we've got to help us, Joseph."

"Of course, I'll be right there," I replied, already on my feet and throwing on my jacket. In the back of my mind I felt a twinge of annoyance, which I quickly brushed aside. Both mum and dad had a habit of reminding me that, as I had no siblings, I was the only one on whom their hopes were pinned.

I ignored that bit of family drama just now, of course.

"I'm on my way, Mum."

At the hospital I learned that Dad's condition was serious, but that he would survive. We also learned that it would be some time before he was strong enough to even consider returning to work. And given the state of his overall health now, it was highly unlikely he would be able to operate at full strength for a long time — if ever.

My mother tugged me by the sleeve, away from dad's bedside in the Intensive Care Unit and out into the waiting area. Her face was carved with worry, her voice distraught. "What are we going to do, Joseph?" she said over and over.

It pained me to see her in distress.

The problem was that there were employees waiting to be told what to do. As I had no siblings, there was no one else to step in and take over dad's business, and there was no money to hire someone. In a short period of time, the business my father had worked to build his whole life would collapse and my parents would be ruined.

Unexpectedly, I found myself in an agonizing position.

I had worked for years to become a Barrister, and I had never in a million years wanted to work in the rag trade. But my parents' wellbeing and future was hanging in the balance.

The next day I was in the poorest area in London, sitting at dad's desk in an office under a railway arch. Outside the office, in the sorting area, a dozen or more men and women in scruffy clothes were weighing and bundling mountains of rags. The abrupt shift from an office full of trig and trim Barristers and clerks and polished mahogany and brass was surreal.

As I shuffled through files in a rusty file cabinet I felt overwhelmed by the sense that I should not be here. I was intelligent and educated, far over trained for the rag trade. The dignity of the law courts and the wig and gown was on the other side of town, far away from the bins of dirty rags I had come here to manage. Again and again I pushed these feelings and thoughts away, as my attention became more focused on what the files revealed.

My dad's business was on the brink of collapse, and it was clear someone needed to step in.

The painful position I now found myself in was, in fact, a crossroads. I so badly wanted to make my mark in the world by levelling the legal playing field for those who needed justice. The situation that presented itself to me now was this: two older people, who had worked very hard all their lives and who needed money to survive, were desperately in need of help. And not only them, but all the employees here at the rag business, too. If Dad's business folded, they'd be forced out onto the streets to show it around the district, struggling to find jobs.

I ran my hands through my hair over and over. *What am I to do?*

In one direction lay my ambition to make a mark in the world of law. In another lay a totally different duty — to help save my family. Was there any choice, though?

At all cost, I had to keep my parents from financial ruin. That was clear enough. As their only son, there was only one choice to be made now – and not just because of the outer circumstances these files presented, but because of early influences that had shaped my thinking and beliefs.

Family had to come first, far and above my own personal drive for a career in the law.

With all my might I would throw myself into the task of trying to save dad's rag business. That was how I did everything. Growing up as a Jewish boy in English schools had taught me to fight. Later, military service would teach me to fight and never quit. Though I'd learned finesse as a good Brit, I had learned to direct my drive and energy into my work like a train at full-bore.

And so my choice was clear. The next day I collected my things from Sir Christmas Humphrey's law office and set out on a new course. It was a path I had never wanted – earning a hardscrabble living in a trade that had nothing to do with my ideal of bringing justice and everything to do with haggling and making as much money as possible. That was all.

What was not clear at the time — not at all — was that this choice, made for perfectly good reasons, was what seemed like a step down would actually become a path that led me to a pinnacle of success and great fortune. In the unlikeliest of ways I would find myself among the cream of London society, among the oldest and wealthiest moneyed families in Europe, in a world of expensive cars and caviar and yachts, among the elite. Quite literally from rags to riches.

And there was also no way to see that one heartfelt decision – to help people who needed help — would be all but swallowed up by the lure of something else, bringing me to the brink of a different kind of ruin, one that overtakes a man who follows the pull of greater and greater success and the promise of more and more wealth.

And so, in a sense, it was one moment in time and one phone call that changed everything. At least on the surface of my life. The changes that would come later, inside me, happened so slowly that I never saw them happening. I would become someone so different from the person who entered the legal profession with such high ideals that, eventually, I would hardly recognize myself. And at the root of it all was a force inside me that, once set loose, would all but destroy everything in my life.

How does a man with good values and a desire for personal success lose his way?

This is the story of a man who did. Me.

More importantly, it's the story of a man who found his way back from disaster…and discovered a treasure beyond price.

All of that was far in the future, however. At the moment, I did what I'd learned to do as a boy, which was to put others first – a value based in our ancient Jewish heritage, which came to me through my grandfather….

Chapter One

TWO ROADS

Could I make it before sundown? That wasn't even a question: I *had* to make it to my grandparents' home before the sun dropped over the hills. And that sense of urgency drove me – as somehow it always did.

It was after 4 p.m on a Friday afternoon, and I sweated as I pumped the pedals of my bicycle. The sun was dropping and I needed to move fast.

I'd dashed home from school stuffed my saddle bag, checked the tires on my bicycle, kissed my mom on the cheek, received at least ten warnings about cycling safety. I was her little boy, after all. Then I was on my way from Streatham in South London to Ewell East in Surrey, 15 miles from our home, where my grandparents lived. This was the eve of erev Shabbat — the Sabbath — and the sun would be going down soon. Since work was prohibited on the Sabbath, which began at sunset, I would have to ride as fast as I could to arrive at my grandparents' home without breaking the rules of Shabbat, which included no bike riding.

But that prohibition was not the only reason I was in a hurry. Grandma and Grandpa Hersh's house had a magnetic pull for me. I loved to visit them.

There was something deeply grounding and at the same time spiritual about Sabbath and the way my grandparents observed it. On Friday nights, my mother's parents sometimes had the whole family over for dinner. Sabbath dinner at Grandma's was not just about the food – though there would be lots of it — it was an event. Many of my mother's kin came with their wives and children. We would elbow-in around the long dining room table, surrounded by walls laden with prints of rabbis, a synagogue, a Sabbath dinner table and a boy at his bar mitzvah service.

Encompassed like this – by family, by images of our heritage – I would feel a deep connection to something wonderfully ancient and greater than myself.

I crested the last hill. The exertion of my ride was making me hungry. I could only think of two things now.

My grandmother's cooking… and being with my grandfather.

Finally, I steered my bike into my grandparent's tiny front yard. Propping it against the wall, I dashed inside.

Grandma was, as usual, in the kitchen, stirring something at the stove when I charged in. The air was scented with the savory smell of roasting beef, potatoes and onions. From the dining room came the sound of talking and laughter, but I was not ready to see the whole family yet. My interest was focused right here.

Turning, Grandma offered me her usual, bright greeting. "Come here, Yoselleh" – she used the Yiddish pronunciation of my name, Joseph – "you must be *hungry*."

And of course I was – *starving*, in fact. For a few minutes I followed her around the kitchen, talking excitedly as she offered me almond cookies and hazelnut treats before dinner.

Through the kitchen windows I could see the light fading, and Grandma nodded towards the dining room, where loud conversations overlapped each other. She lifted the roasting pan, with its delicious cargo, and as we entered the dining room the din immediately quieted.

There around the table were all my mother's relatives – the aunts, uncles, cousins – the fabric from which I was cut.

It was now the start of Sabbath — sundown on Friday evening – and Grandma set down the roasting pan in the center of the crisp, white tablecloth, and lifted the shawl, which had been draped on her shoulders, up over her hair. I slid into my seat, next to my cousin Barry, and silence fell.

Cupping her wrinkled hands around the candles that burned steadily at table center, she offered up the Sabbath blessing.

"Hear, o Israel, the Lord God is one…."

When she had finished, all eyes turned to Grandfather. There he sat, a pinnacle of tradition.

Before him was a bottle of kosher wine and a platted *challah*. Grandpa broke the bread and handed it around, then took the cup of wine, took a small sip, and passed it, as well.

As the bread and wine made their 'rounds, Grandfather prepared himself quietly before offering grace. There would be no rushing this; Grandfather was about to speak on our behalf to the Almighty.

I bowed my head, waiting for him to begin, not so much tuned to the words as to the man who was about to speak them.

Grandpa was an Orthodox Jew, and he walked a very long distance every Friday night to go to the synagogue. I was expected to go with and attend Sabbath morning services, another long walk. Observing the Sabbath was a commandment, and that was that.

"God instructs everyone to rest on the Sabbath day," my grandfather had told me, and what he told me could not be wrong.

The deep sense of trust I had in my grandfather came mainly from one thing: When I was around him I felt special and secure. He was calm and gentle. I respected him like no other man I had ever met. He always seemed very pleased to have me at his side.

"Tell me about your studies, Yoselleh." And he would follow up from there, asking about my friends, my love of sports, my health. As I answered, his eyes never left my face and I knew that he was listening, paying attention to every word I said.

When I'd finish answering he would say to me, "Pay attention to your teachers. Work hard at your studies and do well. You can become someone of importance."

I'd feel a rush of warmth inside. Grandfather cared about me. What's more, he seemed to see something in me and believe in me. I felt valued.

And there was another factor that drew me to him.

Earlier in my life, it had been a mystery to me why my grandfather would disappear to a room at the top of the house in the morning, afternoon and early evening with a Hebrew book in his hand. One day I asked my grandmother about this.

She put down her spatula – she was always stirring something – turned from the stove and looked at me. Clearly, she wanted to say something of importance.

"Your grandfather goes upstairs every day to pray. He talks to God, and he listens to God."

I blinked in awe. I had never talked to God or heard God. But I took careful note of the fact that my grandfather had a special connection with Him. And that he was devoted, not only to me and the family and our heritage, but to something – and to Someone — far greater than all of us. Being near him was like being seated next to a great mountain, with some mystery hidden on its heights, or some depth to him I couldn't grasp.

This man, who so valued me, had found his own riches – not in the hard—knock business world of the rag trade, like his sons and sons-in-law – but in higher things. His ambition lay in maintaining, not only the faith but the great traditions of the Jewish community. To grandfather, we were not put here on earth just to achieve our own goals. We were put here to help each other – and that meant both family as well as the greater community of the Jewish people.

"The great Moses Maimonides said," grandfather intoned, quoting the 12th-Century teacher of the Torah, "'If I am not for me, then who is for me? But if I am *only* for me, then what am I?'"

I wondered what that meant. Grandpa seemed to know, as he seemed to know everything.

And just now, grandpa had launched into the blessing, and everyone had remained quiet and still until the final word – "Amen."

Then there was bedlam.

Everyone at the table began talking at once again. The older folks forked and spooned mounds of food onto their plates, and began digging in as though they might never see another meal. In between forkfuls they bragged on their children, beaming with satisfaction at their offspring. We kids talked about school and sports. The women talked about the price of food and clothes in the market.

Tonight, the men seemed to have a special complaint.

"The Italians – they're bringing all sorts of cheap fabric into the country. How can you make any money off of poor quality rags?"

Rags. The endless topic. Everyone in the family was in the rag business.

I tuned them out. It was always rags, rags, rags. I wasn't interested.

I had turned my attention to the incredible spread of food, dishing as much onto my plate as it would hold – besides roast beef, potatoes and onions, there was gefilte fish, chopped liver, matzo ball soup, pickled herring....

Only later in life would I understand that this over-abundance of food, so carefully prepared was an expression of well being, comfort and hope. They had escaped from a world of poverty and lack in Europe, a place of insecurity, and now they were in a place of plenty. Later in life, too, I would come to understand how fear and insecurity and clinging to worldly possessions can become a driving force in one's life.

For now I was absorbing other lessons. On this day of rest, we were receiving God into our homes, grateful for all that he had done for us. Also that this Friday night tradition was an event which confirmed our roots and our unity as family.

While the bedlam continued I glanced at grandfather several times. Something about him always drew me, though he was often the quietest one in the melee that was our family. There he sat, full of patience and grace, listening to an uncle's complaint or tale of woe, no doubt offering a word of comfort, wisdom, insight drawn from those times upstairs alone with God.

It was too early for me to have worldly knowledge, but I knew instinctively that he was the kind of man that every man should be. In him I witnessed love, devotion, respect, prayer and hard work. I loved my Grandpa. I wanted to be just like him.

I wished then that I knew what he knew.

I wish now he had lived long enough to tell me.

One day, Mum took me to my grandparents' home, and everything had changed. Grandpa was immobile in his bedroom. Most of the family had gathered in his house.

I learned two things.

"He has had a stroke, and he is very, very weak."

I felt anxious.

"He wants to see you, Yosselleh."

I felt even more anxious.

Entering his room I stepped nervously to his bedside. Propped there on pillows, he looked at me with the same kind and loving eyes I had always seen. With effort, he reached out and took his electric razor from the side of the bed and asked me if I would shave him. I saw that his hands were limp and he was too weak to move.

Lovingly, I began to shave him.

Something about his eyes held my attention because they were sorrowful. He had lived in the old world. He had escaped with half of his family from the pogroms in Russia. I was too young to understand why he looked like that, but later understood that he knew he was leaving this world.

When I finished shaving him, he took my face in his hands, kissed me gently on the edge of my forehead above my right eye. That was a special moment I would never forget.

Not long after, my mother took me aside. "Grandpa has gone to be with God."

My legs felt weak. I didn't doubt what she said, but I also didn't know where heaven was.

That evening, everyone was gathered at Grandfather's house — his children and the sons and daughters in law, like a Friday night, but all the family looked very glum. Grandma Hersh was crying uncontrollably. This was my first experience with death and loss.

Everyone carried on, that is, except Grandma. Without him, his wife of over sixty years became quite a different person. I could see that she was very nervous and dependent on her children but with Grandpa gone the children had much less time for her. The respect was gone.

The man who had been the head of the family was no longer with us. There had been something about him that kept everyone together. The effects were immediate and enormous.

For one thing, the family's sense of connection had left with him. Without their father to bind them together, my family would immediately begin to drift apart. Gone, too, was grandpa's wonderful love for his children and grandchildren, and the quiet adoration for the mother of his children. He had been the family peacemaker, an example of hard work, a complete *mensch*. Also missing was his reverence for the Almighty and his values.

Who was I to turn to now for those things?

It would be many years before I understood how great this loss was to me and the path of my life. The one man who had provided any sort of spiritual grounding had just vanished. The influence of my Grandpa left me wanting to be involved with my family and prayer. But that influence was gone, and though his mark on me was indelible and lasting, it would eventually battle unsuccessfully against other influences.

There was my father. But in so many ways, he stood in contrast to my grandfather. Like most of his own generation, who had escaped to the free world, he observed some of the traditions known as the High Holy days. He made sure before I was 13 years old that I knew my portion in the *Old Testament* for the day of my Bar Mitzvah in the synagogue, but it ended there. He worked on the Sabbath giving priority to earning a living and survival. Dad read Hebrew fluently, but like so many people who can quote from the Bible he never taught me the spiritual significance of all that his ancestors had handed down. Somehow, the deeper roots that gave my grandfather his character did not manifest themselves in my father.

I didn't realize at the time that I was seeking a spiritual connection, but that's what my grandfather had awakened in me. Unfortunately, I always felt with my father that I could never approach him about anything. He worked so hard, came home late and ate, and often went out to friends with my mother and I had no time with him at all.

Not that my father was a bad man. He did teach me something of value.

My father worked as hard as any man could work. He collected old clothes from a wide variety of people, sometimes from small tradesmen and sometimes from merchants. They were called "totters" and had small vans or trucks. The rags were graded by fabric quality and then sent to the north of England to be sold and recycled. That is how my father supported us.

At some deep level, I believe, my father was driven to work hard. He had been born in Russia and my mother was born in Russian-occupied Poland. There, he had worked in the rag trade for my mother's father. That was how they met. It seemed to me later that growing up in such harsh conditions had given my father his tough, closed exterior. Nothing got through to him. He was tough. But also, he never gave out anything, at least of an emotional or spiritual nature. He never talked to me about anything, really. He often shouted at my mother, largely because he was intensely ambitious and wanted to climb out of his small world. My father wanted to expand abroad and import cheaper rags, but my mother was unworldly and not keen to step outside what she knew. She felt safe in her modest surroundings and she was comfortable with very little.

Nor was there any kind of spiritual input from my mother's family.

My mother had four brothers who had all worked for Grandpa Hersh in the rag trade. In the old country, and then in England after they emigrated, they were all eager to work hard and make their families secure. My father, who was, of course, a son-in-law and not a son, was only able to pick up crumbs. He realized he would have to start his own business or he would get nowhere.

And so, soon after my mum and dad married, he rented his own space under a railway trestle in Camberwell, a neighborhood in London. And in this building, he worked from dawn to dusk to provide for my mother and to pay for my education. He never talked about the past or how he got to England with his mother, three brothers and a sister. He never discussed his father or other siblings who were left behind. Never. Probably because something awful happened to them during one of the pogroms he and his and her family had narrowly escaped.

It was through my grandfather, then, rather than my parents that a faint connection was made to something greater – to higher values; to God. My father's focus was elsewhere, and as I watched him labor at his rag business, haggling for hours to make very little money, I came to accept that a man had to work hard – very hard indeed – to become successful. To stand his ground and fight and do whatever it took, in fact, to make it in this world.

There was one other thing I picked up in the atmosphere of my childhood. Anxiety about our wellbeing. A sense of insecurity, as if the bottom could drop out at any time. That came mostly from my mother.

My mother did not work outside the home, but she cooked and cleaned, and our modest home was always spotless. If something was spilled, she cleaned it up immediately. She grew up hearing stories from her mum and dad about the horrors and privations of Russia and Poland. They'd fled Eastern Europe, running away from danger, the constant threat of being imprisoned without cause, and the black shadow of death. She was intensely grateful for what she had, but also edgy. Yes, she lived in a free country, had a loving husband, a fine son growing up, and there was food on the table every night. But behind the kindness in her eyes a fearfulness lingered much of the time. Because she'd been born into an anti-Semitic environment, she was always expecting something bad to happen.

Somehow this deep-background anxiety worked its way subtly into my soul, as well, and I would carry it with me for years.

And so it was that, as a boy I'd encountered, briefly, a connection with higher values, embedding in me a sense that I was destined to do something good for others. And at the same time I had it ground into me that fighting with all you had and working very hard to succeed was the way to get ahead in this world – tinged with a sense that the world was just waiting to take me and my family down.

Now the one person who had begun to anchor me in those values was gone, though the impact he'd made would last a long, long time. Had he lived I might have been able to make better choices and avoid the dire course I would find myself on later.

Instead, the values grandfather had begun to plant in me would begin to dim as other influences came into play.

Chapter Two

SCHOOLING FOR LIFE

Strange, how early experiences teach you lessons about life that subtly and inexorably shape the course of your future.

One of my early lessons came from playing marbles.

Most days after school, my chums and I played marbles. I loved the challenge. It was sort of like the haggling my dad did, in a way: I'll put up these marbles; you put up those. If another boy had a beautiful cat's-eye or a shiny black or fiery red marble I wanted to win it. We'd kneel in the schoolyard, taking aim at an opponent's collection, and the shooting would begin. With each win I felt a kind of elation. It was all about seeing who won what in this little transaction.

With each game, my collection grew and soon included small and large marbles of all different colors. I sorted them, much the way Dad sorted rags — which were the good ones I wanted to keep, and which were not perfect. Some were rounded and traveled undisturbed across the playground. Others had slight flaws in them and took a bad turn when they hit a bump in the ground. Those I wouldn't mind losing.

As a competitor I was among the best in class, and with great pride I constantly showed off my ever-increasing inventory.

One day, a tall older student challenged me to a game. I thought that was marvelous. I felt so important. We met on the playground after school and he beat me again and again. For the first time, something kicked-in: a kind of intensity, a drive to win at all cost. I did not know when to stop.

It was almost dark when I realized that I had no marbles left.

When I got home, my mother scolded me. "Where have you been? I've been out of my head worrying about you. You're so late."

I mumbled an apology, and went to wash up before dinner. Mom had made one of my favorite dishes, roasted chicken with carrots and peas.

But at that moment, I couldn't care less about food or anything else. I was miserable because I had lost everything unexpectedly and I didn't know how to handle it. I loved winning and hated losing. Gritting my teeth as I scrubbed my hands, I determined that I would win back all those marbles…and then some.

This is what I learned: I liked winning.

That loss, and others, stirred in me a kind of raw energy, a drive to win at all cost. I learned that I liked that feeling. Actually, I craved it. And in the years that lay just ahead I would need that tough, competitive edge as a Jewish boy, with no experience on the first rung of the ladder in the world.

More lessons in life were just ahead.

Fortunately, for me and many others, the Education Act of 1944 provided a nationwide exam for public school students. Prior to this, there was a great deal of discrimination against those who were non-Anglican, but this legislation gave the brightest students the right to attend the college of their choice.

"Thank goodness we live in a land where the law is on our side," my father said, when the law was enacted. "Without champions in the courts to balance things out, the powerful will always take advantage of the weak."

I had heard enough stories about what had happened to Jewish people on the Continent to understand all that was contained in that statement. Somewhere in the back of my mind I also made a mental note of Dad's words.

Soon after I was admitted to one of England's best schools — Dulwich College. Admission was easy; studying was not easy.

For one thing I didn't have the proper environment. Ours was not a household with books, and neither of my parents had received any education. There was no one to help me with my homework. Furthermore, we lived in a working-class apartment, and one wall of the building was attached to the wall of a noisy tram station, where box cars ran on the rails until after midnight.

As if these challenges were not enough, the fact of my ethnic background came into play.

One day, as the war with Germany was coming to an end, I was walking between classes, carrying an armload of books. One of my classmates bumped into me, nearly knocking the stack from my hand. When I turned to say something, he hissed in my face. "I despise you."

I took a step back and looked at him blankly. We had never had any issues, he and I. What was his problem?

Another boy, a friend of his, was passing bay, as well. He stopped and thrust his face close to mine, his lip curled in disgust, "My father says you're a dirty Jew boy."

I was stunned, confused. Where was this hatred coming from?

"You Jews started this war."

"My uncle was killed in France because of you people."

My stomach knotted with small twinge of anxiety, but at the same time an even stronger anger made me double my fists. What on earth were they talking about? Everyone knew Hitler was a madman. He had sacked Poland, then the rest of Europe, and ordered the blitz on London that took so many English lives. Those events were terrible and tragic, for sure. But countless Jews had been hounded and driven from their homes, beaten, tortured and killed, and the nations — including Britain — had remained silent and unmoved for a long time while this was going on. Where was this unreasoning hatred coming from?

I turned on my heel and walked away, stinging with anger.

I didn't understand these boys. And frankly I didn't care to.

For the first time, but not the last, I learned that making my way in this world would not be easy. Also that in England and elsewhere in the world terrible prejudices against certain types of people existed – and I was among those people.

Mainly, and at some foundational level, I began to see that if I was going to succeed in life I would have to be able to stand up for myself. It was not likely anyone was going to stand up for me.

After that experience an intensity took over. Something in me rose up against the sense that there were people in this world who didn't want to see me succeed. But I had a dilemma: I wasn't tough, and yet I also didn't want to lose this great educational opportunity by running from opposition. I wanted to succeed, become somebody – as my grandfather had said – and make my family proud of me.

One evening, struggling in frustration over my school work as trams thundered by, there seemed only one solution. I had to know I could face down any challenge.

The next day I joined the boxing team, and trained and trained, hitting the bag for hours, jumping rope to build endurance, sparring with opponents until my arms dropped limp at my sides. Slowly, my body became honed, and my instincts for where, when and how to land a punch sharpened.

There in the ring I directed all my competitive energy into every solid punch I threw. And with each one that I landed, and every 'round I won, I was coming to understand what it took to make it in the world – or at least in my world.

In the ring, the raw energy could take me over. Thinking and acting happened by animal instinct. I loved the rush.

There is something for letting your aggression take hold of you: For the next five years I was the school boxing champion for my weight, and winning that title over and over meant I wasn't bothered by anyone anymore. That seemed to prove one thing. Being aggressive and being the best was the ticket. Anything less meant you were second-rate and open to derision and having everything you worked for taken from you.

When the years at Dulwich had passed quickly I felt honed to an edge and ready for greater challenges.

By now, the words of my grandfather – "You can make something of yourself" – and my father's comment about the weak being victims of the powerful had given me a focus. I decided to move on to law school.

When I first cracked open a law book I knew I'd found a worthy calling. By now I had become enamored of the famous 19th-Century Barrister, Marshall Hall. In his biography, written by Edward Marjoribanks, I found myself absorbed by the life of a man who, despite humble beginnings and with many obstacles against him, rose to be a legend in the Old Bailey. Reading about his legal daring and his aplomb – taking on impossible cases and winning — made me want to be just like him.

Three years later I had satisfied the examiners, and all that remained was for me to be called to the Bar. Before I could practice as a criminal law Barrister and carve my mark on the legal world, I would have to complete compulsory military service.

I was about to gain in the service more life lessons that would prepare me for greater challenges than I could then imagine.

Chapter Three

GOING UP AGAINST THE MILITARY

Army service presented enormous challenges for everyone. First, there was the grunt work. I learned to fire a rifle, which I liked, and to take orders, empty trashcans, peel potatoes, and polish boots, which no one liked. I was a good soldier, but restless to get out into the world and start my life and a career in law.

Fortunately, I would not have to wait until my service ended to begin that career.

When I was a private soldier in Aldershot, a large training area for recruits, the word got out that I was trained as an attorney. A veteran Sergeant came to me one day when I was pressing some fatigues, and he looked extremely worried and confused.

"An order was posted in which I was named as Duty Sergeant. I didn't see the order," he continued.

I knew instantly what this meant. He'd done something to trigger a demotion.

"I have been summoned to appear before the Colonel. Look, I've been in the military for over twenty-five years, and now I could lose my rank."

That meant not only the loss of his dignity, but the loss of his military pension, as well.

"Will you defend me?"

Under military law, any soldier can ask any other soldier to represent him at a Court Martial, even a private like me.

I hesitated. This was edgy. To go up against the military establishment would put me at odds with my superior officers and could mark me as a trouble maker.

Nonetheless, looking at the misery on this man's face, feeling the unfairness of losing your pension because you'd missed one order in twenty-five years, something in me rose to the challenge.

"All right," I replied. "I'll do it."

When he left I wondered what on earth I'd just agreed to.

Days later I marched into a Colonel's office – me, a miserable, lowly private — to defend a Sergeant. This was unheard of, and the Colonel's face soured with displeasure.

It was a simple matter really. I pointed out, respectfully, "The orders this man is charged with ignoring were posted at *5:06 pm*, and the Sergeant was off duty at *5:00 pm*."

The room was silent, and no one looked pleased except the Sergeant.

He was released, suffering only a mild reprimand.

Walking back to my barracks I noticed several things.

I felt totally energized by the fact that I'd gone up against the powers above me and *won*. More than that, I recognized how much satisfaction came from helping someone who had no power. I felt a surge from the past, as if I could still hear my grandfather reminding me that we are not here just for our own purposes or gains, but to help others, as well. But frankly, by now I also liked a good confrontation.

I wanted to take on more challenges.

Not long after I applied for Officer Cadet Training School. Eager though I was, it did not go well. Not that I couldn't climb trees or jump over logs, it was just that I thought it was a good idea to demonstrate my officer potential by letting everybody else do it and explaining to them where they'd gone wrong. This didn't go down well with anyone.

The Colonel in charge grabbed me by the shirt and pulled me aside. "We don't need baby Napoleons in this Army."

Undeterred, 3 months later I tried again. This time, the officer in charge informed. "Caplan, you didn't show enough initiative."

The thing was, I'd worked incredibly hard, but this time I'd kept my mouth shut like they'd told me to. Fortunately, I didn't tell him that I could have said a lot about the way he ran things.

Finally–the third time, a year later–I got it right. By then I had climbed strenuously from the rank of private to the rank of full Corporal.

When I completed my training in Officer Cadet School in Aldershot my final challenge was to learn how to handle a sword – and not just any sword, one known as the Sword of Honor.

This blade was awarded to the best officer cadet, and I was thrilled to receive that honor. The Sgt. Major was none too happy, when he discovered I was going to lead his Passing Out Troop in front of the General during the parade. For one thing, I was too short, and the sword had to be specially hitched up onto my Army pants in order for me to wear it. The Sgt. Major always seemed to start his day or end his day when our troop was on parade in front of him by shouting at me, "Step out of your shit bucket, Sir."

And then there were my sword-handling skills.

To put it frankly, I found myself struggling through the practice drills, with the Sgt. Major screaming in my face.

"CAPLAN, I WILL RUN YOU THROUGH WITH THAT BLEEDING SWORD IF YOU DON'T MARCH PROPERLY!"

I was already sweating and struggling to keep pace with the others and I had no sense of timing. I knew I looked like a disaster and not an example of the military's finest.

All this – the challenge and the ever pummeling words — only made me that much more determined to succeed at anything the military could throw at me. I was proud that I had become, like the Sword of Honor, a man of sharpened steel, ready for anything.

A few weeks later, I was posted to Northern Ireland as a Lieutenant. I had volunteered for Cyprus, thinking that would be fun as a young officer. The Royal Army Service Corps, however, sent me to Belfast.

One day I led my platoon of thirty-six trucks on an exercise into the hills. I had overshot our target, my jeep broke down, and it was almost dark. I led the platoon into a village but the village was down a deep dip in the hills, and there was no room for the trucks to turn around. If my sergeants had any respect for my rank prior to this incident they quickly lost it.

Somehow I always found myself shadow-boxing against one thing or another, struggling to achieve and then to maintain a position of authority and respect. All this did was to make me more determined to grit my teeth and succeed.

While in Northern Ireland I was called into legal duty again and again. Now I found myself defending many soldiers accused of offenses under the Army Act of 1882, which was crammed with so much trivia that you could practically be court-martialed for breathing heavily.

Once, for instance, two fellow officers were on the verge of being court-martialed for allowing girls into their jeep and later driving around the base at 1:00 am, drunk and making a lot of noise. A section in the Army Act states that if a senior officer watches a junior officer committing an offense and does nothing about it, then he himself is guilty of an offense as an accessory. When the officers left the General's house party with the two girls, as it happened, the Major was standing by, and like a good sport, he looked the other way.

Here it was, my knockout punch.

I went to the Colonels office and said, "Unfortunately, if these two officers are court martialed it will come out in testimony that the Major saw their behavior and did nothing to stop them." The Colonel gritted his teeth.

The court-martial was cancelled, and the two young officers were each given six extra guard duties.

The army discharged me early in 1957, and I believe that so far as my superior officers were concerned they would have been quite happy to have discharged me through the barrel of a rifle. I'd gone up against them that many times.

So my national service in the army had come to an end. It was a good experience, and I'd helped a few soldiers get out of a mess. Now, as I traveled home, I was looking forward to beginning my own career and getting on with my life.

When my father met me at Victoria Station in London, however, I was startled by his appearance.

He was gray and looked ill. He stared straight ahead, as though he was in shock. His suit was wrinkled as though he had slept in it. He didn't ask me anything about my life in the army, or say anything about Mum.

Back at my parents' apartment I pulled my mother aside and asked about Dad.

"The rag business has put him under a lot of stress, Joseph," she confided. Competition is fierce, and in order to increase profits he decided to cut out the middle man. That meant him taking on more work. And then he decided to expand by purchasing a small factory in Dewsbury."

Dewsbury was in Yorkshire in the north of England, about 200 miles away. Between taking on more roles in the business and travelling that distance over and over again it was no wonder he looked nearly spent.

The next day, for the first time ever, Dad confided in me about the business, and also his financial situation.

"I put my accountant in charge of the mill in the Dewsbury, and the business is crashing. Something is going on there, though," he said, "and I can't put my finger on it."

"What do you mean?" I asked.

"I don't know for sure. But with all the shipments of rags going there, we should be turning much better profits. I want you to go to Yorkshire and see what you can find out."

Dad was a good businessman and I trusted his instincts. I'd come to trust mine, too. And my instincts were shouting that something wrong or unfair was going on.

Before I moved on with my life and entered the legal world I would have to find out what that was. I sensed a challenge.

Chapter Four

FROM RAGS... TO A WIG AND A GOWN

Dad's factory in Dewsbury seemed normal to me at first. I didn't see much of the accountant, but he was there somewhere, presumably, working on the books.

My legal training had prepared me quite well for investigation. I talked to people in the town, like the gas station owner. When I introduced myself and mentioned why I was there, he stared at me a long time before speaking.

"I just returned from the military," I continued, while he stared at me. "And I'm distressed to find my Dad is in terrible condition. Something is clearly wrong here, and we don't know what it is. I'm fearful for my father's health, to tell you the truth."

The man cleared his throat, then proceeded. "One of the workers at your Dad's factory confided something. Don't ask his name, because I won't tell you. But he says that truckloads of rags that are supposed to arrive at your Dad's factory are being diverted elsewhere and they don't appear on inventories. The workers are worried the place will close and they'll lose their jobs."

A bit more sleuthing uncovered an unpleasant truth. The accountant Dad had trusted to run his business had rented his own factory and had his own truck and drivers. Once I'd put it all together I presented facts to some of the workers and to others who acknowledged they were aware of the circumstances. Some were willing to provide written statements.

Returning to London I presented the evidence to my Dad.

"I can't believe I trusted that man, and he's ruined me."

The thought of Dad being harmed sent a jolt of anger through me.

"Call the police," I urged. "Get a lawyer." The man needed to be punished.

Dad shook his head. "I cannot be responsible for sending another Jew to jail."

I felt frustrated, but I understood. Like my grandfather, Dad valued loyalty to the community.

The damage to my dad's business was terrible. As bills mounted and income plunged it crippled him financially. The stress showed in his face, and in his tense pacing. I believe the betrayal actually broke his heart.

Now he would be left to struggle, trying to hold onto a business that was teetering on the brink.

As for me, while I felt terrible for Dad, my hands were tied. I could not do anything to help him if he didn't want to prosecute — and I also had to get on with my own life. My dreams and ambitions lay in the world of the law.

In fact, a great door was about to open for me – but it would take me in a direction of which my father did not approve.

It was difficult for me to explain to my father why I did not want to join him and the rest of my family in the rag trade. For one thing, it would have been like holding up a mirror for dad to see his own life – the long hours, the haggling, the scratching for a penny – in short, how very, very hard the rag business was and, therefore, how unappealing it was to me.

Nonetheless, my father did everything he could to persuade me to join the family business and help him to earn money. I stuck to my guns.

"More than anything, Dad, I want to be a criminal defense attorney. I want to defend people, argue with judges, and banter with juries. I want to help people get a second chance if they've made a mistake."

Dad stared at me blankly. Eventually, reluctantly, he agreed to let me go into law. "But only if you become a Solicitor."

A Solicitor is an all-around attorney, but he is only allowed to address the judge in the lower courts. That was not what I wanted.

"Dad, I want to be a Barrister." I wanted to wear the Barrister's wig and gown, which symbolized that you had "made it" in the legal world. That was how I wanted to make *my* mark and, fueled by legal successes in the military, my drive to succeed out in the world-at-large was huge.

Dad grimaced. "Solicitors make some money straight away," he argued. "Barristers have to wait years before they're even recognized and start to make a decent living."

How could we be father and son and be so different, I thought. I didn't disparage who Dad was, a hardworking man, but what we valued was so different.

Reluctantly, for Dad's sake I took a position in a Solicitors office. It wasn't intended to be a smokescreen, but I didn't stay long. After a few weeks I left the Solicitor's office without telling my dad, and signed up at the Honorable Society of Lincoln's Inn to start my legal studies.

When he found out I'd left the Solicitor to become a Barrister he was not pleased, but it was clear I had made up my mind. In the end, he paid my student fees and I was grateful.

I was thrilled. I had made my break from the rag world and was now free to move toward the type of success I wanted. I had nothing against making money or having financial success, but my eye was on another prize.

Besides success I wanted notoriety.

By now Sir Edward Marshall Hall had become my absolute hero. I'd continued to read about him and the cases he defended and, inspired by him my burning desire was to follow in his footsteps and become a renowned Barrister at Law.

Beyond his successes, some quality about the man, which eluded me, emerged through the stories from his life. There seemed to be something different in the spirit of this man.

I found it compelling, for instance, that when Hall was a young man, his mother sent him the words of the hymn, "Oh Jesus, I Have Promised to Serve Thee to the End."

O Jesus, I have promised to serve Thee to the end;
Be Thou forever near me, my Master and my Friend;
I shall not fear the battle if Thou art by my side,
Nor wander from the pathway if Thou wilt be my Guide.

Though I was Jewish and could not relate to the Christian message, nonetheless I saw in Hall a devotion to something greater than himself. That appealed to me. What I failed to recognize was the fact that Hall's faith was a sort of anchor for him, one that would keep him from being pulled by the riptides of life, of which he would experience many.

Perhaps the worst tide of ill-fortune came just as Hall was about to start his career as a court attorney. His young wife, who was 23 years old, fell into the arms of another man, got pregnant and later died in childbirth.

Despite the betrayal, Hall was broken-hearted, which also spoke to me about the depths of humanity and passion in him.

I could relate to all of these things – devotion to higher purposes, passion, and even adversity. Like him, too, I wanted to set my face like flint to do good. Stirred by my youthful idealism I wanted to be just like him — devoted to justice and what was right.

Though I didn't have the same anchor, or anything like it, Hall's was the prize I wanted: to be known for doing something worthwhile for society. In the words of my grandfather, I wanted to "do greater things" with my life.

Could I hold onto these goals and values in the cut-throat world of law though?

First things first, though I got down to the serious business: where to buy the proper attire so I would *look* like a criminal defense attorney.

Tradition dictates that a Barrister wears a wig, a gown, also a black jacket, black and gray striped trousers, a white shirt with a stiffened collar and a good, somber tie. I would be dressed and ready when success called.

Then there was that other important detail. I had to find a law office where, for £100 and some additional fees, someone would give me the privilege of following them around for a year in the law courts. It is called pupilage, and is similar to being an intern.

I bought a street guide to London, and started at the Fleet Street end of Middle Temple Lane. With no family connections, I knocked on doors, attempting to find a position as the pupil of an experienced attorney, preferably a criminal law attorney. I had to become someone's "pupil," learn court procedure and how to formulate a set of legal pleadings before I could start practicing as a Barrister.

From office to office I trudged, studying the lists of attorney's names etched on brass plates on each ancient-looking door, listed in order of seniority, with the Head of Chambers (the law firm) at the top, and the most junior at the bottom.

Inside each one I made my speech.

"I've been called to the Bar. I've just finished my National Service, and I would like to become a pupil."

Staring eyes met hopeful ones. I didn't realize how unorthodox this was. "Who recommended you?"

"No one, Sir."

"Sorry, no vacancy. Full up."

Slowly it was dawning: having a recommendation was the ticket.

I didn't have a recommendation.

Each time I was turned away I redoubled my courage and told myself, "I will be a barrister. Someone is going to take me in."

At the far end of Middle Temple Lane, on the left hand side, is Number One, just before you walk out of the gate and jump over the embankment into the River Thames. It is the last set of offices on the street. On the brass plate on the door I saw the name Sir Christmas Humphreys at the top.

Humphreys was the Senior Crown Counsel, later to become Lord Humphreys, a distinguished judge at the Old Bailey Courthouse. The Second Senior Barrister named on the door was Edward Clarke, later Sir Edward Clarke.

I made my little speech to the Clerk of the Chambers, who looked at me as though I was someone who had just come down from the moon.

"We are" – I knew what word was next – "full. *But*" – this was new – "I will take your name and phone number."

By the end of my march, Middle Temple Lane had offered me no "vacancies," and after Number One came…. *Zero.*

I went home to in Edgware, the last stop on the Underground, more than an hour traveling time, with no good news. I was depressed and tired, thinking maybe I had made a very wrong move.

When I walked through the door and my mother said, "Joseph, there was a telephone call for you this afternoon, from a Mr...."

She spelled the name carefully, as though she sensed its importance.

I ran to the phone and returned the call — from Sir Christmas Humphrey's clerk.

The short of it is, Sir Christopher had just that day returned from his annual vacation to Tibet and after I'd walked out the door announced to his clerk, "I have decided to take on a pupil."

"Can you come in tomorrow for an interview."

My heart nearly stopped.

It was well-known that Sir Christmas was an ardent Buddhist, and his religious practice seemed to contribute greatly to his calm demeanor and dignity, which added to the stature and ability he already possessed in the legal world.

As I concluded the phone conversation with the Clerk I made sure to keep my voice level, cool and professional sounding.

Then I hung up and leaped into the air, shouting and jumping around for joy.

Having the chance to work with a man of his stature, who was also reputed to be of a kind nature – this was a far bigger break than I could have hoped for.

If only I could have stuck with that course.

Chapter Five

IDEALS...AND AMBITION

Many years can pass before you're able to look back and see clearly where subtle changes within yourself began to send your life on a course you never meant to take.

As a student of Sir Christmas Humphreys I followed him to court day after day. Even before courtrooms full of people and nasty, aggressive Barristers, he was imperturbable, unmoved by anything caustic or sarcastic that anyone would say. He had only one objective: to prove to the jury that the man or woman in the dock was clearly guilty.

Daily, fascinated by him, studying his every move and inflection, I watched him prosecute murderer after murderer. Nightly, I read the newspaper reports of his trials.

For a few days I also had the extraordinary privilege of sitting next to Sir Edward Clarke, a colleague of Sir Christmas Humphreys, who became famous for prosecuting Dr. John Bodkin Adams, one of the first known serial killers. Adams was accused of doing away with 25 of his female patients whose decomposed bodies were found in his garden. My role was simply to look after Sir Edward's papers and books and not say a word. I couldn't have spoken anyway, so dumbstruck was I by his style, eloquence and persuasive manner.

In short, I found myself in heaven. Somehow I'd stumbled through an open door to the future I dreamed of. A whole new world had opened to me, thanks to my great models and mentors, a world in which I very much wanted to play a role.

And here is where the subtle shift came into play. At the outset what I really wanted was to help bring justice for the powerless. But something else slowly took over. Maybe it happened as I noticed how people offered greatest respect and gave deference to men like Sir Christmas Humphreys and Sir Edward. The respect people offered them gave them a kind of power. I didn't want to be treated like a shabby rag merchant's boy, a "dirty Jew," a pushed-around pawn of the military. I had felt so devalued. Now I wanted people to respect and honor *me*. It wasn't that I stopped wanting to offer help to the powerless, but to this goal I added something else: I wanted for myself the power that being respected gives a man.

How subtly do new motives take over.

I worked very hard for Sir Christmas Humphreys. He nominated me to become a member of the Central Criminal Court Bar Mess, a prestigious private dining room. When my time as a pupil was over, Humphreys offered me a permanent office. I was at the bottom rung of the ladder, but it would be the place from which my star would rise. I knew it. I had a few cases, and just knew they would get bigger and more important. One day, people would actually call the clerk to the chambers and ask for "Joseph Caplan."

Joseph. Part of shedding my past involved the name change. I decided to Anglicize myself, thus calling less attention to my heritage. For although I was in a supposedly egalitarian world, prejudices still held sway. And while I remained very proud of my heritage, I *would* get ahead. I allowed myself no other option.

From where I was starting, though – accepting "dock briefs" – it was a long way to the top.

Now a dock brief provides a young Barrister with the chance to represent a client and get experience. Unfortunately, a dock brief comes about when a defendant has no money to employ his own attorney and the State permits him to receive legal representation at no charge. The fee for a dock brief is very modest. A portion went to the clerk, and the remainder was for me – it just about covers train fare and a sandwich. After the arraignment is read, the judge tells him or her to choose from one of the barristers who are standing up in the front row.

The first time I went for a dock brief I felt like I was in a police line-up. I was nervous and excited at the same time. I looked at the other barristers who, like me, were all beginners and hungry for experience. One or two were twitching nervously. Another looked pompous, as though he couldn't care less. Yet another looked deadpan serious.

And then there was me.

I was nervous, yes, but I had also been sharpened by years of dreaming about moments such as these. I was determined to get a case, and win or go down swinging.

My face was set.

The man who had just been arraigned looked rough indeed. Hair barely combed, facial stubble. He looked entirely bored, as though he had been through this drill before.

He looked us over like mutton chops, then pointed at me.

"That one."

So began my climb.

I went for a dock brief many times, because I had no other work. As I stood before the judge and the accused, I would try to appear distinguished by holding the lapel of my gown with my right hand. Other times, I would look away to pretend that I wasn't really interested. Sometimes, I would put a very stern look on my face to give the impression that I was tough.

Once, when I was chosen to defend an accused man, we lost and he was convicted. Later, feeling badly, I went down to see him in the cell.

He looked at me through the bars of his cell. "I know you didn't get much for this job, guvnor, but I've got a smashing job to do when I get out and I'm going to see you, all right!"

In those early days, despite the struggle to get by financially, I began to learn a lot.

First, I learned about life and what a mess it is for so many people. Most, of course, were indigent, which is why they had me to represent them. Losing even a month's worth of pay because they were sent to jail might mean utter ruin. And there was the fact that people were not always what they seemed. So much was hidden beneath the surface. One of the accused was convicted and sent to jail for homosexual activity which at that time was illegal in England. His wife was waiting to hear the verdict. I went to see her in the corridor outside the court. Without thinking about it, I told her that he would be in jail for a short time and why. Until the moment I opened my mouth, she hadn't known that her husband had another life. She became completely hysterical.

On one hand I could identify with the financial plight of these people. My family, while not poor, was not rich either. A problem in business – such as my Dad encountered in Dewsbury – could mean ruination.

But on a subtler level I could not identify with them at all. I had a sort of feeling of immunity — not a class distinction, but I had been brought up "right." The powerless people I had wanted to defend, in my idealism, were now rough and real. They were people who had stepped outside the law. I was, quite simply, not "that kind" of person.

Feeling for them in their poverty ran counter to my sense about them as moral beings, leaving me with mixed feelings.

As more time passed, I built up my share of acquittals at the Old Bailey. Soon enough, better cases would start to come to me and I could leave the lower, grittier echelons of society behind for good.

I would sit all day in my office at Sir Christmas Humphreys' firm in the Middle Temple — one of the four Inns of Court, membership in which entitles the British attorney to practice law – and my heart pumped day by day, waiting for a phone call telling me I could go to work and defend someone of importance. That would get my name in the newspapers. I wanted to plead for my client in front of a jury, argue their case, defy the odds, and get an acquittal, which, if it was the *right* client, might get me mentioned in a headline.

Now I measured success with a kind word from a senior advocate and a successful case. Even an unsuccessful case might bring a commendation from the judge as he told a forlorn client on his way to his cell that counsel could not have done more on his behalf. These were the remarks, whether in court or in our own chambers, which gave me the incentive to carry on — the coin of the realm, so to speak — because there was not much actual money involved, and so every supportive word fed my will to keep going and succeed at an even greater level.

Daily, then, when I wasn't working on legal briefs, I stared out the window at the fine cars – Mercedes, BMWs, Rolls – that passed up and down the street outside the office. One day, some important someone in a car like that would hire my services. Then my eye would stray to phone, waiting anxiously for it to ring, bringing that one call needed to jumpstart my success. "Joseph" Caplan would become a known and respected personage.

Looking back I realize that something that once held great importance for me had faded away. My grandfather had instilled in me the values of heritage and doing what was right to bring goodness to the world. If I'd thought of him at all – and I had little time to – I might have noticed that those values were slipping from my thinking.

But I didn't notice that at all.

And then, what happened to me next fell like lightning out of a blue sky, changing the course of my life forever.

Chapter Six

FROM A WIG AND GOWN TO RAGS

Having found a position with an excellent law firm I felt I was on my way to the kind of service to humanity of which I had long dreamt — though that dream had been dampened by my early experiences in the law.

That was when one telephone call changed everything. I was preparing to leave the office, waiting for the clerk to deliver a case file for my evening review, when the phone rang.

The news was bad and I nearly dropped my briefcase. Dad had suffered a heart attack and was in the hospital.

"Please hurry," Mum sobbed into the phone. "It's bad."

When I got to the hospital, I found my Dad lying in bed with I-V drips in his arms and tubes in his chest. He looked ashen, much worse than when he had met me at the train station the day I came home from the army

He stared at me as though I was a stranger, unable to speak. He raised one hand weakly, then it dropped onto the white sheet that was covering his body and had no more energy to communicate.

My mother more than made up for it, however.

"The business is still in bad shape. He's been fretting and pacing every evening, telling me it's taken a serious nose-dive…And now no one is there to try and save it." Mother was wringing her hands, agonizing. "We're going to lose everything now."

When I left his bedside, I felt a deep pang for my parents. Over and over I asked myself, *What do I do now?*

The next day, in Dad's office, I went through his financial records and discovered that his business was on the verge of collapse.

Mum was distraught. She didn't know what to say to me and didn't know what to do. She was not able to handle it. Family members were there initially, but after a few days, the phone stopped ringing and we were on our own.

As I walked into the sorting area, where men and women were busy bundling rags into bales I found myself wondering what would happen to them if Dad's business closed. Sure, there were lots of low-end jobs for unskilled laborers. But these people, most of them, had worked for Dad a long time. Finding a new job meant starting over at the lowest rung of some other business. Many were middle-aged, with families to support. That would be a hardship.

Not to mention what would happen to Mum and Dad.

As I agonized, old connections to family began to re-emerge. Though I'd pushed away from the family business years before, the deep love for family that came from my grandfather surged in. That, and a sense of desperation for my parents.

There was only one choice, really.

I turned on my heel, went to calm my mother down and tell her my decision.

Later that day I collected my wig and gown from the law offices and told the Clerk of Chambers why I had to go.

It was a very hard blow to the gut. I had worked so hard, had such a lucky break, and been headed in the direction of my dreams…and now life was forcing me to step into a world I wanted nothing to do with. I was angry.

The next day, gritting my teeth, I moved myself to my father's rag factory under the railway arches on Crown Street, in Camberwell, London. Sitting at his desk I felt like I had dropped from some pinnacle to the bottom of the mountain all over again.

There wasn't a lot of time to sit around feeling anything, though. Workers were asking for direction. Loads of rags would be arriving. Creditors would be calling. I had to learn the business from scratch. Fast.

If I'd had any time to think, I might have realized that, when I made the monumental decision, something shifted in me at a deep level. The youthful idealism I'd carried since I was a boy had faded a little in the desire that had grown in me — to be known and respected. Now that idealism was dealt a death-blow. I had to set my sights on an entirely new goal. Making money.

During my first week running Dad's business I forced myself to shake off anger and resentment. My old boxing and military personas rose to the fore. I would win. I would make this business successful, whatever it took. I didn't know if anyone in the legal world would have me back, considering I'd bailed-out on short notice from no less a personage than Sir Christmas Humphreys. What I did know was this: I would not stop till this business was on top and Dad and Mum were secure again.

First things first. A whole new world challenged me — which was good, as a challenge got my blood going. A sweater with holes in the elbows replaced the dignified Barrister's gown. I wore no tie with my shirt, my shoes had no shine and my pants needed cleaning and pressing. If I was going to fit in here I couldn't put on any airs.

Next, just as important, I had to acquaint myself with the people. They were a different breed.

In Camberwell, a poor area in London, the people held on to their way of life, they had nowhere else to go, as there was little upward mobility from this echelon. The inhabitants preserved their anonymity behind rows of terraced housed, narrow streets, and brick walls that showed their age. There were no front gardens, only flowerpots and curtains much faded by the sun on one side of the road and much grubbed by time and dust on the other.

Actually, to my relief, I began immediately to identify with the people who worked for my Dad.

For one thing, the men and women who lived in this neighborhood didn't have a complicated life. For the most part, they didn't do much of anything but work, drink, and make love. They were ordinary people who lived and died in ordinary homes, never to be heard of while they lived and easily forgotten when they died. The occupants lived private lives closely sheltered from the outside world. There was no incentive to either achievement or success.

And yet, beneath the rough surface, these people had dignity despite their circumstances. They were, in a word, poor. But the thing is the poor don't ever use words like "poor" or "poverty." That's a superior way of talking about *those* people, the *others*. They understood deprivation— none of that, very little of this — usually with no anger or resentment. They had grown up with what they had, and if they lost a job and things got worse they just got in line.

There was a dark side, too.

Camberwell was a place where people were, shall we say, "miscellaneous"; they could blend in and disappear. There was an equanimity which everyone accepted, and the dark nights had no difficulty keeping their secrets. Camberwell was part of southeast London where you would not want to be walking alone after dark.

This is where I now found myself — walking the dirty streets of South East London. It was a strange world indeed. The streets were filled with the sights and sounds of horses and carts and old men pushing wheelbarrows — the "totters" who plied their trade in sun, rain or snow, calling out "Any old rags?" Then they would haul their heaps to a guy like me to claim their earnings. Some knew how to separate wool from cotton to get a better price, but most did not.

That's the world that presented itself. In my mind's-eye, however, I looked up through smoke, dust, and fog at a distant dollar figure and better life someday. If the rag business was the slope I had to climb to save us all I *would* do it.

Every morning, now, I walked around the rag factory and tried to understand the new problems facing me. The old arches and cobbled stones rasped at my feet. I was surrounded by discarded stinking rags and employees who were there to work from 8:00 to 5:00 or 6:00. Everyone would be sorting, hauling, bailing, working hard to keep their jobs.

Quickly, I became aware that " Morry's son" – me — was the focus of their attention. I knew what they were whispering. Can he pull this business off the heap?

With my father in the hospital and no one to help me I had no way of measuring the effect of my decisions, other than the occasional overdraft at the bank and the availability of inventory for sale. The money the goods brought in was quickly reduced by paying outstanding bills. And still there wasn't enough.

The pressure was relentless. Two or three or four creditors called almost every day.

"You're a Barrister, aintya?" one man said, sarcastically. "If ya owe money, ya gotta pay."

The mere mention of the word Barrister was a slap in the face. I put the phone down, hated him for that reminder.

Where would all the money come from? How soon before the lawsuits rolled in? As the weeks rolled I soon realized that this was a world where different standards applied.

In the legal world, Barristers were expected to do everything by the book and above board. When it came to money, the highest degree of scruples was demanded.

For that reason, I balked at the little deals that had to be made "on the side."

I was in the midst of a conversation with one supplier, arguing that things had to be correct, watching his face grow red — when one of the old gents who had worked for Dad forever caught my eye.

"Little Mo, that's the way it's done. This business will eat you alive if you don't understand that."

Something began to dawn on me during this stressful time, though. A different perspective.

People measure happiness in different ways, I learned. And those who were working by my side, strange as it seemed, had no worries other than occasional health issues. Even when the husbands went into the wrong bedroom, it was accepted. That's the way they lived. Sometimes dinner would come down to potatoes and greens. They accepted things which would give sadness and overwhelm most people on the other side of the fence, yet for the most part, they slept a lot better than they did.

Though I had pulled myself away from my father's world, and felt apart from it though I was in it, I saw that this was where he earned his daily bread that paid the rent and provided me with ten shillings a week to spend when I was a boy. The labor of these people had allowed me to go twice a week to the movies, and once a week to the local dance hall on a Saturday night, and to buy two coffees — a young man's paradise.

Over the coming months, the gray, damp dirty walls of the factory surrounding me began to look different. At first, I had stared back at them in disbelief. But the more I got used to the place, and its people, the more I felt — what was it? —let's say more *at home* here. For years, what they had yielded had brought me up, got me into college, and given me the opportunity to be somebody. But I'd never thought, as a youngster about my Dad's place; where he worked or exactly what he did for a living. I had taken it all for granted. My Dad had worked hard and wanted his son to use his college degree to make life better.

Now the old neighborhood, the rag works, and the old stone walls were beckoning me back, as though I was obliged to help these people earn their daily sustenance. Every day I became more used to the strange faces, the sacks of discarded clothes, the dirty steel benches loaded with rags. I looked around to see where I was and where I was going to be for the rest of my life.

Inwardly, I was changing, though I didn't see it at the time. My philosophy, my high thoughts and ambitions about "helping society" were slowly fading. I felt, like it or not, pulled in another direction. A new vocabulary emerged: worsted, serge, velour, mungo, and the baler. A new way of thinking emerged. All I could focus on was, "This is now my life. I must make it successful."

As the days turned into weeks, I found myself blocking all thoughts about the career and dreams I'd left; I was too tired every night when I got home. I let go thoughts about the dignity of the law courts, bowing to the judge, the excitement of speaking up for someone in front of a jury whose life was about to move backwards. I let go thoughts that I was moving backwards. My father remained, for some time, immobile in the hospital. My mother was alone at home, fearful, crying every evening and worrying about her husband. Their future. Employees gave me sidelong glances as I passed, as if to say, *My family's wellbeing is in your hands, son. Don't forget that.* People were calling for their money. I *had* to fight for a solution.

The pressure was relentless.

It was one thing to see my world change dramatically, and another thing to hear it from someone else, someone I didn't even know and who couldn't care less about my family's plight or my own grief.

Without my knowing it, the rag trade would slowly, inexorably pull me apart — pull me away from once-high goals and ideals. My father wasn't there. No one cared. No one even asked me how my father was doing in the hospital. I got used to it, but it scared me. I didn't understand why the world was so callous and cold and indifferent. I would walk the gritty blocks to the bus stop to go home each night, alone, mystified by it all.

It began to dawn on me that all during my growing-up years I had been cloistered. Dad had never talked to me about business. I'd only known, from the way he and my mother spoke, that sometimes he did well and sometimes business was no good. But I didn't dare to ask for details.

What I knew now was that we — my mother, father and I — needed to survive. And *now* it was my job to put food on the table.

The world was barking at our heels now. I decided I would have to do whatever it took.

And so I learned how to deal with the ragmen, the totters who brought small packages of rags and metals through the door at prices which we invented as we went along. That is, I learned how make "street deals." Most of what was brought in was hardly worth calculating, so we swept the vendor away with a bulk price without bothering to sort what he had left on the ground.

When a totter showed up with a load of lead one day I asked, off handedly, "Where did this load come from?"

The man looked at me, his face reddened with anger, like I had lost my mind. I realized in an instant I had crossed a line by even asking the question.

My "mentor" shot me a look when the man left. No word was spoken. Did I really *want* to know where everything came from that we were buying for resale?

The stack of debts had only decreased slightly. The harassing calls were still coming in. Dad was only just coming home, after two months in the hospital, with personal bills to pay.

I never asked again.

Very quickly, I found myself taking to the bluffing and bargaining of this world, as if it were sparring in a ring.

There were the totters who asked, with great bravado, for ridiculously high prices, hoping the new young man in charge —me— would be stupid enough to pay.

"Fifty pounds for the lot."

I was ready to hand him the money, when —fortunately— one of my workers, who was standing by waiting to take the goods back to be sorted shot me a forbidding look. I quickly understood his meaning.

"Twenty-five. Take it or leave it," I replied, shrugging indifferently.

I was learning that my profit or loss depended on pricing with this kind of audacity during these transactions.

At the same time, a different kind of transaction was going on in my head.

The man engaging in this kind of business was some new version of me —in transition from the person I had once been. I felt I *had* to adapt myself to a new world and way of doing things, where, in fact, there was no standard at all.

The standard was whatever I wanted it to be.

I thought, *If this is what it takes to make this work, so be it.*

The good rolled in, and I became more brazen.

Now the totters hardly ever argued. I'd won my 'rounds with them, and realized there was nowhere else for them to go. I'd felt cornered when I was flung into this business; now I had someone else cornered. I crawled to the top of some small heap, at least.

I had to admit—secretly liked that feeling.

Chapter Seven

MONEY AS MASTER

Weeks and months went by, and I'd gone from handling legal briefs to handling bales of rags. At first, I'd gone home every day with sore, blistered and cut fingers from lugging the 112 pound bales. I learned quickly to lift a bale with one foot underneath and strong arms, and heave it up onto my back.

I began to pride myself on working as hard as anyone else, even though I was the boss's son. All I knew now, really, was how to make a buck the hard way.

The thing was, I didn't complain or even think much about the radical reversal my life had taken. There would have been no point in it. We — my parents and I, and these people who worked for us — simply needed to survive. We needed money, and there was only one way to get it.

Profit was made by collecting mixed rags, sorting them, separating the cottons from the worsted, and the wool, and bailing them up for sale. A bail weighed 112 pounds. When money came in on-time, the bank loan could be paid and some of the creditors could be made to shut up and sell us more rags for sorting.

Each bale was valued by the quality of its contents. And now and then — another little survival trick the workers taught me — if the cardboard was the right shape, you doubled the cardboard because this added a little to the weight. A hundred of these fractions meant more money, not much more, but much was the need.

This meant payroll could also be met, and mortgages and rents could be paid.

Several months in, this world of rags and scrap metals was becoming my world. The noise from the trains going back and forth overhead was deafening, but I got used to it.

Everybody in the factory worked very hard and was keen to sort their rags, carry their bales and make things happen. There was no jealousy. None of them were grasping. Every now and then there was a fight — sometimes over a girl or a bad remark about a football team — but we looked the other way and let the guys sort it out for themselves, knowing they just needed to express themselves and vocabulary was limited.

At lunchtime, there was no such thing as, "I'll see you in 45 minutes, I'm dashing out for a bite." Everybody brought something for lunch; There was a small room where the girls made tea for all of us. Some of them didn't even take a lunch break, but ate their sandwich while they were working. They were happy to pick up a paycheck on Friday evening, dashing off in hopes of catching a bank still open so they could cash it. After all, there were pubs to visit, and if sometimes a man wound up in the wrong bed that night —well, that was part of it.

In short, I learned that these were people who took pride in what they did, humble as that was. They didn't question who they were or what the next day would bring. They didn't have time for such mental anguishing; they survived on an edge, and they made the best of it.

That made me reflect a bit, whenever I was tempted to feel bad for myself that by coming to work here was I "down on my luck."

There was something else that came clear to me, as well.

From time to time, a family member would stop by. The boy, who looked to be about 10, who would bring his father's forgotten sack lunch, riding a rusted bike with a front wheel so wobbly it looked about to fall off. The girl of 14, bringing her mother's forgotten prescription, who looked as if she would desperately love a new dress to replace the hand-me-down-looking, faded sack she was wearing.

I began to realize that I was not working just for me and my family, and not just for the people I saw every day at the rag factory. Like them, I was tweaking my back and neck, slipping and falling, cutting my hands, and going through all this for their families —spouses and children who were stuck at the lowest level of society.

In a very real sense, this somewhat revived my sense of ideals. These people needed help to make a living, let alone have anything extra to show for their backbreaking labor.

Strange as it seemed, as my clothes got dirtier, the pains went away and I got through the work more quickly. Perhaps I was a joke to these people — I was still a Barrister trying hard to be a workman in their eyes — but I tried very hard to speak their language and to understand their way of life and way of thinking.

Late in December I hosted the annual Christmas party. In some ways it was exactly what I expected.

It began as a raucous affair, with employees swirling around full of beer, smudged lipstick, broken windows, and happiness which comes from working hard non-stop throughout the year and only getting the occasional break.

In another way, it was *not* what I'd expected.

Christmas time — I overheard, more than once —another truck...or two... had disappeared off the roads and reappeared in forlorn back streets, with the cargo missing. ("He got a pay-off for that, I can tell you.") Hearing these underworld dealings discussed made me wonder: Was this just hearsay? Were any of these my people? I realized that, their share of what life had to offer could never grow unless there was some alternative.

As I watched the drinking and listened to the dirty jokes I also looked at the children, who were stuffing as many Christmas cookies into their mouths and pockets as possible.

I felt a twinge of sadness. Of course I would not condone stealing or anything illegal. But I was working shoulder to shoulder with people who had no other skills and very little chance of a better life. And if nothing else, *Christmas* seemed to me the one time of year that everyone should benefit from their hard work. But most of the people who worked for me lived hand-to-mouth, and there was no money to set aside for luxuries like Christmas presents. The children of these workers, who waited for their Christmas gifts, would wake up — not just on Christmas morning, but everyday — to realize that life was not going to give them much and their lot would never do much better. The boy with the wobbly-wheeled bike would not get a new bike. The girl in the need of a lovely dress would not get it. I could almost see why men were driven to do what they believed they had to do for their families.

As the last of the alcohol was drunk and the party ground to a close, I realized that, however difficult the rag business was, *I* was the man making the deals that kept us all going. Something about being *that man* sat well with me. But it wasn't enough to really help these people rise from their circumstances.

What else could be done?

As the new year dawned I knew Dad's business was going to make it. I had paid off some of the creditors, and I'd struck up new partnerships to spread the load and increase sales. Dad was still weak, however. And as for me, there was now no question of going back to the law, and there was no time to stop and think deeply about what I was doing or where I was going.

Something inside me had shifted, though. The world of the deal was now my world.

Not long after I met a man — the most unlikely man to alter the course of anyone's life, but meeting him did just that for me. Maybe it was because I'd stopped putting up a resistance to learning anything from men like this man.

H.R.J. Slack, otherwise known as Reggie, was a mechanic, who stopped by a few times a week just for a laugh with the guys and a slap on the tush for the girls. If Reggie wasn't real, you'd want to invent him.

To describe Reggie as a self-employed mechanic operating on a bomb site on the corner of Camberwell Road would be to say as little as describing a house as a house or a garden as a garden. At 5 feet, 4 inches in height, he was one of the tallest men that I'd ever met — an immensely thick set man whom God had blessed with a forever smile. And there was far more to this man than met the eye.

I began to learn from him about *attitude* — that is, attitude toward life and people.

Reggie lived by choice in the way of poverty because it didn't matter to him. His large hands were always covered with the grease and that came from hard work —not that he made a massive contribution to the Exchequer or that he was particularly reliable. Reggie didn't even have a proper business. He never went out to collect the monies owed to him, although now and then he might receive a partial payment. Then he might even pay his rent, if he was in a good mood. His appearances in court on default summonses and judgments were so frequent that the dialog with the judge was more like a Sunday afternoon chat between two pals over the garden fence. Reggie was paying so much a week on so many judgments that he must have been costing the state money just to administer his debts.

At the base of it all, these were the two attitudes that struck me most: Reggie was his own man and he would cut his own course in life; also no obstacle could stand in his way and nothing got him down.

We became friends, and in the months that I came to know him, he taught me to laugh when I didn't think I had anything to laugh about anymore. I couldn't exactly adapt to his personality and treat pressures and adversity like he did, but he was the kind of person who made me realize that *disaster* — which I felt I'd experienced — and death are a long way apart.

And I learned one more important thing from Reggie — about *character*.

I learned that it isn't the important or the successful people who make the most lasting impression on a man. It is the people who you know instinctively are *genuine*. Their lives may be mucked up, but what comes out of their mouth is what they mean. They are not devious, they don't pretend to like you if they don't, they don't want to impress you or anyone else. For the most part, they don't want to learn anything either. They just want to work, get their paycheck, make kids, and stay healthy. People like this have a sense of grounding or commonsense about them, perhaps because the earth beneath their feet is all that's holding them up. Not money or luxuries, just the pavement beneath their shoes.

So this was Reggie Slack. His life was a complete mess. Nonetheless, he was the kind of man who lived life to the fullest on less than nothing, and who would not lie down and die, no matter what happened.

Of course we went into business together.

As a former Barrister I knew how to use the kind of language — barrister-speak, if you will — that would help Reggie collect everything I could collect on the money his customers owed to him.

I began to spend time at the banged-up office typewriter, pounding out letters demanding payment, which was a rather unusual way of collecting money in that part of the world. In this way, the debtor did not know that the man contacting him was not, in fact, active in the legal system. It just sounded like I was.

As the letters went out on Reggie's behalf I started to receive many calls that made me think that there were easier and safer ways of making a living.

"What you want from *me?*" the voice shouted.

"The money that you owe," I would answer calmly. "All of it."

"I ain't got it. And I ain't payin'."

In the same calm tone I would state, "A court will determine that, sir. You have till Friday or we will see you in the dock soon after.

I learned something about myself. If bringing some financial justice for Reggie meant bringing the hammer down on other people — well, so be it.

I didn't know it then, but I was learning skills I would need later: to corner people, challenge their excuses, persevere, insist, refute…and *get what I wanted.*

At a rough guess — there were no records, of course — if Reggie was paid all of the money he was owed, including all the services I had begun invoicing for him, he would easily be able to track and collect on money owed and clear up his debts.

But that never happened. Not because he threw money away on nonsense.

This brought up another thing I admired about the man.

Reggie Slack was a natural-born benefactor. He valued people and gave what money he had to those in need. Maybe that's why we got on. He helped to revive the idealist in me.

Not long after meeting Reggie and working with him, I noticed something. When I was down, Reggie came around to enjoy a laugh. The deadness in my soul would lift, and the physical exhaustion that sometimes overtook me weighed less heavily.

I would think, *A man like this should live in a utopian society, where money does not exist and people just get tickets for their hard work and a broad grin. Then I'd smile and think, Reggie would be giving the tickets away for nothing.* His heart was *that* big.

Years later, Reggie called and invited me to his daughter's wedding. Camberwell High Street is not fashionable like Berkley Square and doesn't take kindly to large cars or chauffeurs.

The wedding was like most weddings — predictable, repetitive, inconsequential. The pastors usually look as if they have another appointment and want to get it over with.

On this day, the most unlikely young people, the groom, the best man and the ushers, were dressed uncomfortably in ill-fitting tuxedoes which had been worn so many times that you could clearly see that the threads were stressed and the silks were faded.

But Reggie's daughter and son-in-law were getting married, and he was — moreso than usual — beaming.

After the wedding ceremony, Reggie took me to a house, which was clearly, to him, like a palace. It was one of those row houses on a narrow street which only had room for a horse and cart years before. He proudly showed us the home he had given "the kids" for a wedding present. I kept my feet close together on the runner as we climbed up the stairs to the second floor, not wanting to mark the wooden floor on either side of the carpet, which he'd had polished to a shine.

We looked at the living and dining rooms, "scooped out of a saucepan," as the saying goes, but newly furnished. We surveyed the bedroom and the teaspoon kitchen. Reggie was so proud of all that he showed me — it glowed on his face. He had done the very best he could.

As he displayed his world I thought, *Out of the little he possesses — has any man given more than what he's given?*

I would leave that day, and remember Reggie fondly as someone who taught me that you can be a decent human being without much money.

Reggie would disappear from my life, along with his quirks, his mistakes, and his mixed manners…and his wonderful simplicity. He had no masters, or mansions, but he had his independence, and freedom of action and thought. He was a grubby, bloody marvelous human being. He was honest, he loved people, and had no fear. He had the one thing so many of us strive for all our lives and never attain.

He had peace.

If only that simple kind of existence had been enough for me. I was soon to find out it wasn't. Another door would open and my path would shift again.

Chapter Eight

THE CHRISTMAS CLUB

Gradually, my father recovered and came back to work. He took over his business again, with his own ideas.

He never said, "Thanks, Son, for keeping things going and giving up your legal career." My ideas and my leadership were not acknowledged.

My mother, who would have thought that I was wonderful if I did nothing in my life, constantly told me, "You're a good boy." But from my father – not a word.

I very quickly felt like a fifth wheel. What was my place here in Dad's rag business now?

Fortunately, love and support came from another source. A very lovely one, in fact.

Valerie and I had been married for some time. She was very patient with me as, clearly, I was the type of man who was driven to work hard, leaving home very early and returning very late. From the beginning, she took that in stride.

We had met at a hotel in Bournemouth, a seaside resort in England I often visited with my grandparents, and we had quickly fallen in love. She was an art student, and at the time we met I was studying law. She was pretty and always spoke to me in a loving sort of way. When she looked at me, she was never distracted. She was also intelligent, but she never pushed herself or her opinions forward. Women loved her because she was not competitive, and she was the perfect team player. One of her most endearing charms was that she focused on people and their problems.

Now that Dad was back, Valerie and I talked a lot about the future and the work I was doing in my father's factory. In her eyes, my time there was over.

One morning, over a quick breakfast of eggs and toast, which I hastily threw down, she watched me silently until I looked up at her.

"What is it, Val," I asked, pausing.

"It's not you, Joseph."

"What, love? What's not me?"

"The rag business, of course. You know that, don't you? And now that your father is back you know there's no place for you there, and you must move on now."

I put down my fork, clasped my hands and looked into her clear eyes. I felt nothing but love and concern from her. She not only had my back, she was usually right.

Inwardly I did know it was time to pack up working in the rag business and start something for which I'd been educated.

"I want to wait a bit and be sure Dad is going to be strong enough to make a full comeback. It will only be a matter of time."

Valerie sighed. "Fair enough. Then you'll go back to the law."

It was half-statement, half-question.

I took in a breath before answering. "Things are different now," I offered. What I meant, but didn't say, was that *I* was different.

"What does that mean?" she replied. She'd stood up to start clearing the breakfast things, but her eyes had never left mine.

How could I tell her? She'd married a man who was aiming at a career in law. Now that man had changed. But that man didn't know *how* to tell her how he'd changed or *why*. That man didn't know why himself.

Truly, it was like I'd lost track of the man I had been. Some sort of inner drift had happened in the time I worked at Dad's business. I didn't want a legal career anymore. This was the impact of everything that happened since my father entered the hospital with a heart attack and I'd had to commandeer his world.

Only later, in deep reflection I had no time or skill for at that moment would I understand some things.

First, I hadn't so much as commandeered the world of rag men and dark deal makers. It had subtly commandeered me.

Second, there was a driving force buried so deep in me I couldn't see it. It stemmed from this: Some of the men in the rag business still disliked me, because I hadn't been able to honor all of my father's debts. And in my mind's-eye, whenever I saw their smirking faces, whenever I heard their sarcastic voices in my head, I winced. I felt small and petty. I hated that feeling. It's called dishonor. Shame. For so many years I'd wanted to be honored. Now there were people in this world who could look at me and say, "That man did not live up to his word. He is nothing in my eyes."

Something inside could not let that be.

"I" is like an axis, around which spins the world of many men. I would not be dishonored. *I* could not tolerate the feeling of shame that came with that. I would be somebody – a man everyone would look up to.

Maybe it was the old, aggressive spirit rising up in me in response, but I felt that my whole personality had been invaded and I wanted to answer back to my detractors. And in the world I lived in, there was only one way to do that.

Make more money.

By this time, my old value system had been flattened. There is no other way to say it: The rag trade was a sleazy industry; that's just how it was. I dealt with scavengers all day, and a good portion of the men selling us stuff had likely stolen it and I knew that but there was never any way to tell who and what.

If I had thought about how I'd changed since leaving the legal profession it would have been this way: it was as though I had been in a bad car accident, and my spirit had been injured and I was in shock. I had no one to blame for this, as I'd gone along with every little under-the-table dealing and kept my mouth shut, when it was likely hot goods were passing through our hands.

What had crept in was this – a skill at justifying things. That was certainly not something I wanted to say to my wife. In fact, I'd more or less buried it from my own mind.

I'd learned enough about this world at the lower end to know that everybody was doing everybody. The guy who brought in a questionable lot had been kicked or stepped on by someone else. It was his way of evening the score in a world below the legal system. No one was going to stand up for the wrongs done to him, so he had to even things up himself – a sort of frontier justice system.

That had made sense to me from the beginning. No, it didn't seem "right" in the ultimate scheme of things. But neither I nor these people were living and operating in an ideal world. We were fighting our way through a very gritty, tough, dog-eat-dog world.

Somewhere in the back of my head I'd accepted as my operating truth this concept:

This is not the world in which the spiritual values I'd learned from my grandfather could hold up. In the world I had to live in, different rules applied.

With my parents' wellbeing and with my honor and dignity at stake I no longer felt as if I had time or the luxury to think about higher purposes again, or to figure out what I was "meant" to do with my life.

What Valerie didn't say, though she might have, was that I was not exactly the same man she had married. And it was true.

When I left for work that morning, however, I felt as if I had to find something new to do with myself, now that Dad was back. But I felt a bit lost… again.

Some weeks later, Valerie – who never pressed me about my work — pressed me again. "Please go back to the law, Joseph. Not so long ago that was all that mattered to you. Why are you letting those dreams go? You hate going to work every day, and that's a bad thing."

I stood up and carried my tea cup to the kitchen sink. I couldn't answer her. I was angry at what had happened to my father. Every day this anger rippled through my mind. My motivation had been drastically changed by these circumstances.

Valerie was exactly right about one thing: I hated going to work every day, now that Dad was back and I was a third left shoe at the back of the closet. I might have left the rag trade sooner than later, had it not been for one small event.

In those days, in the poorer parts of London, people joined a Christmas Club. They would save a little money out of their paycheck each week. This was a self-imposed discipline so that at Christmas, they would get their savings back with a small amount of interest, and have money for food for the Christmas season and presents for their children.

When I first heard of it I liked the idea. I liked it very much. I realized this was a way for that 10-year-old boy to get the new bike and that pretty young girl to get the beautiful dress her parents could not otherwise afford.

So I printed up business cards and started offering them around. I began by knocking on people's doors, folks who had known my family through the rag trade over many years. They liked the idea of saving money for Christmas, too.

Every week thereafter I picked up each saver's money at regular intervals. Most of my customers were factory workers, their wives and friends. I used their money to provide loans at interest. All the loans were risky and unsecured. But the rate of interest on the loans was high and usually made up for the loss caused by those who did not pay back.

Behind the Christmas Club, though, lay another idea. And a new goal.

The concept of the Club originally came to me from a tailor shop on the High Street in Camberwell, a few minutes from my father's factory. I saw the ad in the window. You could buy a suit from them on a twenty-week repayment program. That worked out fine for the tailors. If you borrowed money for, say, a suit at 15 percent flat and repaid it weekly over 20 weeks, the actual interest rate on an annualized basis would be much higher. The reason was that the borrower paid back every week, but the interest didn't go down and the lender could use the repayment again and again.

Suddenly, something made sense.

This is how money lenders make their money.

The concept seized my imagination. This was what I could do with my future.

So, while the Christmas Club would benefit everyone who took part in it – and kids could have a better Christmas – making money, and a lot of it, could benefit *me*.

From that day on I went to work in a tiny office in the rag factory, with just enough room for a small desk, an occasional basket of rags, and two chairs. But in my mind's-eye I saw myself as someone else now. I'd proven I could be very tough at making deals, and that I had no problem asking, even pressing people, for money. I would be the man at the top of the heap again, not the bottom of it. Not the top of the legal world, though. I would climb my way up the financial world. I would be Joseph Caplan, financier.

It occurred to me from the outset that the only difference between a Christmas Club runner – which I was about to become — and a banker was volume. Running a Christmas Club would always have its financial limits. I could only make just so much money with it. I wanted more. And I knew who I could team up with to get it.

Everyone knew Sidney Keston. He had been in the rag trade all of his life. He was old enough to be my father — a bit of a heavy-set person, with kind eyes. He always looked tidy and clean shaven, and his suits were a bit loose fitting, but he was not the sort of man who cared about looking spruce. He had a way about him that gave people confidence, because he was honest. Just as I'd learned from Reggie that people can detect a buoyant and unbeatable spirit, I learned from Sidney that people can detect a deeply founded honesty. It was in the eyes, and in the conversation. If you asked anyone in the East End of London to select the most trusted man in the neighborhood Sid would have won hands down.

If you were going to run a business in which you asked people to trust you with their money you needed someone like Sid to front it.

Sid and his son operated a rag factory and he had his own Christmas Club. Surrounded by so many people, all of whom had a need for one thing or the other, he had also become a money lender. Sid didn't know about licenses, and you needed one to be legitimate. It was one thing to slip some bales of rags or a truckload of scrap metal under the table. No one was looking, really. But handling money – that was a very different matter. You had to be a different kind of person to be a money man.

I made my pitch to Sid: my bit of education joined up with his people-person skills — how could we lose?

Suddenly Sid and I were in the Christmas Club business. Together, we built quite a sizable portfolio of business people, some bosses, some workers without realizing that what we had created was a mini-bank without checks.

Our little money lending business rapidly took shape. We put our customer base together; more people saving, more people borrowing. This was the beginning of a relationship which would carry on for years. I would learn a lot about being a money man.

First and foremost Sid taught me that to be in the world of finance you had to understand people's relationship with their money. Everyone has a certain way they think about, feel about, and relate to their money. It was important to know this about them. I made a mental note of that.

Sid didn't just collect money from people; he became a part of their lives. People simply told him everything about themselves. They confided in him and confessed to him. He was like a priest without the collar. He always knew what was going on in people's lives. People trusted him completely. Sid knew if a man was going wrong or if a man gambled. He knew where that woman went, where the man went — and where their money went.

I made a mental note: Team up with the right people — the ones who can give you entree into their world. If you want access to their money, know and understand what makes them tick. Talk to them and gain their trust at a very personal level, and they will trust you with their money.

The other thing I learned was that you had to be the right kind of person in order to gain access to people's money. Find the right people to associate with and you find your way into the right pockets. I made another mental note.

Sid was, in fact, a legend in the East End. He was the only money lender you would ever meet who gave as much as he got and earned every penny he made without a bad word or an enemy. People loved to give him money. They knew their savings were safe. He had compassion, a deep understanding of how people lived and died and a great desire to see people happy and successful. He was a genuine person, which in all generations, at all levels of business, is rare. There was no jealousy or envy in this man. He drank more whiskey with his many brief social contacts than you could ever imagine, but it seemed to have no effect on him. He found time for people's funerals, as well as their weddings.

Sid figured so prominently in my life that there will never be adequate words to describe him. He was a man of character who looked ordinary and spoke in an ordinary manner. I looked up to him because he did what he did with integrity. I made a third note.

Sid was the very embodiment of the word *respect*. However successful or unsuccessful people were, he never put them down he just gently gave them advice. Most people will tell you that respect and trust have little place in business. The old image of two people shaking hands and being bound by an agreement is just for the movies and for days gone by, but for Sid it was his way, and in the coming months and years I would do very well by doing things his way.

Now I was on my out of the rag trade, and that was all that mattered to me.

One day, in 1960, I moved my modest activities from the rag factory to Coleman Street in the City of London. The rent was £10 per week. I was ambitious, eager... and scared... all at the same time.

My cousin, David Share became my partner in what we initially called *The Share Loan Club*. We feverishly collected the Christmas Club contributions and turned that money over, and over and over again. It was easy to lend money, especially to people in the rag trade, because they always needed money and they didn't care how much they paid for it.

Valerie, amazing woman that she was, put up with my penchant for hard work and long hours. I worked every hour that it was light and many hours when it was dark.

As for business acumen – well, I was learning fast.

I never knew a time when it was hard to lend, even when bank credit was easy. Ordinary workers and even bosses felt more at ease dealing with people they could talk to — people who drink shots of whiskey with them after work and knew them by their first name.

In fact, the loan club didn't do very well at the outset. We had to pay ourselves something to keep our homes going. If we weren't making much money, we weren't losing it either. There were no other employees. I did the typing and answered the telephone. David delivered checks and picked up checks.

Despite the struggle – another struggle in the long string I'd faced — a new sense of life started to take hold of me again. I had something to work for and a new hope for the future.

Soon, the Christmas Club was doing well. But I was already thinking ahead – far beyond Camberwell. In another part of London, the financial district, lay my future. I could taste it. We'd hardly made a dent in what could be done with our little venture. How could we make this grow? – that was the question.

The City seemed to hold my answer.

The City is the financial center of London, the equivalent of New York's Wall Street. Fortunes had been made, stolen, and lost here for centuries. I had no idea what I was going to do, but The City was where I knew we needed to be if we were going to be successful. Not just a little successful, but greatly successful. That was now my ambition. I felt that I'd lived twice over already by the age of 30. It had to come right. And making the leap out of East End to the City would put us in the right place to do the right kind of business.

The two-room office we rented to start our business was in an old building. It wasn't much to look at, but I was beyond determined. The Christmas Club wasn't growing fast enough for me, and a new ambition was taking hold.

I wanted to give money out – a lot more of it — and have some sort of legal protection while doing so. I discovered that to do this correctly, there were laws in England which made it mandatory for a person to take out a money-lending license in order to make loans legally. Otherwise, if forms were not signed and the borrower given a copy of those forms, he need not pay back one penny under the law. Hardly any of our clients knew this, but the risk bothered me greatly. I was working so hard; I didn't want to make a mistake and see it all blown away by an unscrupulous borrower.

With this in mind, I took the necessary legal steps and became a licensed money lender.

At the same time I began to learn about the occupants of this famous square-mile of London, known as The City. All the people around me were looking up to somebody who had a better job, or who was in a larger firm, or more important. Very quickly I learned what the financial establishment thought of a licensed money lender.

We loaned money to people, who for the most part, were eager to borrow. It is easy to criticize a money lender because the interest rates are very high. The risk of the money lender not getting his money back, however, is much greater than in traditional banking. This created a pressure inside me that began to occupy my mind. I had to provide for Valerie and me. And I had to *not lose.*

I concentrated on the movement of money. I'd had enough of everything else. I wasn't looking for people, places or things, I just wanted to put other people's money into the bank as fast as I could; three, four, even five times per day to meet checks, to save interest, or to give out a loan a day earlier.

One day, I had a discussion with a group called Independence Finance Company. Unlike us they did not have access to the general public. They had funds, but no market for those funds. Independence loaned us money based on a percentage of some of our loans, which they took as collateral. We hardly made any money doing this, but it made our balance sheet bigger and impressed our bankers.

That was a breakthrough.

I layered on the cement, so to speak, and grabbed at the next brick I needed to build my career.

A career in finance. There it was. Dad could have the rag business back. The path I'd been searching for ever since leaving the world of law. I'd found myself again.

Now I was in the money game— right up to my eyes in it. Maybe I was at the bottom of the heap again, needing to climb another slope up to success, but I was ready for this. More than ready. Hungry for it.

I knew just one thing. Whatever it took we had to get bigger, and I was beginning to see ways to make that happen.

And so, driven by renewed ambition, I was eager to take another step forward into the business world.

Or, as I would come to think of it later, *the abyss.*

Chapter Nine

THE CLIMB BEGINS

My life was now wrapped around this thought: I would become big in the world of finance.

The odd thing was, I had complete confidence I could do it. I was very aware that I was a novice… but at some core level I had the confidence that I could figure out how to make the world of finance work for me and make a great deal of money at it.

Looking back, I believe it was more of a confidence in my own work ethic and utter tenacity. When I made up my mind to do something or be something I went for it and didn't quit until I'd reached my goal. So it wasn't *hubris* – or not only that — it was knowing myself, really. I was a fighter and I knew I would fight for what I wanted. And I was tired of waiting for my chance to prove myself. At the base of it I just had a special kind of hunger – to *be* someone.

I was ready. Now, after all the years of waiting, what I valued most was personal achievement. Somewhere in the back of my mind, the goal of leveling the playing field for people who lived close to the paycheck was still there – but I was unaware that a new goal was subtly taking over. All I did know was that now there would be no stopping me.

In November 1961 I made a first move toward traditional banking by purchasing a small company for £21,000. The company was then known as London and County Advance and Discount Company, and to swing the deal I borrowed £5,000 in my own name and £5,000 in the name of two relatives, with the balance to be paid later.

It was an inauspicious beginning, for sure. There wasn't much, on the surface of it, to indicate success was "in the cards."

We were now located at Howard Street, Strand, London, closer to the financial district for sure, but we might as well have been lightyears from the respectable financial institutions.

For one thing, London and County was a few thousand pounds in the red. The loans averaged £50 to £60 per person, repayable over 12 to 24 months at money-lending rates – not exactly a money-making scenario. I purchased it partly for the name, and partly because it had been established as a company in 1869 and "vintage" rang a bell of confidence. It was really nothing more than a very small, old-fashioned money-lending company that was going nowhere.

For another, there was a great divide between a money lender and a banker and somehow that failed elevator highlighted the difference. Banking was respectable and money-lending was contemptible in the eyes of the public — and certainly in the eyes of the City.

Also, our office on the third floor back was as much as we needed – at least it was a start and a bigger office than the last one – and our only real contact with the banking world were the bank messengers, who had to climb three flights of stairs for two weeks because the elevator was out of order.

Finally, there was this: I didn't know anything much about banking.

This is where something else came into play, however: I'd come to trust my own instincts. Somewhere inside I just *knew* this was the platform from which I would launch my rise to success. And one by one, ideas for expansion and improvement began to emerge, as if from nowhere.

From the outset I realized the only possibility of further growth was by offering savings accounts, and issuing check books to customers. To make that happen, however, we had to relinquish the title of licensed money lender, with the accompanying disadvantages. If you don't have a money lending license or a banking license, a borrower is not obligated to repay a penny: that was the law.

I took the plunge, like a man jumping off a diving board without knowing if there was any water in the pool beneath.

In May 1962, we abandoned our money-lending license, which laid our breast bare to attack. We had to qualify for a banking license, which was issued by the government. I took this risk, knowing that from a legal point of view we were now in a no-man's-land, and all our money as well as the money people had invested with us was in jeopardy. The law had not provided for anyone moving from traditional money lending towards conventional banking.

We printed our own checks for the first time. To start with, only a few customers accepted them, because they were different from the well-known household banking names.

But as word spread about what we were doing, more customers began opening checking accounts.

And there we were. At risk… and plunging ahead.

From this first bold step to prove myself in the financial world, our business began to expand at a rapid rate. Inwardly, a new image of myself started to come clear.

My next step was to focus our vision on small businesses. Many small businessmen were uncomfortable sitting in the office of bank managers at big banks who had rules and conditions. Often, the bank manager wanted to know a client's life history for something as small as a £1,000 pound loan. For many people we became the alternative to a traditional bank.

As our reputation for working with the everyday man and woman spread our customers relaxed and felt more and more comfortable with us. By sheer gut-instinct we had tapped into a new market which was potentially large indeed. We did not have the funds necessary to meet the demand for customer loans, however, as we were struggling just to keep up with the weekly cash-flow. On one occasion, we had to empty our own, as well as the secretary's pockets, in order to meet a customer's need to draw his money out in cash.

Still, our profits had begun to move upwards – rapidly — and people were taking notice. The press, which somehow caught wind of our quick climb was calling me "Midas."

The simple secret was this: In our service to the small business owner and the common man we were unique. And despite what the press was saying, the fact that

I could offer a way to even the playing field for the so-called "little man" gave me satisfaction. Still….

To be called "Midas" helped the new image I had of myself to come into much clearer focus. I liked the sound of it for one thing. Midas was, of course, a king, and one with an incredible gift, at that. With his touch, he could turn anything into gold. One of the things you want in business is to be able to project an image and create a sort of mystique about yourself. It has a sort of mesmerizing effect on people. They start to see you as the image you project.

I wish I had known at the time that you can't let yourself get lost in what the press is saying about you, weal or woe. To do so is to lose sight of who you really are beneath the bigger-than-life business image you project. If this happens you – the real you and every good thing you live for – can become lost.

The pace of business was quickening now, and I had to be laser-focused on London and County.

"Joseph, will you be home for dinner tonight?" Valerie asked one morning as I was leaving for another long day.

"Not likely. I have meetings all afternoon and one early this evening."

Our son, Justin, was a toddler, and she looked at him as she spoke again. Not one to nag, she simply stated a truth. "We miss you, Joseph – Justin and I."

In my mind, everything I was doing was for them, and while I wasn't perturbed at her statement, it did trouble me… a bit. I thought, *She has no idea what it's taking to make this venture a success. Molding a business is like building a house. Every brick has to go on one after another. If you miss a brick, there is a gaping hole.*

"What about this weekend, Joseph? Will you be free to spend time with us this Saturday? If there's nice weather we should take Justin to the park. You know how he loves to run."

I sighed. "I will try," I said. "I'll really do my best."

Then I walked out to another intensely full day. Knowing what every entrepreneur knows. You want to be there for those you love. But you are torn, because you also have to be there when the telephone rings to answer it. If you want to build up a business from nothing, there's no time off, because if a potential customer can't reach you they will call the next guy in line….

If I had been honest with myself – yes, I was committed to success for the sake of my family, and to help so-called "lower end" customers, but also for another reason that was becoming all-important, as well.

There are those who make a case for keeping the pressure out of life, but they don't build empires. You have to be discontented and hungry to build something. You have to want it so badly that when you go to sleep at night your brain is whirring and your head pounding. And when you wake breakfast is unimportant, because all you can think about is the first phone call you need to make, deals that need to be made and money that must come in.

And so my life was caught up chasing after an image that sometimes rose from the recesses of my mind.

Valerie, I believe, sensed a subtle change in me. Quietly, she urged me to move in a better direction than the one I was planning – toward a goal I began to voice. She did this without demanding. Her gentle words were given with so much love that even if I thought she was wrong I sometimes heeded her advice.

But as it would turn out, not often enough.

And the image of the man I wanted to become continued to become clearer.

Whereas I was "just a money lender" to the big financial people in The City, the press had called me "Midas," and I saw myself standing at the top, respected by the London financial world.

Enter, Trevor Pepperell.

At the time we met, Trevor was administering two small Savings and Loans and I was also fascinated by the way he did business – mainly because he was a study in contradictions.

For one thing Trevor had a great intellect, but not a "business brain." He could also work harder than anyone – that is, when he worked, which he very seldom did. He was positive in his thinking, positive in his thoughts, positively ambitious, yet I never saw him sit at a desk through all the time I knew him, except to answer the telephone. All in all, I'd never met anyone in business who was so disinterested in money or material things who, nonetheless, had a greater ability to make money.

For another thing, Trevor had allowed a strange confluence of voices to influence how he did business. On one hand, he came from a Quaker background and held a strong human ethic. On the other hand, contrary to his Christian heritage, he was constantly focused on getting advice and direction from someone he called "The Witch," a woman who read tarot cards and dictated his approval or disapproval of major business decisions over the telephone.

Now the fact is, I didn't take Trevor's strange habit seriously. I didn't see the fact that I ignored his affiliation with "The Witch" for what it was – a step away from my own spiritual moorings in the Judeo-Christian tradition and a willingness to play hunches perhaps a little too loosely… and more than that a belief in my own ability to "scry the signs," as it were and chart my own course. In a different way, perhaps, I was doing exactly what Trevor was doing: In my desire to rise quickly I was willing to make decisions more on speculation than on a sound foundation.

And so, Trevor became an influence, a huge influence in my life, as well as a friend. He was ambitious for the sake of achievement, and if I slowed down, or showed caution, he pushed or pulled and got me on the move again. We could have saved ourselves a lot of trouble and disappointment if we had been more circumspect and diligent.

Not long after we met, Trevor hired me to be the Receiver of the Savings and Loan. My job was to collect the money due from delinquent mortgages. I would work with the accounts receivable in order to bring accounts of those who owed money up to date.

The two Savings and Loans he managed, the Eagle Building Society and the Law Mutual Building, were small and up to their eyes in arrears and administrative problems because he didn't administer. This suited my work ethic perfectly.

Now, county court forms for stamping, acknowledgements to the savings and loan, preliminary letters to borrowers, certified copies of borrower's accounts, as well as many other forms of documentation which are necessary in an institution ultimately controlled by government statutes — all of these documents burned through my typewriter with a fury. I began to bring in money for Trevor. Lots of it.

And not incidentally, a lot of money for me, as well. I was earning fees for collecting arrears that supplemented the financial side of my life, which I badly needed, and with no risk. To do something without risk, just by tearing the guts out of a typewriter was really worthwhile. I typed and typed and I kept on typing. Nothing distracted me. Every letter I sent out seemed to me to have that "Midas' touch" the press had identified, because the payments continued to pour in – back into Trevor's Savings and Loans and into my pocket, as well.

And here is the thing: Somewhere along the line at this point in my life I stopped looking at the names of the people I was chasing for money... stopped wondering what neighborhoods they came from, better or worse, and whether or not they were struggling to make a living like the men and women I'd come to care about at my father's rag business. The letters I wrote were not to *people*, per se, but to names on a list.

So it was that on my climb to the top I stopped caring about who or what had an influence on me, as long as that influence pushed me toward success. And I stopped thinking, really, about people at some fundamental human level. What did I care who they were, as long as they paid their mortgage arrears and I collected my fees?

Now, as payments came in I poured more and more collection letters into the mailbox with energy and enthusiasm. And I could feel it now – my climb to the top was accelerating.

What could go wrong?

Chapter Ten

ANOTHER BEND
IN THE PATH

When you are not keeping your eyes on a fixed point – whether that's a trail marker or a set of values – even the smallest encounter can pull you, slowly, slowly off-course.

The encounter with Raymond Nash was no small thing.

One day I received a call from someone, who asked in a throaty, superior tone, "Are you the Receiver?"

That was the term for a collections agent. "Yes, I am the Receiver," I replied.

"I have a message for you. Stop sending your letters or your right ear will be cut off."

I should have been scared, but instead I was indignant. Angry, I started to shout, "Who do you think…."

All I heard in return was a dial tone.

I was furious. The man must be mad. The court had appointed me. It was beyond my understanding that anyone could behave like this. I had official documents to show that I representing a bonafide business institution, protecting them from the problems brought about by mortgage borrowers who had not kept their payments up to date.

I went back to work and forgot about the call. And the letters demanding payment continued to fly out the door.

When the second call came a few weeks later, I was ready for the man.

"Why are you continuing to write letters?"

"I can assure you there is no question of ignoring the unpaid mortgages. This is a public savings and loan and I have been appointed receiver" —the sound of the word pleased me – "to protect its funds."

There was silence, and I sat back in my seat like a commanding officer who had issued an order.

The phone changed hands at the other end, and this time the voice said, "We're going to cut off both your ears. Go away."

I was legalistic, crisp, specific, determined, and unafraid. They did not know who they were dealing with. "Pay up," I said, and dropped the phone in its cradle.

The second call had identified the specific properties with which they were concerned. Far from deterring me, the registered letters poured out again, final demands, formal notices insisting that the defaulting mortgage holder must bring his account up to date or legal action would inevitably take place leading to foreclosure.

Later I would realize it was the challenge itself that helped to blind me to what came next. There are people who, when you wave a red flag at them, lose a measure of rationality and charge at it. I was one of those people.

Threaten me? I felt alive and excited, like I was fully in my element now.

Shortly after that, a meeting was hastily arranged. "The boss wants to see you," was all I was told, and given an address, day and time.

"The boss," it turned out, was a man who went by the name Raymond Nash. When I checked him out, what I learned gave me a moment's pause. "Nash" was born in Lebanon, and I would never learn his real name. I discovered later he was well known in certain quarters as business man with many "interests" and that he was feared by some, admired by others.

Something about having a face-off with Raymond Nash spelled success or failure to me. If I could go up against a shadowy and powerful man and win, I believed, I could face down challenge.

A few days later, I found myself sitting in the law offices of Shurman and Bindman. The office was, like all solicitor's offices, depressing and faceless. When I arrived, the room was already overcrowded with savings and loans representatives, clerks, and strangers.

I was on-edge, wanting very badly to *win*.

Twenty minutes after the scheduled time for the appointment with small talk abounding throughout the room, the door to the office was unceremoniously thrown open, wrenched against its hinges, as two large men stalked into the room. They took a quick look around, turned and nodded, and then "the boss" appeared.

Raymond Nash was dark complexioned, solid in his shoulders and his stance told you he had an immensely powerful build. His face was young and hard, with a firm jaw full of determination and authority.

"Which one of youse is the Receiver?"

"I am," I said boldly.

Everyone else in the room stared at their hands or fiercely studied bits of paper. Clearly, this was an off-the-record conversation that no one had witnessed.

Nash fixed a hard-eyed glare at me. For a moment, I felt like a student who had worked hard at his homework and had gotten it all wrong. Then he crossed the room, sat next to me. "Explain to me the job of a Receiver? And tell me how you have the guts to do what you do, when you have to deal with a guy like me."

He said the last two words very low voice, wanting me to know was something way beyond the ordinary with a guy *like him*.

This was it. Either I met his match or, I suspected, I really might wind up losing both ears.

I didn't miss a beat, having rehearsed my lines carefully. Staring him in the eye, clearly and concisely, I explained who I was and what I did. I carefully put the case before him, recalling my days as a barrister when I would try to impress a judge or jury with the logic of my arguments. If he owned all the properties, whatever names they were in, they must be worth a lot more than the mortgages.

As my closing line I said, forcefully, "A man in your position who claims to be the owner of so many houses should not be wasting your time letting arrears accumulate and running the risk of losing your properties by legal process. Which I assure you can happen."

Nash's eyes had left mine, and he was now staring straight ahead. Then without looking at me he suddenly stood up.

At least four other people also stood up with him. It was too unexpected, everyone waited expectantly.

He announced: "Me and the Receiver have settled everything."

Then he walked out of the room without looking back.

The Savings and Loan representatives sighed with relief and crowded around me to inquire what I'd said to him. The lawyers, who always assume that the law is on their side, lost interest in me completely and left, calculating their fees as they went along I'm sure.

I had won my first *big* financial battle.

Contact with Raymond Nash did not end there.

A couple of weeks later I was back in my office, when one of Raymond Nash's adjuncts called — this time, with a tone that was completely relaxed and light. "I say, old boy, you seem to hit it off with the boss the other day. He would like you to have lunch with him at his house on Reddington Road in Hampstead."

I wasn't all that enthusiastic. Noon was a bad time of the day to cross town. Mainly, I was still struggling my way toward earning a living to support Valerie, Justin and me, and usually didn't take a lunch break.

Nonetheless, I took down the details.

I am not quite sure why I took up the offer to meet Nash for lunch. He came from a shadowy world, though maybe that was it. Men like him can think that men in legitimate businesses were brought up in more genteel and civil circumstances and don't know how to play hard. Perhaps, having come from the world of the rag business, I wanted to show him – or myself – that I was no lightweight. He didn't intimidate me in the least.

I'd never been to Reddington Road in Hampstead before. The houses were large and unimpressive, and I found the place – an old Victorian that had seen much better days. The front garden was a shambles and faded curtains hung limply in the front windows. I didn't know what to expect.

As I approached the front door, a large servant who had no facial expression opened the door.

I walked in…very cautiously. The room was full of a mish-mash of furniture of many styles, all worn and faded, and also crowded with an over-abundance of other guests. Nash owned a good many properties, so why was he living here? An answer occurred immediately – *To keep a low-profile and draw no attention.*

The guests, who stared at me silently as I entered, seemed as miscellaneous as the furniture. Some were Middle Eastern but wore Western clothes, some wore wonderful Arab robes, and others were obviously English. Since the host was not yet in sight I took a moment to nod and murmur greetings – and to notice who was present.

There was a Member of Parliament present, who would subsequently become a cabinet minister. A tall man, he peered down at me and made me wonder, not for the first time that day, what he and I were doing there.

Suddenly one of the large servants banged on a gong. From out of the walls it seemed, "the boss" appeared, with a young, prepossessing Middle-Eastern man in an immaculately tailored Western-style suit at his side.

"The son of the King," muttered the adjunct, between his teeth, staring straight ahead.

We were ushered into the garden where a long table had been prepared. The guest of honor sat on the right of our host and I – to my great surprise – was seated on his left. Instantly, servants appeared with whole lamb on huge silver platters.

It was a magnificent sight to me, and I felt like I was entering a new world. There was other food I had never seen before, conversation I'd never heard before. I just wanted to listen and learn about things I'd never known before.

After lunch we were steered toward a large living area. I moved a little around the room. Then I made the comically tragic mistake of admiring the enormous clock resting on the living room mantle. It was eastern with ornate brass figures on it. I dissolved with embarrassment as with the greatest difficulty I persuaded my host to prevent two of his servants from removing the clock and presenting it to me as a gift.

This was indeed a whole new world, made up of powerful men making business deals over dramatic lunches. A far, far cry from soup in the lunchroom at the rag warehouse or a half-sandwich at my desk at the savings and loan.

I was mesmerized. For me, there was some kind of magnetism at work here. Had Nash known this? Was it a sort of test, to see how I would respond?

I left that day feeling very much in-charge of my world. But was I?

And what did he want from me?

The luncheon at Nash's home was the first of many meetings.

Perhaps he had recognized the hunger that was driving me – for money and the position of power it would give me.

I quickly became a familiar visitor of the household and was introduced to the spectacle of my host weight lifting and demonstrating his physical skill in a room that was fitted out like a small gym. Here, we talked about my career as a boxer back during my school days, my military training, and the rag trade. It seemed to me that Nash was impressed by the fact that I had fought hard to get where I was in life. That seemed to forge an otherwise unspoken connection.

And something else was going on in his head – but what that was I did not know.

I found out as time went by that Nash had a wife, an Irish woman, for whom he had no emotional connection really. He made it clear that he had liaisons with other women, for whom he had no feelings at all. For him, they were the alternative to food, work, or sport. Their existence was necessary, but not important in his plans. It was apparent that the exercise of power and the excitement it yielded offered all that he needed.

As I got to know Raymond, I realized he had a reserve of energy which knew no bounds, both physically and mentally. His life had a purpose and it was solely this:

To make money. A lot of money, for himself and a lot of other people.

In London, his empire included nightclubs, discotheques and gaming houses. They were symbols of his ability, controlled with power, determination and intolerance. They reflected a permanent purpose and personality that demanded respect, and obedience. His leadership was undoubted and unquestioned by those around him.

One time, with a few of our friends, Valerie and I visited a club in London called Beyond the Fringe. It was the kind of place where you paid a lot of money for not very good food and a smutty show, but it was fun. The club was packed and no tables were available. We were waiting to be seated when, quite suddenly the head waiter appeared.

"Are you Joseph Caplan?"

"I am," I replied, surprised. I had never been to this club before. How did he know me?

"Come with me," he said, turning on his heel.

We carefully excused our way through the crowd, following the head waiter to a table up front, where people were seated. The waiter leaned over, said something to one of the men – who looked at us curiously, then got up and motioned with the others to get up.

"Here is your table," the waiter said, turning to me.

Within seconds, the people had disappeared, the tablecloths were changed and bottles of champagne were placed in the center.

The head waiter whispered in my ear, "With the compliments of Mr. Nash, Sir."

The people with us seemed highly impressed that I had such "clout." As for me, I'd had no idea that Raymond owned that club.

I never asked him how he found out that I was there. I wasn't sure I wanted to know. And I continued to wonder what Nash wanted with the likes of me.

As was true with Trevor and his occult associations, my growing affiliation with Raymond Nash signified another step on my path. In one sense I felt I was headed up, into the world where powerful men made amazing business deals in back rooms. And in another sense – I would see much later – I was headed down, losing track of an inner compass of values that had once guided me.

If I'd had the least clue where this path was leading I would have taken a different course.

Chapter Eleven

"THE MAN"

A few months after I met Raymond Nash, he invited me to spend an evening with him. I had no interest in becoming like him, and could not fathom his interest in having a friendship with me. Clearly, he operated in a very different world, one that I did not want to move into. What I did not realize was that, just by our association he was having an influence on me.

When the Rolls Royce drew up at the restaurant address I had been given Raymond stepped out accompanied, as usual, by two personal body guards. I was surprised to see them dismissed, together with the Rolls, and relieved in a way to see Nash. This was Soho, an area of London that accommodated drugs, prostitution and various types of subcultures I knew little about.

At the table that evening, Nash's conversation was animated and difficult to keep up with. Like so many powerful men, he liked to talk and explain, leaving little room for reply or discussion. I tried to stay interested, but was more fascinated by watching the way people doted on him.

It was clear to me that the waiters were especially attentive to Nash. He seemed to glower at them as they approached the table, as though he suffered their existence and plates were moved very carefully and quickly on and off the table.

It didn't surprise me as we left the restaurant that Nash was not given a bill and did not ask for one. As we moved towards the exit, the head waiter nearly slid on his backside to get to the door and open it for him. The waiter's eyes were riveted on my host until he was well past him, ahead of me and out on the pavement step. I was dismissed politely with, "Good night, Sir. Thank you, Sir," and unseeing eyes.

Everything everyone said to Nash, and the way everyone deferred to him said it clearly: Raymond Nash was "the Man."

And everything those same people said and did in relation to me said: "…and you are not the Man."

If this was one of the points Nash was trying to make by demonstrating his power to me, he'd made it quite strongly.

It was dark now, as we walked along the Soho streets together Raymond said little. He seemed preoccupied, and also eager to show me something.

I felt a sense of apprehension.

After a five-minute walk I saw a building with a cinema-style ticket booth and we turned rapidly into a foyer, which was small and crowded. Suddenly, he had disappeared through the double doors of the building.

I told the human wall in front of me that I was accompanying him. They stared at me without interest from a great height. After a moment, someone came out and spoke to them, and the human wall gave way to a door that opened to let me into a much more private inner room.

And there I was – wherever *this* was.

It wasn't easy to see much, as the room was dimly lit, there were about 60 young men and women packed onto a dancefloor beneath the flickering chandelier lights. Pounding music was throbbing from a kiosk set on a small platform in the middle of a large room. Everyone was rolling around in time with the music, or leaning against the walls, entering that extraordinary world of intimacy that arrives with the night.

Everyone was ogling someone, and everyone was drinking something. Some of the girls were leaning on shoulders. Some of the boys were staring at butts. They were carefree and emancipated and for all of them, there was no outside. I saw

Raymond talking to the girls in the kiosk and I walked toward him squeezing past the couples dancing. Most of the girls looked as though the messiah had come. Most of the boys looked as though they had conquered Troy.

The noise was loud, the lights were low. The heat was unbearable and smoke filled the air. I found myself wondering if I should even be there, but I quickly dismissed that thought because I wanted to be there. For a brief moment, I found myself seized in the arms of a girl who looked desolate and abandoned.

What was I doing here?

To my relief I saw Raymond, standing at a flight of stairs. He indicated that I should follow him. It suddenly became clear that the weeks of lunch and dinner meetings had all been in the interest of checking me out. And there was no doubt that some sort of initiation had begun.

I extricated myself from the forlorn girl and followed Raymond upstairs.

On the upper floor, we passed room after room of gaming tables. All roulette — *no chemin de-fer*, no chips, cash only. Every money gatherer was a woman and every player was a man. No women at all were playing at the tables. Raymond was studying my face inquiringly. It became clear to me that he had something on his mind.

"Well, what do you think, Joseph?"

I've never seen anything like this before. I knew what he was looking for – my moral reaction. Yet I found I could not tell him what I was thinking.

I was conscious of the fact that the gambling I was looking at was illegal. It was clear to me, from the tense atmosphere at the tables, and the appearance of the players, that what was at stake in most cases, was a week's salary, perhaps the wife's savings or borrowed money. Most of them would be losing. Some would win, but they would come back again and become losers. It was quick, it was easy, no one would see them there, the soft drinks were free, no alcohol. It was hot and exciting.

"It's fascinating," I replied, remaining intentionally vague.

Raymond smirked. "The girls like to stare at the money, watch the men sweat with excitement, take their jackets off, take their sweaters off and suffer. It gives the girls sexual excitement. You see that one?"

He pointed with a slight movement of his hand towards a girl sucking soda through a straw. "She waits for me every night, whether I get here or not. In every place, there is a girl for me."

He visibly drew back his broad shoulders as he said that, smiling with satisfaction.

I thought of Valerie at home, and my little boy. I had not done anything to violate Valerie's trust in me, nor would I. But I felt uneasy.

As we walked by the girl to leave the room, I saw her look down as though she were a starlet brushed over by the producer at an audition.

On we went with the tour, and Raymond continued to glance at me to gauge my reaction – which I held in check, fighting to keep any expression off my face.

Why did I care what this man thought about his endeavors? In fact, I had crossed the line in the past in minor ways – or at least that's how I'd thought of trading in obviously stolen goods. I'd justified it by telling myself that was the way business was done. That it was none of my affair where everything came from. I wasn't the policeman or the priest or rabbi. So Nash's game was different than mine. What right did I have to judge him? Still, I wondered: What did he have in mind by bringing me here to test me in this way?

As Nash led me on and on, not only through this building but others, I couldn't keep track of the myriad of rooms. I guessed there were three or four terraced houses tight together and inter-linked by passages and stairways cut through outer walls. Eventually, we came to a doorway, and Nash ushered me inside.

"This the control room," he said, smiling.

Seated at tables were about a dozen men, busily writing out data on legal pads. From every one of his units, he explained, whether it was gambling, discos or nightclubs, the returns were telephoned-in here to this control room at regular intervals.

"Each night of the week has a different intake pattern. We know about how much income to expect. If anything was wrong, if the numbers aren't right, my managers know instantly. If anything looks wrong, my men are quickly at the scene."

I nodded, realizing how many thousands, or tens of thousands, of pounds came into Nash's hands every single night. When I looked at him, he was beaming, clearly very proud of the range and efficiency of his system.

I was very aware, as he turned his eyes to me – with the smile now gone – that he had trusted me by showing me this place. And somewhere in the back of my mind I was also aware of those first threats that had been made by his lieutenants. *Open your mouth and we will cut your ears off.*

Throughout the rest of the evening, we moved from place to place and the gambling scenes repeated themselves in one form or another again and again. Finally, the tour was over.

I waited for Nash to say something, anything, about why he had showed me the secret heart of his operations. No explanation was offered.

A week later, we met at Nash's home. He offered me everything that most young men dream about. Women, wine, unlimited money, authority, travel, an opportunity to use all my legal knowledge and talents assisting him to keep control of his business and expand it further.

It was obvious, however, that he would also control me.

Here was a Rubicon. By crossing it, I knew, I would not be able to return. If I was in I could never get out.

I gave Nash my answer – carefully and respectfully, but clearly. It wasn't so much that I came from a different culture, that of a barrister and a would-be banker, and wanted to follow my own ambitions. That was part of it, of course. It was simply that I knew that his way of life and the world he represented was not for me and Valerie and never could be.

When I got back home to our modest apartment in St. John's Wood, Valerie would greet me at the door, brush my cheek with hers, take my hand, usher me in as though I was a guest.

I looked at her and thought, I am sure that I can't be part of Nash's world, however profitable.

Nothing would transpire from our relationship — not in terms of doing business together. Nash continued to live in his world of illegitimate business and I pressed further into the world of legitimate banking and investments. I could have moved in his direction and enjoyed all the benefits that flowed from his exciting life, but our worlds were far apart. And other than a strange connection of friendship that remained, my ambitions would lead me down a different path.

I wanted to be my own master.

Something did happen because of my contact with Raymond Nash, however. Seeing his world, something had rubbed off. An attitude. A bit of desire. I'd loved seeing how the room focused on him when he walked in. I loved the thought that a man could be, not only successful, but a big man in the eyes of others. I didn't need or want to be showy, but the idea of being "the man" had definite appeal.

And something else had taken place. A secretiveness had taken hold. I'd become used to making decisions alone. I was never interested in Trevor's witch, and now I never confided my doings to Valerie either. That meant I was no longer allowing people who were closer to my past and closer to my old way of thinking and being to comment on my decisions and actions.

At the same time I was allowing myself to spend time with more and more people – not just Nash, but others in world of legitimate business — whose thinking and lifestyle would have strong influences on me. If everyone we meet is, in a way, a kind of signpost, pointing to a way we should think, act, and be, then many signs and signals were coming at me, from free-thinking and powerful people whose words and actions said:

"Life can be whatever you want to make it. Whatever success you want is within your reach."

The gravitational pull to people who thought and lived like this – with eyes fixed on power and wealth — was now irresistible. In my own way, with my own type of empire, I wanted to be "the Man."

Chapter Twelve

THE GOLDEN DREAM

Meanwhile the money-lending business was growing. I was busy putting money and people together from morning until night. We moved to more prestigious offices at Nos. 2 and 3 Norfolk Street, in the Strand neighborhood of London. Now, for the first time, we occupied ground floor premises. We looked like a bank: We had a large counter with deposit slips and other banking paraphernalia, and we were handling other people's money. Just like real bankers.

As the messengers from the major banks came in every day, they looked around in disbelief at the new premises.

"I admire your pluck," said the National Provincial Bank messenger. "Good luck to you."

He had no idea the kind of "pluck" it was taking to build this business. The lengths I felt I had to go to.

Sometime earlier, Raymond Nash had introduced me to a man named Peter Rachman who wanted to sell me one of his businesses. I can remember my first meeting with him as clearly as if it were today. We met in the large lounge of the Grosvenor House Hotel in Park Lane, an area of London which houses the most expensive nightclubs, restaurants, and hotels.

The waiter indicated to me which entrance Rachman would be entering from. When he arrived he was preceded by body guards who studied the area with experienced eyes before he appeared.

Then I saw him. And recoiled a bit.

He was a small man with a pinched face. His head was bald from the center to the sides, with the fringe around the side. He wore horn-rimmed glasses and he had eyes that could burn a hole in a piece of metal. His suit was well fitted and his speech was extremely demanding. When I heard him speak, I wanted to listen to everything he said. I knew I would be hard pressed not to agree with his suggestions even if I didn't like them.

Rachman's eyes darted around the room. He was restless. I imagined he moved at great speed from one place to another to clinch deals, issue unpleasant orders and accomplish what most men would be ashamed of. Peter was surrounded by an air of mystique. He was always under surveillance but avoided any clash with the authorities.

His home was on Winnington Road in Hampstead, London, where the houses were large and expensive. Rachman had earned the dubious title of leading slum landlord in London and was credited with many other fringe activities that surrounded this way of life.

Everything to do with this man made me feel uncomfortable, even though I was young and eager to do almost any kind of business which would advance my name and make money. So I would keep my distance, even if I wanted access to his money.

Though we felt just like bankers what we were doing was different – and that was starting to gain a lot of attention. We talked more about business and less about rules and regulations and the word was out: If you want to do business talk to Caplan and his people. Because of that customers were now coming and going all day every day.

To keep up, I was working every minute of every day, too. I was excited and didn't stop. Together with my team, we were making things happen and I could taste success.

The truth is, what we had going for us at this early stage was, in a sense, "window dressing."

London and County had been incorporated in 1869, which gave us the air of an old, established institution. Playing off that, we found a large, vintage portrait in an old art shop in the Portobello Road Antique Market in London of a gentleman of about forty or fifty years old – stately and important-looking. This we hung in the foyer, in the splendor of his 19th-Century frame, and promoted him to the role of "founder." A number of customers told me that there was a likeness between him and me, assuming that I was somewhere down the family line.

Though we looked the part of an established bank, what we needed was more capital – lots of deposits, and more stature.

Here is where my ambition found an edge to walk. It was risky, but men like Nash had shown me that if you want to get somewhere fast you take risks.

Here was the edge: We had no license and no credentials as a bank. The truth is, we were in a legal no-man's land. Even so – this part was legal — we began to advertise for deposits, offering a little above the interest that the big banks paid. To do so, we circulated millions of deposit forms in a mass mailing, together with postage-paid return envelopes.

Overnight, the return envelopes poured in, filled with deposit slips and checks.

Opening these envelopes every day was one of the most exciting experiences we ever had. All this meant we had more money to lend out, and suddenly we were on a rapid-growth curve. Soon we were able to give out more overdrafts and this led to larger secured loans, which told me that profits were on the way.

Now we were really ready to take off.

The Corporation Act granted banking licenses to companies which had reached a certain level of bona fide banking activity. In due course, we acquired no less than four banking licenses – because now there were four divisions active in the financial markets and earned the right to have their own license. This recognition by the Inland Revenue permitted the company to pay interest to depositors gross instead of deducting tax.

Which is exactly what people wanted!

With happy clients sending in others, with licenses now in place, I had now built a solid base for that empire that was starting to emerge from the mists of my dreams.

In 1966, very shortly after we began, we started making a profit and were ready for the next big step.

We acquired a controlling interest in G. Eberstadt & Company, which managed investment portfolios and dealt in foreign securities. London and County purchased Eberstadt because of its overseas connections mainly in Europe and North America. I saw this acquisition as another step in the direction of orthodox banking and ultimate recognition as a bank.

Just as important, I was introduced to someone who would become a legitimate and very powerful mentor. Someone I would grow to admire greatly.

One of the principals of G. Eberstadt & Company was Charles S. Warburg.

Charles was born in Hamburg at the turn of the 20th Century. The history and traditions of his banking family started in 1798 and will never end. Originally established in Hamburg as M.M. Warburg & Co., it was one of the most revered institutions in the world of banking. The Warburg family was particularly close to N.M. Rothschild & Sons in London in the middle of the 19th Century. The Warburgs had earned world-wide respect throughout the generations.

My pulse raced when I was first introduced to Charles Warburg. He was appointed to the board of London and County to keep oversight on our company after the acquisition. Charles would show me the meaning of the word banking in the orthodox sense – and how could you ask for a better mentor in the banking business than to be coached by one of the oldest, first families of finance in Europe? Beyond that, Charles was "old money" and old-world class all the way.

Finally, I had found a worthy influence — a man of great knowledge and distinction. I felt beyond fortunate.

Charles' personal lineage intrigued me.

His early childhood was one of great privilege, given the great wealth of his family. As he grew up in the street know as Warburgstrasse, (named after his father), in Hamburg, Germany, he became the natural heir to the bank which had been established for well over a century. Paul Warburg, one of his family members was a founder of the Federal Reserve Board in America.

At the outbreak of World War II, Charles was in England. He was interned on the Isle of Man, a small island off the English coast, until his parentage was established. Then he became an interpreter with the British Intelligence during the war. This was a man who loved and served Britain.

Perhaps the whole aura of the Warburg dynasty is summed up by a conversation which took place in the Vier Yahrezeiten Hotel following one of my business trips with Charles to Hamburg. We had just ordered drinks in the lounge from a waiter, whose wrinkled face, stooped shoulders, and gray hair reflected his age. He acknowledged the drink order in German.

"Yes, Herr Rothschild," the waiter acknowledged.

Charles replied in German, "My name is Warburg."

The waiter stepped back respectfully, gave a slight shrug of his shoulders and said, "The money is the same."

Not only did Charles Warburg's stature lend us class, it lent credibility, of course.

Charles Warburg was "a banker." A banker in London is someone who other people call a banker – because it is a reputation and a way of being, moreso than just a career. He was cautious and dignified and knew banking inside and out. It was some time before I could understand his initial reticence to offer insights and advice, and the truth is the relationship resulting from the acquisition his company did not immediately add anything to our financial growth.

What I did gain, immediately, was a glimpse into a world in which I now longed to create my own empire. If Nash's world was the dark side, this was the light side – and I wanted to climb to success here.

Eberstadt was the kind of business where you made and lost money in seconds. In a tiny room, the dealers would have contact with every European center. By contrast, we at London and County were children playing an adult game. We didn't have enough clients just to depend upon commissions, so we had to take up a position in the bonds ourselves, purchasing the bonds for our own portfolio and hoping they would increase in value.

As compared to what we were doing, the odds in roulette are better. But, again, I was determined and more than ready to walk this edge.

In time, this, too, paid off. And London and County continued to grow.

Gradually, Charles Warburg let me into his world.

A year or so after we met, Charles and I visited many of the banking centers in Europe. There were hardly any reputable major or private banks where the principals or their successors were not known to him. Whether we had an appointment or not, the mention of his name brought instant recognition.

Besides getting myself introduced into this rarefied world, here was the other reason for our visit. The pound sterling was a very weak currency at that time.

Part of my ambitious plan was to use the Warburg connection to negotiate foreign currency transactions. We were already actively dealing with European banking companies in the Eurobond market. Adding this new dimension would be a logical increase in the growth of our international activities, however, the profitability in this area of banking is based on very narrow margins.

I found that traveling with Charles was comfortable. He had opened up and was easy to talk to, offering advice – finally – from his vast knowledge of the banking world in which I wanted to play a part.

On one foray, Charles and I went to Amsterdam so he could introduce me to bankers on the highest level there. One morning, Charles and I were standing on a bridge over one of the rivers that lace the city. I was watching boats pass underneath us, and looked up to say something to him – but stopped.

Charles was staring motionless, at a shop window some forty yards away. Something was on his mind.

"Charles," I inquired — but before I finished my sentence, he turned slowly to look at me, and I could see tears in his eyes.

"My sister and her daughter were hidden in a cupboard by the Dutch during the Nazi occupation in 1942. They were fed and protected by them. They sometimes had to urinate in the cupboard. Their lives were saved but of course, many were not."

Then he dropped his head and walked back across the bridge.

Silently I followed him to our next destination, and could only imagine the horrors that he held inside his head.

Yes, the Warburgs were a wealthy family, but the truth is *every* Jewish family was scarred, directly or indirectly, by the horrors of Nazi Germany. My childhood knowledge of World War II revolved around stories about the battles and the radio reports I barely understood. As a child I didn't understand the loss of life, bereavement, or the consequences of war, and just wanted my country to win. I could comprehend the demise of a large group of people as a child, but the destruction of one individual with whom there was a heart connection – well, this was beyond my experience.

Though, clearly, it was not outside the experience of the quiet, sorrowful man beside whom I walked, respectful of his need for space and privacy. *Who* he saw behind those gray eyes, dying in the concentration camps, he never said.

The mood passed, of course, and later that day we met with some of the boldest, most successful men in the European banking world.

I was truly on my way up, on the right path, and in the company of the right people now.

I could not go wrong.

Chapter Thirteen

PIONEERING

In the early winter of 1968, a regional director of Barclays Bank, called me. I was flattered, but couldn't make head nor tail of it. We were only a small company by their standards, although by now they'd seen us around for quite a few years.

"We have a customer who has a problem," the man began.

It was not the first time I'd heard this. There had been a number of occasions when the large banks, suffering from head office restrictions on their lending capacity, had referred business to us. It wasn't usually successful. The customers they sent over often had problems which we could do without.

"Who is the customer?" I asked, fully expecting he was about to invite me to take over a 500 or 1,000-pound overdraft for someone who had either gone over their limit or for whom a branch manager was unable to obtain head office consent.

"Jack Sampson, Chairman of United Drapery Stores," he replied.

I sat up. Was he serious?

United Drapery Stores in Great Britain was similar to Sears or J.C. Penney in the United States. The idea of a £500 million group requiring any help from us was not something I expected.

"What sort of problem has he got?"

"They've got a bank in the Whiteley's Store in Bayswater, London. Apparently they're having some difficulty in running it. They've offered it to us, but it's not really our cup of tea. We don't run branches in department stores, so we thought that you might like to buy it from them."

My pulse quickened. On one hand, this was beyond my reach. On the other hand *this* was an opportunity. I couldn't measure the financial implications at that moment, but I certainly could measure the potential.

"When can I meet Mr. Sampson?" I asked, using the measured tones of a man who never does anything impetuously or quickly. I hoped the answer was "this afternoon."

"Well, I'll tell him you are interested, and no doubt he'll give you a call."

When the conversation ended I felt that a crack had opened in the sky and heaven was about to shine down.

A few days later, I was seated at a meeting with Jack Sampson at his head office on the High Street in Kensington.

United Draperies was a large and successful retail group that owned countless small shops, stores, and a variety of groups all over the United Kingdom. And yet their offices were in a modest, older building – which, to me, spoke well of their business practices. Jack Sampson was a small man with a friendly smile and eyes like darts, and as we shook hands I knew I was being examined.

This could be a lucky break, but would I pass inspection?

The moment we sat down at a conference table, Sampson looked me in the eye and said, "Joseph, people have told me about you and they say you are heading in the right direction. Tell me what you're doing."

It's great to have people saying good things about you – but hearing that from a man at the level of Jack Sampson was a delightful surprise.

After I fumbled through some words of gratitude, he plunged into his agenda. Whiteley's was one United Draperies largest stores, with a bank on the second floor in the Bayswater neighborhood of London.

"The previous manager lacked experience, and things are rocky. Now we have a new manager who's doing a good job, but the whole venture is a headache for us.

We're a clothing group, after all, not bankers. Perhaps you'd be interested in taking it off our hands."

I *was* interested, and could have told him there and then, but that wasn't the prudent thing to do.

Our next appointment was at Whiteley's store, where, at the back of the second floor was a hut, with a plastic window. Behind it were old files, a couple of filing cabinets and about thirty or forty accounts. The accounts were mostly from store customers, with a few lending accounts. It was easy to determine that the previous manager clearly didn't know what he was doing.

My mind did a somersault: department stores, thousands of customers all over the country…. Where do people go after traditional banking hours end at 3:00 p.m.?

The answer — a new idea — was staring me in the face.

That was when branch banking was born. We would offer longer hours on weekdays and on Saturday mornings.

My next visit to Jack Sampson was quite positive. I was forthright and clear cut on my observations.

"I've had a look at your bank," I told him. "It's not really more than a mess with a handful of bad customers. If it wasn't for the chance of association with you and your group I wouldn't touch it with a ten-foot pole."

In no time at all, Sampson was working out a deal. They would guarantee the bad debts, but something new had to happen. We were to build a bank, a real bank, on the first floor of Whiteley's for all to see.

Within two years, the bank would have over a thousand customers and nearly £1 million on deposit.

A vision now exploded in my head.

I saw a way to make vast amounts of money quickly. I could see 50 banks like that in department stores throughout the country. That's where the money was, in people's pockets, walking in and out of department stores up until 7:00 p.m. on Fridays and all day Saturday. The shoppers were a captive market. People were there because they were buying for the weekend, visiting the food department or purchasing household items such as a vacuum cleaner or a washing machine.

Whichever direction they took, there were placards that said: "Bank." Customers began to open new checking and savings accounts.

The word spread. The idea grew and this was only the beginning.

There was only a small obstacle in my way: the need for cash – a lot of it.

People who start a business need working capital to buy furnishings, equipment, and so forth. I didn't have any. That meant I was borrowing money from the bank to purchase what was needed, and then paying the bank interest on everything. With that kind of tight rein on me I learned how to employ every penny available without wasting a minute of a working day.

I didn't realize it at the time, but the pressure on me personally began to build. For some reason I loved it. I thrived on it. I should have paid more attention to this, but I didn't. My eyes were on a vision that now held me mesmerized.

Now, every bit of my mental and physical focus was pumping into the business. "Banking hours" for me meant getting on the last train home. We used every penny we could lay our hands on all day, every day. We didn't let the money rest, because we didn't rest.

And so some kind of energy had taken me over, and I could feel myself starting to run on pure adrenalin. I would not stop till I'd reached the goal I could now envision… could taste.

I wanted to be a banker — a very successful banker.

I could now see myself as a man with a very large personal fortune.

Chapter Fourteen

RAGS TO RICHES

It was Spring 1969, and the stock market was strong. Now was the time for London and County to take off; I could feel it in my pulse.

We had started out as a unique, potentially successful financial company with banking ambitions… a company run by a man now driven by a clear vision. And because of the way we had developed our money lending company into a small bank, the enthusiasm of the stock brokers who handled the shares couldn't have been higher.

In this atmosphere of general excitement about the economy, the press coverage we now enjoyed brought more depositors and investors, which gave us the ability to expand at a far more rapid rate.

Then came a day in May, and what I had been driving myself for… *happened*.

After months of preparation, a detailed prospectus was published, and – for the first time in over 50 years — the stockbrokers launched our shares, and a small company was listed on the stock market as a bank.

Throughout the day I watched the stock exchange, and paced. And paced. Throughout the morning and afternoon investors poured more and more capital into our small venture.

When the dust settled, the public had bought our stock at a price equal to 42 times our projected earnings, compared to a norm of 16. In short, the stockbrokers, people in the City of London, and the general public were all anticipating a spectacular future for the company.

United Drapery Stores had received their shares into the Pension Fund and, on the first day, they were the big sellers, making over a million pounds profit. Our shares closed in the most hectic of dealings, at thirty-one shillings — nearly three time the issue price.

In one day, many people picked up handsome profits, and the kid from the rag trade in Camberwell in the gritty East End of London was worth £4,000,000.*

I was still in my thirties and just starting out. And I was suddenly a wealthy man.

That glorious day in May, after the market closed, I called Valerie.

"Our life has changed forever," I said.

I had no time to say more, as bunches of admiring fans were knocking at my office door and calling, with wild congratulations.

Finally, as the furor died down, I was finally alone in my office, and the phone rang.

In a bright tone, the receptionist announced: "Sir Isaac Wolfson on the phone for you, sir."

I could not believe my ears. Sir Isaac Wolfson — owner of the Great Universal Stores, one of England's largest department stores, the owner of the Anglo-Portuguese Bank and of real estate all over London, a huge benefactor to the State of Israel and perhaps the greatest corporate giant of all time — *this* man was on the phone, calling me.

I stood up at my desk with the phone pressed into my ear.

Sir Isaac, a legend many times over, and one of the richest men in England, didn't waste a moment. "Caplan, I'd like to congratulate you on your success in the stock market today."

My jaw hung open, as he went on to speak to me about the future. "It's clear you have remarkable prospects."

"Thank you, sir," I replied, stunned beyond words.

* About $100 million at today's value.

The great man went on. "Would you like to come and have a cup of tea with me?"

"Thank you, sir."

I was no longer alone. The world was at my door.

The following afternoon, the great man told me what a brilliant future I could have if I threw in my lot with him.

In the end, politely, I declined. The offer was a bit was too quick. I would be a very tiny part of his empire, and having been through the rapids alone I wanted to paddle my own canoe for awhile.

What I knew, however, was that I had made it.

Now life was different. So many people were hanging on every word that came out of my mouth. Now, too, I began looking for further acquisitions, more publicity, and ways to grow faster. I was being asked my opinion on everything — politics, economics, the prospects of major companies on the stock market. I learned to give intelligent answers, sometimes thinking, *I don't know what I'm talking about.* But it didn't matter. People were listening to me, and I loved it.

In September 1969, we excited the City by announcing a substantial investment in our Bank's shares by Banque de Paris et des Pays-Bas (Suisse) S.A. They purchased 10 percent of the equity in our group at 32 shillings 6 pence.

The prospect of co-operation and support by the biggest banking group in Europe, and the evident faith in London and County that was shown by their move, indicated a new surge forward and the ability to broaden our activities in the banking investment sector. The following day, the shares closed at 50 shillings 6 pence. We now had more capital, a better rating, enhanced respectability and the prospect of financial backing and a further increase in deposits.

If my pulse was fast before it was racing now.

As time went by, I was to visit Sir Isaac a number of times at his magnificent home in Grosvenor Square in the heart of London.

In the foyer, in a fish pond sunk into the floor, were rare and beautiful gold, black and white koi.

"Gefilte fish," he said, jokingly, ushering me in.

Sir Isaac was a collector of many treasures, but I found his superlative collection of 19th-Century gold snuff boxes from different countries particularly astonishing. This was interesting to me, since I also collected snuff boxes, but in a much more modest way.

On one occasion, he took me to the lower ground floor, walked over to a refrigerator, opened the door and said, "Look, Joseph, it is full!"

I smiled.

Sir Isaac was worth countless millions. And yet, like my parents and grandparents, this extraordinary man put the highest value on food because it represented freedom and security

Not long into our acquaintance, Sir Isaac again approached me with an amazing offer. He wanted to appoint me head of his Anglo-Portuguese Bank. In return, he would purchase 51 percent control of London and County.

Again, this was all happening too quickly for me. I had only just tasted fame and fortune. I wanted more and wanted to retain control of what I had created. It had come from humiliation and despair, and I wasn't ready to let go of it.

What I did not recognize was the fact that, while I was indeed maintaining control of my rapidly growing little empire I was also keeping out important people like Sir Isaac, whose wisdom and insight might have spared me what was to come.

Later, looking back, I would see that this was the best time in my career. The value of the London and County group was increasing all the time — and I held 22 percent of the shares. We hadn't upset anyone, and according to the press I was "the new Midas."

Everyday was a dream come true. I had invaded the City. From far and wide people came to London and County. I had climbed up a ladder and people were pushing me to keep climbing.

Within a short time, other companies would try to take us over. Clearly, our growth was still around the corner. Everyone wanted to catch a ride on the bandwagon.

What could be better?

Ironically enough, I was also discovering that a tycoon's life was full of complications. This may sound ridiculous, to offer a complaint about walking into the financial and social stratosphere, so to speak, but it was truly not what I'd expected. I wasn't unhappy about it - but it was unexpected.

For one thing, there was no privacy. The round-about of social life, the entertainment, never stopped now. I had to be available. Everywhere we went, Valerie and I were now treated to champagne and canapés, as a prelude to meals served with impeccable taste… and guests chosen to impress each other.

For another thing, everyone with whom we hobnobbed was serious about only one thing: money. Conversation circled around stories about the stock market, rumors, takeovers, and investment tips.

And so, while everything was looking superlative, underneath there was a shift in the way I felt about my work. Whereas there had been an initial excitement about my success, now I felt uneasy all the time.

What if I missed an opportunity to invest and advance London and County? What if the wave of attention and interest that was bringing me this newfound success ebbed away – and I was no longer the celebrated man of investments?

However far we traveled on holiday, whatever we did, or saw, I could never relax; the feeling was always the same. I was on a precarious climb but I didn't know it, and a moment's inattention could make the difference between failure and success.

Here was the thing: Whether I was excited by new gains or anxious about losing them I *liked* the edge.

For now.

Chapter Fifteen

FAILURE/SUCCESS

There is a popular saying: "Live and learn." If only that were true.

By December 1969, London and County was planning its next big move – opening businesses in Malta.

Malta is a small island in the Mediterranean, close to Libya to the south and Italy to the north, and at the time it seemed ripe for business opportunities. We were to be the first Merchant Bank to open in Malta, and with distinguished Maltese nationals on the board, we intended to offer 50 percent of the bank to the Maltese as soon as the anticipated Banking Act of Malta was enacted. Along with opening a bank, we decided to form a diaper manufacturing company for distribution all over Europe, as I was advised that the cost of labor would be very low.

The board of directors for the new bank would include the Right Honorable Lord Bradbury, whose father signed England's paper currency, known as "Bradbury notes." He was a fine, upstanding man and friend, well respected everywhere. Another distinguished board member was Baron Salvino Testaferrata, who hailed from a Maltese family that dated back to 1,000 A.D. in Rome. Thus, a solid Board of Directors gathered together every few months on that historic island, much loving the ancient nature and class of that beautiful place.

Malta intrigued me, not just for its business prospects but its character. The Maltese are gentle people with an impressive history that goes back hundreds of years. I enjoyed meeting them, they were simple, uncomplicated people with hardly anything in material possessions. They were eager for work and I believed that my company would do well there and at the same time do something worthwhile for their island.

In that sense, it felt like something of the old Joseph Caplan was still alive and well, and wanting to make a positive contribution.

After negotiations, the government of Malta made a huge factory available at no cost to what had now become the London and County Group, because of the prospect of income and employment for the island. The directors discussed the manufacturing cost, the distribution cost, and the ultimate potential. If we manufactured diapers on a large scale, because of the low overhead and labor costs, it had great profit potential.

I was about to see, however, that in business you can be treated to special surprises.

For one thing, Muammar al Gaddafi became a big influence in Malta. Gradually, a climate of uneasiness began to take over.

For another, what my representatives did not research was the fact that different countries require different diapers, and, therefore, different machinery was needed to manufacture them. Germans, for example, were much more demanding regarding the quality and efficiency of diapers.

The last thing I expected in Malta was to be a victim of local politics. Everyone was so laid-back about politics when we first began our investment there. And then things changed. The Maltese parliament consisted of only 46 people, who were divided equally between Labor and Conservatives. Since the island was frequented by many British tourists, bringing in pounds to spend, British traditions were honored.

Shortly after that, representatives of our 900 workers told me that they had joined a labor union. I was invited to attend a meeting in the factory, where the workers were represented by three men from Libya… and suddenly there were heavy demands. The significant increase in everyone's wages would wipe out our profit. I said no – and although we'd employed many people who were happy to have jobs, the factory closed down.

Some 900 Maltese citizens lost their jobs… and I lost a great deal of money.

The last straw was the bank. With fear of Gaddafi's influence growing, British emigrants were leaving and tourists were not coming in. And with a tougher business climate, deposits and investment moneys were not coming in either.

The bank did not take off.

All in all, the Malta investment cost a good deal of money, took up a lot of my time as well as that of some of our directors – and it put incredible stress on me and on the London and County Group. And here is where I should have learned something.

I'd been travelling from home more and more, missing time with Valerie and the children – we now had two, as our daughter, Julia, had been born. When I was at home I tried to cram in as much as I could with them. And somewhere in the back of my mind I knew that I was missing important moments in their lives, and that a few hours here and there did not make up for absenteeism. But in the front of my mind, held in my mind's-eye, were images of the life I could give them – with the best of everything money could buy – if I stayed at my task of making money, a lot of it. They might not have much of *me*, but I was determined they *would* have what I never had growing up – which was the good life.

If I'd allowed Malta to teach me anything, it would have been this: I'd invested time, effort and energy, and spent a lot of emotional capital that the venture didn't pay back. Investing a bit more time, energy and interest in my own family would have had better "dividends," so to speak.

The other thing I might have learned was that I wasn't the "Midas" that the media continued to make me out to be. There is a saying, however, that applied to me: "The problem with self-made men is that they always make the head too big." I liked being known as "Midas;" it was great for attracting the attention of wealthy and powerful businessmen, who saw me as their ticket to making even more money.

What I did learn, about myself and about my quest for success was that, even if I encountered something that blocked or resisted me I would not be stopped.

Some driving force had settled in and taken control of my decision making and my energy. I would make it to the top echelon in the financial world. There were so many signs that huge success lay just ahead. Failure was just not possible. I liked my own raw determination.

Despite the failure in Malta I was in the throes of building fame and fortune, rapidly, in many other ways. If anyone had irons heating up fast in the fire it was me. During that time, Robin Sallinger, an attorney, came to see me. Since the Spring of 1969, business in England had been nothing but golden. Now, it was early 1971, and Sallinger came to tell me he was representing Jeremy Thorpe and to ask if we would consider offering him a seat on our main Board.

I was excited at the prospect – at the doors that would open if we associated ourselves with this powerful man.

Thorpe was the head of the Liberal Party, as well as one of the Queen's distinguished Privy Counselors, in company with other senior political figures and nobility. His party had received 19 percent of the popular vote at the last general election. He was a charismatic person and many thought that he would increase his party's strength at the next election and perhaps one day he would become Prime Minister of England. He was certainly a threat to both the Conservatives and Labor party who held about 40 percent each of the electoral vote. The Prime Minister, Ted Heath, offered the Liberal party a coalition with a cabinet seat for Thorpe — but Thorpe could sense a bigger future for himself and his party and turned it down.

I was not a political person, but the bare fact was this: having Thorpe on our board would be a huge asset. In short order, he joined us as a non-executive member, with salary.

In many ways, Thorpe was exactly the kind of man anyone would want representing their business. Not only was he very well and powerfully placed, with the promise of more power to come, he was always impeccably dressed in pin striped dark trousers, waistcoat, white shirt and a formal neck tie. At a personal level, he was positive, encouraging and expressed constant enthusiasm about our progress. He was intelligent and affable, with great wit and humor, a dashing and vibrant young politician.

In public, he also presented well. He was dark haired, tall, lean and handsome, appearing in press photographs in energetic shots, playing tennis or vaulting over some fencing in London. Thorpe was the sort of man you'd invite to your dinner party, confident that he would be witty and an amusing addition to any gathering. He was a barrister by profession and was educated at Oxford University.

Here again, were lessons I'd have been wise to heed.

Thorpe was not a sharp businessman. That, I ignored, not even pausing for a moment to consider why I'd have someone with little or no business acumen on the board of a growing business venture. There was a reason for this.

From the first day, it appealed to me that Thorpe was like me — a climber. Only, he was climbing the political ladder and I was climbing the financial ladder. And it appealed to me that, given his position close to the Crown, Thorpe could easily open the way to the higher echelons of British society.

We quickly found ways to make our association with him as visible as possible.

He officiated at the opening of branches of our Banks in different parts of the country, with the result that he gained publicity for the Group as well as the Liberal Party. He was the key figure when we opened our new head office on Euston Road, London, and he accompanied me when I went to meet the directors of the Leopold Joseph Bank, at the time that London and County positioned itself to take them over.

Another adage says, "Be careful what you wish for."

There was no cautionary tension in the pit of my stomach to warn me that a person whom I considered one of the keys to my ambition would contribute significantly to great trouble ahead for me. Had I vetted-out Thorpe and not rushed into our association I might have discovered that he was being quietly investigated by his own Liberal Party and the government with regards to a shadowy area of his personal life.

What I did know was that Jeremy had experienced great tragedy, and that gave me and the public a great sympathy for him. His wife Caroline had died in a car crash, with their two children in the car. He never talked about the tragedy and we thought it best not to ask about it.

At first, of course, having someone of such stature on the board was grand, and opened the door to an upper world where the elite hobnobbed.

Valerie and I were invited to his wedding at the Royal Albert Hall to Marion Stein, who was the former Countess of Harewood and also a renowned concert pianist. Her Majesty Queen Elizabeth showed favor to Marion. The Queen's cousin, the Earl of Harewood, had treated her very badly when they were married. She was quite a lot older than Jeremy, but even so the Queen gave the couple her blessing. In fact the Queen was the matchmaker. She gave them a beautiful "grace and favor" home in Orme Square London, which Marion could occupy for the rest of her life.

We were entering at the edges of a world where such boons were given.

If I had learned from the failures of Malta – if I hadn't rushed into the association with Thorpe – things may have gone differently for me later. But all I could feel was the racing pulse of my own success. And all I could see was that I was approaching the stratosphere now – thinking about the way that Thorpe referred to me as "my lord."

In allowing him on our board I had not overlooked the possibility that given his position one day he could grant a knighthood. Indeed, as a self-made man, the head was becoming too big.

Sir Joseph had a nice ring to it.

Chapter Sixteen

THE LIFE

The famous Cote d' Azur on the south coast of France probably owes its origins to the relaxed and less heady days of the early 19th Century, when King Edward the Seventh and his entourage used to visit the area of Nice and Cannes. To this day, that part of Nice, which proudly claims some of the most famous hotels in the world, is called *Promenade des Anglais*. Between Cannes and Monte Carlo, before you step into Italy, there are many villas which can be rented for the summer. The choice of food in this area is amazing, from the taste of moules, calamari and langoustine, to spaghetti, fettuccine and cannelloni.

The alternative to renting a villa — if you've got the stomach, the urge and the money — is to rent a yacht complete with crew. But of course food and extras aren't included. This casual and calm way of enjoying the summer vacation has appealed to an international set, made up of Europeans, Middle-easterners, Americans and, of course, the French themselves. All the "beautiful people" are here.

With my skyrocketing successes, Valerie and I were now able to leave behind the intensity of the banking world and rest ourselves and our souls on one of these yachts for a short time.

In this fabulous setting I thought, Y*es, this is it. This is the life. I've gotten where I wanted to be.*

On a yacht, looking across the water as far as the eye can see, nothing challenges you. As your craft plows through the sea, you become lightheaded and indifferent to the world you've left behind.

It is not easy to describe the sight of the blue, blue sea or what its calm does to you. The sea is wide open and free, and it freed my soul. I could sit on the deck for hours, stretch out my hands as far as my fingers could "touch" there was nothing but ocean. Sometimes the waves would roll from the bow or the stern and the spray would tease the deck. The water on my lips was better than champagne. And sometimes when the sea was calm I would sit on the bow, looking at the sun teasing the wash of the waves, as it sank below the skyline and ushered in the night. The world around me became a sort of holy place. It cleaned my hands, my body and my mind.

There were moments, too, when I realized the toll the world of business and banking was starting to have on me. Realized the nagging sense of fatigue I had come to live with all the time, physically and also mentally.

I felt that, if I could be there forever life would be alright forever….

Unfortunately, you *can't* stay in these moments and these places forever. And the life that goes on there is not real life, as people know it.

As well, when Valerie and I were there long enough, we began to get glimpses beneath the surface of this beautiful world with its beautiful people and what they were really like.

The yacht circuit's main preoccupation was entertainment and pleasure seeking. The harbors in the South of France had the best food in Europe, the shops sell the best wine. The best champagne and caviar are free of tax if you have a yacht. Because of this, you buy twice as much of both. You also need to eat, however, so you buy salmon, salad, the best bread in the world, milk, coffee, fruit, nuts, and cream. Not only that, but incredible lamb, steak, all kinds of seafood, lobsters like you've never tasted before. The local fish called *le loop* was my favorite. The trouble with this way of living is that after awhile you take it all for granted and you forget that most people don't eat or live like that. You lose contact with the real world and reality.

It all seems worthwhile, because the crew does all the work unless you're an enthusiast. If the sea is not in a bad mood that day, you get your money's worth as the bow of your boat plows its way through the water at 12 to 20 knots. It makes you feel that everything is going to be all right. While you are at sea, the "real" world vanishes and you sink into a sublime illusion that nothing bad can happen in your life.

We "did" the Coast that year — San Tropez, Antibes, Cannes, Nice, Ville Franche, Beaulieu, San Remo, and other exclusive ports. We visited harbors like Millionaire's Bay on the Cote D'Azur, where the rich have yachts as well as villas. We traveled in our yacht, the Hona Lee II, as far as Corsica and Sardinia. You play the games that everyone plays. People there have all the time and money they need. There is even a dress code for boarding a yacht. Many of the people who own these magnificent, money-wasting machines spend much of their time on the water, in a world all their own.

There were many glamorous parties in these villas full of those "beautiful people," especially during the summer. We sailed our yacht to one of these parties. While the crew stayed behind, we lowered our small boat and rowed over to a cove. The rock face was spattered with people of all kinds, many with bottles at their knees and glasses in their hands.

It was a large villa owned by a banker friend of mine. I looked around and looked around again. I whispered to Valerie pointing out some of the well-known people from banking and politics. She whispered back, "Who are all these women? They don't look as though they belong with the men."

She was right, of course. I was probably the only man there with his wife.

A few times, feeling at least like an Admiral leading the fleet, I would arrange to meet friends or associates in the ocean or at a harbor on the Cote D'Azur – then order my captain to get us there. He would get out his compass and his ruler and calibrate the instruments in the right direction, and tell me how long it would take to reach the meeting point.

Everything was under control, organized. I felt important. The worries of London, takeovers and mergers – stresses which had begun to surface — were brushed away by the wind and the steady slap of the water against the side of the hull, as the yacht of which I was so proud divided the waves and moved forward.

The world of the poor barrister and the struggling rag merchant were so far behind me now I felt I was no longer the person I once was. I couldn't, and didn't want to, remember that man and what he had lived for.

I was the captain of my own life and destiny now.

Back in London later that year, my taste for "the life" brought even more new pleasures.

As my association with Joe Allbritton, and certainly with others like Charles Warburg and Sir Isaac Wolfson, had shown me, when you have real money there are no boundaries. Extravagance is taken for granted. After all you work for it, it's your money, why can't you spend it?

It was my 40th birthday. Valerie and I were planning two parties at home; one for our whole family and the other for close friends and a few business associates. Incidentally, the wife of one of our friends brought me, if you can imagine this, a gold toothpick. Her note read, "What do you give a man who has everything?"

That week, Brian McMenemy, the bank's general manager, told me that we had to meet. "It's a birthday surprise, sir, and you will be very pleased." My chauffeur, Dougherty, one of the players in this little conspiracy, drove me to Jack Barclay Rolls Royce in Berkeley Square.

When I entered, everyone was beaming, especially the floor manager and his staff.

And there in the showroom was my precious Valerie holding a birthday card - and standing next to a "new" Rolls Royce Phantom. I'd commented that the new Rolls was too flashy for me. The sleek lines of the older Phantom were beautiful. Valerie had been listening!

I opened the door and slid inside, nearly numb with the surprise on one hand and my heart beating with delight on the other. This was too much to take in. The leather interior looked and smelled like new. There was a screen between the chauffeur and the back seat. The Phantom had a bar in the rear and an intercom for contact with the chauffeur.

And so we drove home, the world stood still, and I thought I must be one step closer to heaven.

I could have almost anything I wanted.

I felt no barrier could stop me now. I was being welcomed into worlds where I never dreamed I'd gain entry.

One such was Annabel's Night Club, the most exclusive club in London. The club was owned by Jimmy Goldsmith and Mark Burley. It was, of course, a member's-only establishment that catered to many celebrities. It remains the only such club ever graced, on just one occasion, by Her Majesty, Queen Elizabeth II.

By now I was very well known in London — but I was unable to become a member of Annabel's. That was because I was a Jew. Yes, that was sad but true. However, I had money, so, I had friends.

But I wanted to get my foot in the door, and in order to do so I had to make the following arrangements. The man-about-town who organized this for me made it very simple. If I paid for two call girls, one for him and one for the Colonel who was on the membership committee and paid for a lavish champagne dinner, he could arrange for me to be accepted as a member.

And so, to be part of this circle, that is what I did.

When Valerie and I went there that first Saturday night, I was a little uncertain because I didn't know what to expect. The entrance to Annabel's was quite narrow. From the looks on the faces of everyone, they all seemed so happy. The decor was the most tasteful and expensive that money could buy, though I was surprised at the small size of the interior. It was very crowded and very intimate. The dance floor was small, the music was good and the food was superb. Everything went well. It all happened the way my friend said it would.

So, after all, I *was* another step closer to heaven. The fact that I'd had to pay for it didn't matter.

I was not to be denied access anywhere.

Did I say closer to heaven? Maybe in the eyes of the world. Maybe in terms of worldly success. At home, this was not exactly the case.

I had neglected Valerie. I was consumed with my work. It wasn't that I didn't go home every night or that I was involved in any activities which a decent woman would object to. It was simply that I was absorbed from morning until night with creating and recreating corporate entities which I could add to the portfolio, increasing the Group's revenue and growth.

It was time to give my marriage some attention. It wasn't that my love for Valerie had cooled in any way, I loved her very much. Regrettably, sometimes she almost became like an *object d'art*: part of the household which I could touch and admire, always there, always faithful, always eager to listen and happy when I was home.

So, touched by conscience, I planned a surprise for her. I felt bad about my neglectfulness. This had to be something big.

One evening after supper I approached Valerie in a casual, off-handed manner. "Darling, I have arranged for us to have a weekend away with Pat and Derek. I won't tell you where we're going, it's a surprise."

As the date neared, she asked, "Is Dougherty going to drive us to the airport in the Phantom?"

"I'm sorry, darling," I said sheepishly, "It just seemed a good idea to give him a few days off." And so we found ourselves sitting in the lounge at Heathrow, waiting for the flight to be called. At the appropriate time, we got up, I took Valerie to the gate and put my hand over her eyes just was we entered the plane, so she couldn't see the destination.

Onboard, we settled in our seats, and after a few minutes the flight crew announced that we were departing for…Nice, France.

Valerie looked at me and beamed with delight. "Where are we staying in Nice?"

"That," I replied, "is another surprise."

We de-planed on a quiet day, amid the usual group of all different sorts of people lining up to show their passports at French customs, and then we walked towards the exit.

Suddenly, Valerie tugged on my arm and said, "Joseph, I just saw Dougherty!"

"You're seeing things, dear."

She shook her head a little, but moved on.

We collected our baggage and headed outside.…

…and there indeed was our chauffeur, with a bunch of flowers and my 1964 Rolls taking up a great amount of parking space.

Part of my plan, to show Valerie how much she meant to me, was to ship our Rolls from London to France for the weekend. I didn't think about what an incredible extravagance that was, just that Valerie would be stunned and maybe understand how much I cherished her.

We greeted Dougherty. He knew where we were going, and about twenty minutes down the coast, proceeded to drive in the direction of Beaulieu. I'd booked a suite at *L'Hotel La Reserve*.

The suite had a bedroom on either side of a living room. The furniture was a little faded, in that genteel way, which said, "We are the finest hotel in town, we don't have to be flashy. We are not Hollywood." After we had unpacked and began to talk about dinner, there was a knock at the door.

The waiter came in, wheeling a trolley. "Bonjour, Mesdames et Messieurs."

Valerie was looking very pleased indeed. *I was making points.*

I mentioned casually that I had ordered champagne and caviar to get our evening started. After the waiter left, with a good tip in his pocket, I said to Valerie, "Darling, why don't you serve the caviar."

The caviar was in a large silver tureen. She picked up the little silver spoon and then balked. "Joseph, there is something in the caviar."

I replied, tongue in cheek, "Shall I send it back?"

She dipped the spoon in…and out came an elegant diamond tennis bracelet.

That gift from me to Valerie did not make up for my obsession with business, and it didn't make up for coming home late several nights a week, but it certainly made our weekend trip extremely pleasant.

My chest swelled a bit more. I loved the fact that I could lavish my wife with trips like this, and with beautiful gifts.

As well, I reveled in the fact that now everyone, from the chauffer and bellman to the hotel management did exactly what I asked, when I asked for it.

I was powerful.

And then came Dell House, Totteridge Green, London.

Dell House was built in 1930, set in about three acres. It was a stately place — and I bought it.

As you entered the front door you could see a long corridor starting with a wood paneled study. Then the large living room with the windows from end to end looking out onto a terrace, beautiful brick fireplaces, Roman statues all along the corridor and an antique table containing the 18th and 19th Century snuff boxes I had started collecting.

Early each morning, in Dell house, I would get up, look out the bedroom window at our swimming pool, the small judo gymnasium which I had built, and the beautiful lawns flanked by trees which led to a forest as far as the eye could see.

Downstairs, Maria, our house help, would cook a simple breakfast. Very English. Egg on toast with tea and sometimes baked beans. At about 7:30 am, I would step out of the front door. In the center of the courtyard was an antique, thirty-foot column with a bronze figure of a man on top.

The chauffeur would be waiting with the Rolls Royce Phantom engine quietly turning over. Reclining in the backseat of that car was like being in the sitting room of a luxury hotel suite. The interior was trimmed in a highly-varnished cherry wood. There was a sound-proof screen between the driver and passenger with velvet trimming around the window. The outside windows were tinted to complete privacy. I would begin my business day by reading the *Financial Times* headlines and my business files in the splendor of that backseat.

Dougherty, our chauffeur, lived with his wife and children in the cottage on the grounds of the estate. We spoke very little as we drove to the Head Office on Euston Road. Dougherty had formerly worked for Her Majesty, Queen Elizabeth II, in the chauffeur pool and they do not talk when they drive.

As we pulled out of the drive I could not but think that, despite my negligence at home, I had done well by my family at least monetarily and in terms of lifestyle.

And surely that counted for something, didn't it?

Chapter Seventeen

ALMOST SUCCESS

Something wasn't going quite right with my plan to climb and keep climbing the ladder of success.

From the time I'd left off being a barrister and entered the business world what I'd wished for was "enough money." Enough money to keep my family secure, comfortable and free from the worries that had plagued my grandparents. Enough money to feel successful and enjoy life.

By now I'd worked hard to make that wish come true. It had... and it hadn't.

A vague uneasiness stalked me almost every waking moment. I told myself that this was because of the intense focus that the London financial world was suddenly paying to my actions.

The British press didn't tire of commenting on our acquisitions. The growth of my London and County Bank was constantly talked about in the City of London. People were now clinging to my coat tails. The kid from Camberwell and the rag business was making good. The press loved everything, our takeovers, acquisitions, our growth, our prospects.

If there were clouds on the business horizon in England I paid little attention. Some of the establishment didn't like me, but what could they do? It was happening.

My dreams of huge success were coming true. It was a moment of glory.

As the Chairman of what was now a large group of companies, I was approached with many business propositions. When American bankers from Texas offered London and County a business opportunity, it brought me in touch for the first time with a different way of life. This was to become one of my greatest experiences, as I learned more about Americans and their enthusiasm, open-heartedness, and hospitality.

Joe Allbritton, the President of the Houston Citizen's Bank and Trust Company, asked to meet with me in London, and I was delighted.

When I first met Joe, he seemed like a caricature from British magazine Punch. He was short, neatly dressed with a warm, effervescent American drawl and an oval young face. He looked forty, though he was over fifty years old, and the sort of person you could meet at a dinner party and describe him as a nice guy and say, "Let's invite him over." Joe was formerly an attorney and had entered banking. With steady success, he was reaching the peak of his career.

We had many meetings, in London, at his permanently-reserved suite at Claridges Hotel, and at my office. It was sometimes hard for me to follow his conversation. He was so animated and pronounced the future as if it had just taken place. At the beginning and the end of almost every sentence, he used the expression, with great warmth, "mahhh friend."

The Americans, I learned, are great whiskey drinkers. The setting up of whisky glasses is a necessary precursor to discussion. We talked about his bank buying 25 percent of London and County. The merger would have brought much needed dollars into England. He was so enthusiastic that when we got to the point of agreement, he also gave us an option to buy 10 percent of his bank.

This was the man who was sitting with me at a bar saying to me, "Joseph, I am so lonely, team up with me. We can do so much together."

You can't refuse a man like that. His personality reached out. His offer was typical, in a way, of American enthusiasm.

So in February 1973, Valerie and I traveled first class to Houston, enjoying champagne, canapés, smoked salmon, caviar, and eye shades for sleeping.

We were tired, yet very excited at the same time, when we touched down in Houston. The airport was a superb example of modern America, in every way with a marble esplanade and as you walked through the huge airport, and you got the feeling you were looking at a fragment of the power and the strength which characterizes the greatest country in the world. The American attitude of achievement reached out to me.

A bevy of representatives of the Allbrittons converged on us the moment we left the airplane. In the terminal, our luggage disappeared within minutes. We were ushered out of the airport by beaming, chatting executives and guided to a modern, English Rolls Royce waiting to conduct us to the hotel. Joe had purchased the Rolls in London during his last visit and shipped it to Houston. He said to me later, referring to the Rolls, "We wanted you to feel at home."

I'd learned enough about Allbritton to know his personal fortune far, far exceeded mine.

Real money has no boundaries, I thought.

I liked that thought.

Every American, I learned, is an inbred tourist and guide, when it comes to his own country. With great pride, modern buildings were pointed out to us as the Rolls Royce moved smoothly towards its destination which was the Warwick Hotel on the edge of town. I checked in and was shown to the "room" I had booked.

Now for business travel, I was on a budget of £20 per day. At that time, the British government restricted the amount of sterling leaving England. I was really nervous about the cost of my stay in Houston with Valerie. Even with the full allowance, it wasn't clear to me how I was going to manage. I had specifically asked the travel agent, to get me the most modest room available. The elevator zoomed up to the top floor and our executive guide gave us a cheery farewell, saying, "If you need anything at all, just call. Look forward to seeing you later."

When they showed us to our "room," it turned out to be a luxurious suite. The mistake was obvious. I was about to reach for the telephone and explain to the desk clerk that I hadn't booked a suite, when Joe and his wife, Barbie, knocked at the door and came in to greet us.

If there was ever a woman who was made for her man, it was Barbie. She was wealthy in her own right, independent in her intelligence, yet she chose her moments to complement him with her conversation. Her demeanor was calm and confident.

We greeted each other warmly. She was really delightful. I explained to Joe the "little mistake" the hotel had made with the room.

"Don't you worry, Joseph," Barbie laughed. "This is *our* guest suite. Our apartment is right along the corridor around the corner. You and Valerie just have a rest now. As soon as you feel like it, you come right on in."

With the introductions and greetings over, they quickly disappeared.

A short time later, as we walked the corridor to meet our hosts, and our eyes were pulled from left to right. There were works from Renoir, Rubens, Goya, and Rembrandt displayed. I would learn later that the unknown buyer who, six months earlier, paid the highest price ever for a Rembrandt, was Joe Allbritton.

There was no business discussed during the evening, although meetings were alluded to. We just had a very nice time with two very nice people. The next day, we were whirled around Houston by one of Joe's executives. The new buildings, the new housing, it was something to see. What we received was hospitality combined with the objective of showing a future partner what life in America is really all about.

One evening, Valerie and I were asked to dress for a formal dinner. When we arrived with the Allbrittons at the restaurant, we were introduced to the Mayor, Louis Welch. There were probably at least fifty men and women present with Valerie sitting at one end next to Joe. I was sitting at the other end next to Barbie. When dinner was over, the Mayor made a speech and then presented me with a certificate and the key to the City. I became the only Englishman since Sir Winston Churchill's grandson, also named Winston Churchill, to be honored in such a way. Clearly, Joe was influential as well as successful.

The days went by quickly. We were having a farewell dinner with the Allbrittons on our last night in town. Their bank was financially sound with unlimited local backing. I was clearly well on the way to another press announcement and more success.

As the dinner came to a close, Joe presented me with a gold ring in the shape of an oil well. "Joseph, this is your first oil well."

Barbie presented Valerie with a diamond broach saying, "You have given me and my friends a wonderful example of the character of an English lady, by the way you speak and the by the way you dress."

All the while, of course, in this lavish and relaxed atmosphere, we were discussing the deal Joe was proposing.

That deal would have brought approximately $50 million dollars in fresh capital into England at a time when the Bank of England was yearning for dollars. I was dismayed when they vetoed the transaction. It was a huge setback. I thought it was a no-brainer.

Subsequently, the Discount Office — the official contact channel for receiving directives and passing information to or making requests to the Bank of England — explained to me that I should take on an Exchange Controller, and a Foreign Exchange dealer. I was advised to pay the highest price and get the best. It was, I was told, a loss making exercise, but when that area of activity had been established in the Bank long enough — and that meant *years* — they might then consider granting us the limited authority to deal in foreign currency. And then more years after that, this might be extended so that we could engage in international currency dealings.

We were not yet at that stage. Nowhere near.

Thus our negotiations with the Houston Bank and Trust Company came to an abrupt halt. Success on the international level had been so close I could taste it, but it would have to wait.

This episode showed me several things.

First, it gave me a bird's-eye view of America's wealthiest state and the people who prosper it. The Allbrittons and other Americans I'd met were lovely people. Joe and I would have done well together, because I knew I could always trust him and the synergy was there. In fact, they would never get into the British banking market and I would never be able to team up with a solid banker from the USA. But I loved it there! Secondly, I saw that both Joe and I, like other very successful businessmen I was encountering, were, as the expression goes, "lonely at the top." Every decision – every important hire, every acquisition – rested on our shoulders in the final outcome, no matter who advised us. Not only that, our businesses were like demanding mistresses, in need of constant focus and attention. There was no headspace and no time for much else.

Joe and I would stay in frequent contact after that time, each following our own destiny. And I would chomp impatiently at the bit for success at the level he had achieved.

And so the trip to America ignited even more jets for me.

Each morning shortly after 8 a.m., as I entered London and County's newly built head office on Euston Road, the place was already alive with activity. Managers, tellers, busy calculating and checking and supervising.

Valerie had decorated the impressive entrance with elegance and simple splendor. The liveried doorman would tip his hat and smile the same smile every day, like a light that is never switched off.

I would greet the staff, then walk up the stairs to the executive offices. Sometimes I would stop and look down, satisfied by all the banking activity and then continue on my way.

Despite the establishments limiting us, despite setbacks like Malta, I could feel, could taste, that we were on the road to huge success. Success beyond our wildest dreams.

My secretary, Kathy Black, was always there before me. Kathy was a stunning redhead. She would greet me with urgent or priority phone calls, provide me with a quick outline of the meetings planned for the day, just like you see in the movies. Her standard question was, "Would you like some tea?" She was Australian, and the Aussies and the British love their tea in the morning and at 4:00 in the afternoon.

With that I faced the mountain that was my pathway to the top. By which I mean, a mountain of files, holding information about deals to be made, potential acquisitions to analyze. There could never be too many files on the desk for me. My legal background had trained me to summarize a project and decide whether or not we should agree to fund it.

At 8:30 a.m., the bank directors would meet in my office, which had ample space. They would carry notes of their own projects and plans for the day or the week. The accountants presented their cash-flow reports. The corporate directors put forward their suggestions for company acquisitions. I knew before 9 a.m. each weekday everything that I needed to know concerning our group of companies.

Business lunches were dreadfully unhealthy but very traditional. London and County had its own director's dining room complete with chef. There was a less private dining area for the executive staff and a another dining room for junior level executives and the bank managers.

When I went out for a business lunch to somebody else's office, it was always preceded by a gin or whiskey and concluded with brandy or port. I know now that there were a number of decisions which would have been better made without the drinks.

Here was the thing about the course I was on: I'd taken a turn on an unexpected turn of the path in my private, personal life.

Monday through Friday took every ounce of my available energy: Bidding for companies, making deals, and probing propositions, placed a daily demand on me. There was no set time for going home at the end of the day. Finishing a day's work depended upon the deal of the moment and whether it needed more attention. Often, I'd return after the children were in bed, to share a late and quick bite with Valerie before collapsing into bed.

Sometimes I had to get home by 6 p.m. – but that was usually to be present at one of our own dinner parties. Our elegant dining room table would be set for eight to 12 people – some personal acquaintances but most were "friends" from the business world and, occasionally now, a high-placed government friend or a celebrity. People whom one might think of as "useful" acquaintances. In this way, the business world began to penetrate even into our personal world.

Yes, there were holidays and weekends away with my family. But even then, what was going on at London and County came along with us. There was always a file – or two, or three – slipped into the briefcase or phone calls to be made.

"Excuse me, dear. I won't be a moment," had become a gloss on the fact that I could disappear from Valerie and the children for an hour... or so.

Very quickly – but strangely unnoticed – stress had taken over my life. Our lives. But for me at least, that was compensated by the excitement, the publicity, and the ongoing rise of my career.

Or almost compensated. I was not paying attention to the toll it took on me to keep an eagle-eye on the fluctuations of the stock market. Every tick *up* was cause for elation. And because people expected so much from me, every tick *down* now put my nerves on edge.

I felt the pulse of every investor who had entrusted us with their investment capital.

Increasingly, I felt the need to get away. Away from it all.

We were seated in the VIP lounge of Terminal Three at Heathrow Airport. I was already up to my eyes in tension. When we checked in, we found that I'd forgotten our vaccination certificates which were required in order to travel to a foreign country. It was a Saturday, the only day of the week that you can fly on Qantas direct to Acapulco.

When we'd left Dell House – our home in London — an hour before, it was because I had come to a point where I was unable to handle the state of my nerves.

Now this.

I called for a car and driver, and send it rushing to our home in Totteridge, on the perimeter of London. Then I began urgently trying to reach Carmen, our maid, to tell her where to find the certificates. I thought they were in the study. Dear Carmen still refused to learn any English, even after 10 years in the country. Of course it is only fair to say that, likewise, we had not made any effort to learn Spanish. Valerie had a way of steering a middle course to communicate with Carmen. They had their own sort of language.

By the time I hung up from the call home, frustration compounded by frustration, I could only hope that Carmen knew *someone* was coming to pick up *something* important from the study.

Meanwhile, the flight was delayed by the weather. More frustration. I needed to be in the air. Away from here.

Why does my life always have to be full of tension, even when I'm going on vacation? It was strange that I didn't notice who had ramped up the pressure in my own life – namely, *me*. It was as if everyone else had done something *to* me.

I alerted the lounge staff that I was waiting for a call, then sat brooding about the prospect of reorganizing the flight and notifying our American friends, who had invited us to stay at their villa in Acapulco. At that moment, it was all too much for me.

Here was the other thing I didn't see about my situation.

I had become the top man by priding myself on tackling mountains of work. Now, within a short span of time, I'd become weary of people putting mountains in front of me and expecting me to continually produce mounds of wealth for them.

Something very deep was missing inside me. I had homes, car and a wonderful wife. I could go where I wanted, when I wanted. What I felt inside was only restlessness. And beneath that, a constant low-level anxiety.

What an odd position to be in: sitting in the VIP lounge in Heathrow, feeling miserable.

Valerie nudged me out of my gloom. When I looked up, she nodded across the lounge. There sat Jacqueline Kennedy Onassis in a mink coat, very near to us with her two children and a nanny.

Valerie leaned down and whispered to Justin. "Why don't you play with the little boy?"

Justin replied, "Why doesn't he play with *me*?"

Just then, my call came through. The vaccination certificates couldn't be found in the study. Then I remembered that they must be in the safe. I have never before tried to explain in English to someone who doesn't speak any English how to open the combination of a safe. Valerie did not know the combination. Between us, we managed. It took 20 minutes on the telephone. I wasn't keen to give the combination to the limousine driver, so Carmen took on the task.

Meanwhile, I was chasing the clock. My chest felt tight.

Fortunately, outside the fog was thickening and I was notified by a flight attendant: "Mr. Caplan, I'm sorry to tell you that your flight has been delayed."

I put my arms around her shoulders and kissed her on the cheek — she had no idea why, of course – and felt my blood pressure dropping.

I called the car hire firm to tell the driver where to find us. "I'm sorry, sir," was the reply, "he is delayed in the fog, as well."

My stress level went through the ceiling. Almost instantly I felt a headache coming on.

I worried myself all the way through lunch.

Eventually the certificates did arrive and I over-tipped the messenger.

I was so relieved when, at last, we boarded the plane. *Now* I could relax. Leave it all behind.

The first thing we felt when exiting the plane in Acapulco was the warm air brushing our cheeks and an anticipation of the rest. In the airport, we walked across a big, wide-open space where palm trees and a little breeze welcomed us.

The days in Acapulco consisted of swimming, water-skiing, and scuba diving. There were endless buffet lunches which caused us to linger and stare in bewilderment at the amazing variety of fresh and delicious food that entice us to fill our plates. Under the arbors of palm and banana fronds and sprays of bougainvillea, we feast off chicken, fish, beef, tortillas, succulent fresh papaya, grapes, melons… more than anyone could ever eat.

And in the warm night, high in the hills, there was the parade of men young and old, of beautiful young girls — undressed to win — and older women — undressed to compete — all with champagne in their hands and food constantly replenished by their side. The swimming pools yielded to diving and laughter, and incessant music drummed from the speakers…along with the ceaseless introductions and re-introductions.

I was glad my family was enjoying themselves.

I was there… and not there. I wanted us to be left alone.

When our holiday was over and time came to drive back to the airport, down the shoddy road flanked by lovely resorts, you could still feel the warmth of the sunshine.

I had believed that, for a few precious days, my money could buy me freedom. But it hadn't. Most of the time I'd thought about my deals. I'd spent money to be able to relax, but it didn't happen. I was too occupied with my business, and with the stress that never left me now.

How ironic, I thought.

I had become too successful to enjoy the spoils of my own very hard work.

Chapter Eighteen

HOLDING IT TOGETHER

I was now working a punishing schedule, by anyone's measure. With great success came great unending demands. Phone call by phone call, meeting by meeting, as my success rose I was headed downward in other ways. I was slipping under the avalanche brought on by my own success — though, in fact, I did not see it that way at the time. Or, frankly, see it at all.

But Valerie did. She had reached the point, as a loving wife who knew I had run so hard for so long, that something or someone was very likely to make me trip and fall over. She also knew that, given the speed at which I had been going for years, if I fell over it would take a long time to get up. If I could get up at all.

And one other thing: She knew that the two of us had drifted from each other.

After dinner one night, in her quiet way, she reached across the table and took my hand. "Joseph, do you realize how things have changed between us? I know that you love me, but in the early days when our life was more simple we use to take walks, hold hands, and chat and chat. We don't do that anymore, not because you don't want to but because you are so busy. I miss that."

It was sad but true. We now saw each other in the early morning and late evening, as I was coming and going. Mostly going.

"You and the children mean so much more to me than everything else put together," I replied. *Why did those words have such a hollow ring?* "But I'm cycling down a hill and I don't think I can stop."

Not only was I busy, I reasoned, but Justin was now away at school, which gave me some excuse for not being in touch with him and doing things that teenagers like to do with their dad. And then there was Julia. I had spent much more time with her as a baby. Now I didn't have much time to spend with her either. She had gone from toddlers' clothes to a little girl's pinafores while I wasn't looking.

Here's the thing: I kept *intending* to slow down, take more time to be with them. But I just... hadn't done that. There was always the allure of *the next big deal*, to seize and pull me along in its wake.

That evening, we decided to plan a Christmas holiday in Florida — to get far, far away from the office, the telephone, the takeovers, the decisions, the very problems which had created the barrier that now stood between us for the first time in all our years of marriage. I felt myself relax a little, felt my heart warm.

How had I nearly let go of this sense of connection to Valerie and my own children? *Why* had I done it? It wasn't the money exactly. It was something else, but I wasn't sure what.

I was hoping that, for two weeks at least, the City of London would vanish and Valerie and I would become close again.

When the plane thrust off the ground a few weeks later, I squeezed Valerie's hand and smiled at her, feeling that I was leaving everything behind. She smiled back — a *faint* smile, though. I swallowed hard.

We were off to Florida, having registered at the fabulous Breakers Hotel, which is perched on the edge of the Atlantic Ocean, with golf, tennis, amazing restaurants, long corridors, high ceilings, countless paintings, and spacious rooms. It was gratifying to be headed to this world-class resort for many reasons.

In years past, the Breakers had only admitted through its grandiose doors, members of 400 selected White Anglo-Saxton Protestants. When John F. Kennedy became president, he instructed that the hotel should be sued for discrimination under the Race Relations Bill. Now, its grand doors were opened to any guest with deep pockets and the owners sold out.

As we checked in, I felt a surge of pride: the place was typically all-American, in the nature of a huge palatial home, and all around us were the tanned, the lovely, and the privileged. Outside, the beaches and pools and excursion guides awaited. We followed the young man who wheeled our luggage to our room and found ourselves in an utterly delightful solitude and luxury.

Valerie seemed delighted, but also strangely subdued.

I looked at her and smiled. And this was the minute my adrenalin dropped and exhaustion took over. I dropped onto the bed and was soon out cold....

When I woke I felt physically rested; a bit at least. But at a deeper level I felt... *uneasy*.

Valerie was seated beside me on the bed, reading, waiting patiently.

I reached out to take her hand. She drew hers back. Calmly, carefully, she chose her words.

"Joseph, when you come home these days I hardly know you. You don't talk about the children. You don't talk to me about the future, which you always did. You're like a man obsessed with a vision — but I am no longer part of that vision."

I felt an ache in my chest. A hollow feeling in the pit of my stomach. Was I losing her?

"I know you're right, Valerie," I stammered. "I'm only trying to finish what I've started. I know that I'm doing too much, and when we get back I'm going to stop buying, stop pushing the boulder up the hill, give you and the children more time and get back to a normal life."

"I know how tired you are," Valerie said, leaning in to rub my shoulders. "But I can't say I understand what that means – to 'finish what you started.' For some time now money has not been an issue. I sense that you're pushing yourself beyond your limits. For what?... For *what*?"

When she finished she was in tears. "It's not that our life is empty, Joseph. Far from it. But it's full of everything *except* the love of a man and a woman."

At that, she choked up.

Hot tears were stinging my eyes. Emotionally, I had abandoned her and my own children. I felt like my chest was crushing from the pain of that thought.

I wished I knew the answer to her question. "For *what*?"

We did have enough money. I could have sold out my interests and we could have lived quite comfortably. *What was I reaching for? When would I be successful enough in my own eyes?*

Valerie finally slipped her hand in mine. I was grateful. She wasn't going to say, "We're through." That felt like a miracle. With all the luxuries that were surrounding us, we remained there in our private sadness.

For many long minutes I lay there, silent, pondering what she'd said. The beautiful room, the lavish hotel, the fabulous setting — all of it paled. I saw myself as so many businessmen I knew — doing what every successful businessman has to do to make it or be taken down by the competition. A man gets consumed by success and the desire to prove to himself and to others that he can work and make money.

Valerie had just given me a wake-up call. And I wanted – I so badly wanted to open my mouth and promise her that I would change *right then and there*. While I did not want to lose her and our life together, there might as well have been a mistress involved in my life.

The truth was, I wasn't ready to chuck it all and *fully* stop my climb to the top. It was as if success had become a mountain peak that kept moving further away the higher I climbed. As if the kid from the working class could not succeed *enough*.

Still, of course, Valerie's words had begun to soften me…and I took satisfaction in realizing I did in fact care about my family, and that there was hope for me as a family man, as a husband. That day I made a promise to myself that I would demonstrate to Valerie and our children that I was not all business – "Mr. Midas," the Money Man, the guy everyone looked to, to make money for them.

However.

The very next morning I was roused suddenly from a deep sleep by the phone ringing.

This has to be a mistake, I thought. At my side, Valerie murmured. The phone kept on ringing.

My arm reached out automatically to answer it. It wasn't the sleeping that mattered, but the state of mind. I was trying to get beyond the business barrier. I'd been brought 'round from a state of unconsciousness and pleasant oblivion.

Beside me, Valerie sighed — as if she knew what was going to happen before I placed the receiver to my ear.

The smooth, distinctive voice of John Bentley was at the other end of the telephone. John was a young, brilliant, entrepreneur who in the previous ten years had built up some substantial and profitable companies.

"Joseph, I'm sorry if I'm disturbing you, but if we can agree to the deal now I'd like to issue a press statement today."

"John," I croaked, "how can I concentrate on a seventeen million pound deal from here?"

"Well, I thought we'd agreed on all the main points," he replied.

"Yes, we've agreed on a number of points, but it has to be subject to contract. I need more details of your tax schemes and your toy deal with David Alliance."

"I've sold the toy business," he responded quickly.

"That's fine," I said. "Send my lawyers the details."

I knew on such a quick deal there had to be conditions. I had mixed feelings about the deal. On the face of it, the tremendous upsurge once again in capital assets and income seemed compatible with the trend of our past expansion. I wanted to leave the door open. I felt the surge of uneasiness I'd been trying to shake return with a vengeance. I could not afford to take my eye off the ball for one minute with this deal.

"I'll do it straight way," he said. "You don't mind if I keep in touch? There's no one in London at your office who will give me a decision."

For a split-second, the promise I'd made to Valerie not 24 hours before went through my head.

And was gone.

"Yes, of course," I murmured.

John hung up, satisfied he'd gotten what he wanted. My attention.

I laid back in the bed, knowing what Valerie knew – that she would have to wait for what she wanted. What my business got and she didn't.

Within twenty-four hours is was to learn a hard, unpleasant truth: My inability to give him a firm "No" until the formalities had been finalized had just wiped a couple of million pounds off the stock market value of my company.

All I wanted at that moment was peace. Solitude. To be left alone. And I wanted to show Valerie that our time together was a high priority. But now our chance to experience private joys was now highly unlikely.

Within perhaps minutes of hanging up John's call, the rumor passed around the Stock Exchange that London and County may be bidding for Bentley's Barclay Securities. Their stock market price picked up like a flash. I was news and £32,000,000 buying £17,000,000 was news.

The immediate drop in our market price reflected the normal selling by genuine or nervous holders when a large share exchange is in prospect. It is well known that shareholders in the smaller group, recipient of the bid, sometimes sell their shares for no better reason than, having backed one man, or one type of group, they simply do not wish to be shareholders in the larger group. Bentley certainly had a personal following, and with big Jim Slater (Slater Walker) in the background the market was only to anticipate the impending deal, even though the terms were not known.

Suddenly, in our "vacation hideaway," a series of phone calls from Bentley's people poured in, but each conversation failed to take the situation much further. I needed a lot more information before I would be prepared to issue a press release.

My moment of inattention had loosed a tidal wave.

The Economist was saying, "Bentley, Stripper for Stripping." And the Investor's Guide was saying, "Even Joseph Caplan of London and County who has taken whiz kid Christopher Selme's Drakes, has shied away from buying out Bentley."

It was generally accepted that I'd pulled out of the deal. Now I felt the pressure to return to London to convince the stockbrokers and everybody else concerned that I had given a firm "No" to acquiring Barclay Securities.

Still, Valerie and I made the best of the fact that we were 5,000 miles from this morass. We talked for five thousand hours every day. We went back five thousand years. We cried the bad year away and laughed the New Year in. The course of my life was back under control. I felt as if I was ready to return home and handle my life and my business in a sane and more balanced way. By the time we stepped on the plane for London, the course of my life and my marriage with the woman who loved me was back under control. A new kind of calm and a different strength of purpose moved me.

Back in London I got hit straight between the eyes, in the back *and* below the belt all at the same time.

The Annual General Meeting at London and County was like being thrown back in the boxing ring. It isn't often that the Chairman or the Directors get asked difficult questions at a company's annual general meeting. Most stockholders do not understand the workings of corporations. They don't like to rock the boat because they have stock in the company. They wouldn't want to say anything negative about the company's progress when the press is on hand.

I sat with Jeremy Thorpe on one side and Robert Potel on the other. Potel was a new director, the chairman of Cubitts Construction, the 2nd largest construction company in the UK in which we had acquired an interest.

We appeared to survive an endless barrage of prepared questions from the floor. In particular, there was someone whose inquiries showed he had prepared himself to cross-examine me in detail. We later discovered that he was an employee of one of London's large stock brokerage firms.

We complained to the senior partner of that firm, who appeared to have no knowledge of the employee's interest in our company. Indeed, they were quite aghast. I crawled back to my office, full of gunshot wounds, but still breathing, holding onto the belief that we were through the worst.

How wrong I was.

Looking back, I can now see how the London and County Group's commercial decline was about to be accentuated by the persistent comments in the press and by a bear market that was almost upon us. A bear market is, of course, a time when stocks as a whole continuously lose value assisted by professional sellers who seek, later on, to buy them back at a lower price. Few of my colleagues either recognized or took seriously factors pointing to the approach of the bear market that would soon manifest itself dramatically.

Perhaps if I had not been so stressed I might have paid more attention to the signs, as well.

When the furor settled, Valerie and I planned another getaway, in a way, to make up for the getaway that hadn't been one.

For nearly two weeks, my "only" contact with the office were daily reports and almost daily phone calls. By now I noticed very clearly that even when I was away from the office I wasn't fully with the people I loved. And though I *tried* to get free of the business world my mind was always preoccupied with takeovers, the press, people — things that I thought mattered so much.

Inwardly, I began to think that trying to change things was fairly hopeless. The situation was what it was. Period.

Why was I not fighting as much for my family as I was for my business ventures?

So it was, though. And now we settled back in our first-class seats, full of the heat, sunshine, the fun of glass-bottomed boats, crab races, endless throbbing music, and the best lobster and shrimp in the world – on our way back to London.

A cabin steward passed by and, even though it was Saturday evening we were handed the Sunday newspapers — the availability of which was made possible by the time differential. I flipped to the financial section and was quickly lost in the paper.

During recent months, I had been exploring ways of improving our standing in London's banking sector. I had no illusions. Like a restaurant the *Michelin Guide* wouldn't care to visit twice, London and County was unrated. And yet our assets were growing rapidly — too rapidly perhaps — and we needed cheaper money to utilize them to the best advantage. I didn't need to be born a banker to realize that among the quoted banks in London, there was no hope. They were either too large, or their shares were too tightly held by institutions who would certainly at this stage, have no reason to look at London and County.

I had discussed the matter at great length with Charles Warburg. We narrowed down our efforts to increase our stature in the City to two or three private banks — that is, those who were authorized by the Bank of England to deal in investment currency or foreign exchange and hold limited non-sterling currencies. This *had* to be our next step.

The jet engines began their accustomed hum, the voice over the loudspeaker gave the polite instructions and a welcome: "…douse cigarettes…fasten seat belts… we will be arriving on Sunday morning in London…."

But suddenly my attention was riveted as I stared at the City columns.

"Leopold Joseph Bank to go public on Tuesday."

We would arrive on Sunday.

I stared again to be sure.

"Leopold Joseph Bank to go public on Tuesday."

I switched-on like the Boeing's engines. In a few minutes, the thrust of the 727 took us off the ground, and me with it.

By the time we reached London I was intoxicated with the prospect of perhaps buying five, six, or even seven percent of their shares on the market, and maybe after six months or a year, announce a ten percent holding. The shares were to be offered to the public at thirty-four shillings, and 40 percent of the Bank was to become available on the stock market, valuing the Bank at a modest £3.5 million.

At that time, our own stock market capitalization was standing at just over £29 million. It had to be right. I could see the day in the not too distant future, when we would be more acceptable in size, and status in the City of London and in Europe. Then we could enter into discussions, which could lead to cooperation between our aggressive domestic business and their modest, but well-established foreign business. In the current market with the exclusive Bank of England's authorization we would be a much more versatile bank.

Monday morning came and my pulse was still racing. Our banking directors quickly studied the issue and fully supported me. I carefully consulted three separate stock brokers. The orders went out.

Since the issue was twenty-three times over-subscribed, that is to say, of the 587,354 shares offered to the general public, there were applications for twenty-three times that amount, it seemed unlikely that we would be able to buy many of their shares.

The following day — the Tuesday of the sale — the opening bell rang, and dealings in the shares began.

A stock market drama took place in the seven working days which followed. It was the opinion of many financial analysts that we had made banking history in a storm of bidding and dealing—and also that I had made my first powerful enemies including The Bank of England and people in the establishment who had looked at me from afar and were now not so far.

The press enjoyed every moment of it.

My next leap up that alluring mountain peak of success had happened in just seven days. We had acquired an astonishing 25 percent of Leopold Joseph, merchant bankers, at an average of 39s. 10 ½d. compared with the issue price of 34s.

I hadn't yet decided where the money was coming from. And the huge question remained — how would the Leopold Joseph board react?

When the news was announced that London and County had become the largest shareholder, it merited front-page coverage in the Sunday *Observer* and headlines in every City column throughout England. The Leopold Joseph shares charged up to 50s because of our involvement, and the possibility that we would bid to take over the whole bank. Their directors included Conservative Member of Parliament Anthony Berry whose family was connected with the *Daily Telegraph* and *Sunday Telegraph* and Jonathan Guinness of the Guinness family. Another well-known share holder from Europe was Baron Alexis de Rede. We had made a huge profit and a huge impact on the City in under two weeks.

On February 6, 1971, the *Daily Mail's* major headline read, "Battle for Leopold Joseph — We look on as they celebrate decimalization with the first takeover battle for a leading merchant bank in City history."

On the following day, their headline, and their placards throughout London, which were, no doubt, written by a different editor, "What is Caplan up to?"

Up to my eyes in delight, was my answer.

CHAPTER NINETEEN

POWERFUL ADVERSARIES

The sequence of events that avalanched in on me, left no hours in the day for me to relax.

An article in the Sunday *Times* spelled out the precarious – and potentially great – position in which I now found myself.

Sunday Times, Feb 14, 1971
Everything that a Raid on a City Should Be

'Joseph Caplan of London and County Securities is a quiet man. He is really not much like the dynamic brass-faced portrait that hangs in his Basinghall Street office, which gives the impression that he could sprint a mile, throttle a bear and sell someone a half-interest in the House of Parliament before breakfast. At 38, his dark hair softly turning grey, he is discreetly clad in banker's pinstripe and seems almost apologetic that there has been so much fuss over his latest coup-buying a nifty 25% of merchant bankers Leopold Joseph through the market.

Yet this daring attempt to gain control of a city merchant bank launched on the stock exchange only three weeks earlier has the makings of a city classic. To have bought such a strong position without any outsiders (and few insiders) suspecting a thing is a remarkable story but it also leaves an extraordinary situation where the Joseph board is implacably opposed to its biggest shareholder and the public has virtually ceased to hold shares in Leopold Joseph again.

Caplan, a business-minded barrister, unashamedly started at the fringe with an HP company call Dallance Finance. He transformed London and County from losses to 275,000 pound profit by bridging the gap between local bank branches and merchant banks with pricey overdrafts (5% over Bank Rate) for firms wanting to borrow 10-25,000 pounds at a time of growing squeeze. But unlike many "West End" bankers, he made the grade. He now has backing from United Drapery, which chipped in 350,000 pounds plus the Whiteley's in-store bank and ended with a 22% stake. After nine months of looking he finally decided that like-sized Joseph's big foreign business and coveted Bank of England authorization was just what he needed for expansion. The Banque de Paris et de Pays Bas, one of the largest and most prestigious banks in Europe, supplied the cash.

Caplan left things rather late. He had originally planned to make an approach to Leopold Joseph after it had completed its 1970/71 financial year on March 31. But when he and his wife returned from a winter holiday in Mexico, he discovered that Leopold Joseph was already on the launching pad and scheduled to take off on the Stock Exchange. Still slightly dazed from his long-distance flight, he held a snap board meeting at London and County at 3 pm on Monday, January 19 — and within two hours the directors decided to go ahead and purchase Leopold Joseph shares in the open market.

At 9:30 the following morning Caplan and fellow director Charles Warburg called on LJ chairman Sir Hugh Weeks and board director Heyman to disclose their holding (as statute required) and talk terms. It was not a meeting of minds. Joseph's directors appear to have been stunned and angry that their successful flotation could have been so dramatically turned upside down so quickly. By Monday they had not just recovered poise; they were able to ram out a statement rejecting "any proposals" that Caplan might make.

Now the war of nerves and wooing began. The board will have to do well if it is to keep all their support—it is only a pity there are now so few outside shareholders to get any benefit. Caplan is now on the classic raider's knife-edge. At the moment he has 800,000 pounds tied up which, even with cheap money from Paribas is producing no return But he seems no more depressed in rejection that he was elated in success.'

The writer was correct about one thing at least: I was now on a knife-edge, and felt it intensely. The shot of adrenalin I felt when we vaulted to this great success in seven short days continued to race through my system. The business was all I could think of especially as the press calculated that we had made 400,000 pounds profit on the purchase.

The rush of increasing my personal fortune in such a short time, and the rush of improving my ability to succeed in banking, were fantastic. Now I needed to manage this success.

The London banking world was humming with interest and speculation.

If this was a great coup — and indeed it was — the sequence of problems that followed took up every hour in my day.

First of all, I had to raise the money. I quickly solved the problem by calling one of our Institutional shareholders, Banque de Paris et de Pays-Bas in Geneva. Exchange control permission was quickly obtained as we were taking a loan from a shareholder.

Second, it was necessary for me to see the head of the discount office at the Bank of England, James Keogh. I'll never forget that interview. It was as though fate was being spun out for me and I was cooperating with fate by doing everything right.

Keogh, popularly known as Jim, said to me, "Well, you've done it!"

What he said was very clear and I felt very good about it. We both knew what it meant for us to be the largest shareholder in an authorized bank.

He then turned to Charles Warburg and discussed with him how Sir Sigmund Warburg had obtained authorization from the Bank of England by acquiring, years earlier, control of Seligman Brothers. At the end of the discussion, the scar of the Houston bank episode had gone. The irritation of someone on the other side of the fence, having told the press that I was a back street money lender had gone. We left Jim Keogh's office and walked past the large, faceless, counter, which had never had anything to offer a visitor except a polished bell reminiscent of the Victorian era, and a large notice which stated, "Bank Rate: 8%."

The sound of our steps on the stone floors, which led down to the main exit of the Bank of England, onto Threadneedle Street in the City, past the two tall uniformed ushers, was like music in my ears. I was hardly conscious of the traffic outside, and the dust that the narrow street always threw up at pedestrians. I crossed the road as though my life was protected, and returned to the office to plan our next move.

The next problem was dealing with the press. The press can be irrational, irascible and sometimes irresponsible. We tried to take it coolly and told them we were not planning a buy-out. I was surprised that the reaction of the Leopold Joseph Board, as reported in the press, should have been instantaneously antagonistic towards us, when they hadn't even heard our proposals.

Charles arranged an appointment for me with his cousin Sir Sigmund Warburg, so that I could tap into his wisdom. In the true style and tradition of great merchant banks, S.G. Warburg and Company on Gresham Street, did not have its name outside the door. They were just there. Charles announced us, briefly, to reception, and we took the elevator to the Director's floor, where we were expected.

Looking at the two men together, they could have been twins. Their faces were lined by time and experience. Both men gave the appearance of being tall, because of the impeccable cut of their dark grey suits. They spoke with the same intonation, very slightly high-pitched English, emanating from a German-continental background. Deep in their eyes I could read somber, reflections of the past. They had both seen a lot in their lives; two generations of banking. During the War, the Nazis took over their bank, leaving only one manager behind who was not Jewish. The Warburg's cousins seem to represent something significant which had come out of history. What separated them was not their appearance, nor their background in real terms, but the difference between their recognized achievements. Sir Zigmund had built up a great merchant bank in Europe, known as S.G. Warburg which continues until this day.

Sir Zigmund looked at me with a slight smile, mingled with a clear-cut somber expression.

"You will not get the Leopold Joseph board to agree to your bid, Joseph." he said.

Such was my respect for him, and so profound was the way in which he made his remark, I knew without hesitation at that moment, that this attempt to climb further up the City of London financial ladder would not succeed.

Even so, I replied, "As you know, we are now the largest shareholders. Their record is not impressive. They are not thought of in the City as progressive. We are growing, and from outward appearances, they are not growing. How, in the interest of the shareholders, can their board refuse to cooperate with us?"

There is trusting. And then there is too trusting. I would now learn that boards of directors are rarely mindful of the interests of their shareholders in public-quoted companies.

"You know Baron Alexis de Rede is a distant relative of mine," said Sir Zigmund. At that point, he looked at Charles, and his face, which rarely disclosed any form of expression for more than a second or two, concluded with distaste, "He will not agree to your bid. Neither will his friend on the Board Prince Rupert L. Weinstein, be likely to welcome you, or agree to any interference with the present management."

I do not know if I concealed my disappointment, but at the conclusion of our meeting, Sir Zigmund promised to call Sir Hugh Weeks, the chairman of Leopold

Joseph, in advance of my meeting with him. That was scheduled to take place on a Friday, a few days later.

On the following Friday, we agreed to meet the Board of Leopold Joseph at their bank. I couldn't think of a more appropriate colleague to accompany me than my co-director, Jeremy Thorpe. He was the leader of the Liberal Party, a fellow barrister, and skilled in negotiations. I felt confident and buoyed by his presence.

On arrival, we were shown into the boardroom, and shortly thereafter Sir Hugh Weeks appeared. Sir Hugh was also a Director of the Industrial Commercial Finance Corporation which held 8 percent of the Leopold Joseph stock. Two of the managing directors, Louis Heyman and Richard Cox-Johnson, were also present.

Heyman looked as though he had just been put through a washing machine. As they saw it, suddenly their jobs and their future were in danger. I could almost hear their private conversation. ("These people, these upstarts will take over our lives — all that we've worked for. And they know nothing.")

As we entered the room it was clear that Heyman was engulfed in rage. Cox-Johnson looked as though he would like to keep his lace shirt cuffs well away from me, in case I should dirty them. Sir Hugh Weeks looked tired, confused and plainly irritated at having to contend with this unexpected invasion from the "back-street" nearby.

I had briefed Jeremy Thorpe, and our objective was limited to establishing a relationship, to suggest an exchange of directors, which may lead to a full merger at a future date. I was determined to remain calm, dignified, respectful and naturally addressed my remarks to the Chairman.

"As you know, we have acquired the largest shareholding in your bank and we should consider the merit of an association, whereby we could be of benefit to each other."

Cox-Johnson said, "What could you possibly do for us?"

I didn't reply, but I didn't like the comment. I thought, *These people really hate us.*

When I had a moment to collect myself I explained that our domestic lending business was growing, that we were planning to extend the number of branches in the United Kingdom. I pointed out that since their foreign business and their access to financial markets as an authorized bank was not available to us. There was clearly a considerable growth potential if the two banks were to merge.

As I spoke I looked around the table inquiringly having intimated that I thought that we had a great deal to offer each other. I was talking with the words of a successful entrepreneur, however, not with the words of a banker. Their faces were glum and uncompromising. I tried to continue.

Louis Heyman interrupted, "You want our authorization." He was referring to their permission to deal in foreign exchange. His voice was angry and unpleasant.

The Chairman came to my rescue. "I think we should let Mr. Caplan finish what he has to say."

Heyman would have none of it. "There's nothing to talk about."

Jeremy Thorpe indicated to me that the discussion was going nowhere. Sir Hugh Weeks didn't in fact say another word, even as he shook hands on our departure.

From this moment, the opposition in every direction began to build up against London and County, except perhaps the *Guardian* newspaper. On February 9, 1971, the *Guardian* stated, "[Caplan] may have some hope that the mysterious Bermuda shareholdings might finally succumb, especially if the market price now dropped sharply." Palmer Company was subsequently transferred to a trust, however, and was well disposed to the directors, as events subsequently proved.

The *Daily Telegraph*, was inevitably skeptical. "The Bank of England may not welcome a stranger into the foreign currency and treasury bill dealings."

The *Times* was even more aggressive: "If Mr. Caplan decided to hold onto its 25 percent stake into accompany, the Leopold Joseph Board may decide on other ways out of an uncomfortable position."

I could sense the ranks were closing against us. Soon I would find out that the door was bolted shut and no one was going to keep their word. My attempt had awakened powerful adversaries.

When I revisited James Keogh, the head of the Bank of England's Discount Office, the following day I said in the course of discussion, "We bought the Leopold Joseph shares on the open market."

Stiffly, he replied, "That may be so. But I have to protect the sitting tenant."

I reminded him of his conversation the week before, when he had compared my bid for Leopold Joseph to the time that Sir Zigmund Warburg had taken over the Seligman Bank resulting in Warburg obtaining authorization — but to no avail.

That conversation was the tip of the iceberg, in relation to the trouble coming our way.

I received a call from Geneva from the Banque de Paris et des Pays-Bas. Although they not obtained Exchange Control permission from the Bank of England to finance the transaction, they now told me, "We are unable to provide the funds which were discussed."

I was shocked by what they said, I sent one of my senior colleagues to Geneva to find out how on earth they could suddenly deny that they had supported us financially with this investment, and how dare they, as a leading institution, threaten to dump our shares on the stock market if we did not comply with their request and replace their funds elsewhere. Their excuse? "It is our Head Office in Paris. We are very sorry."

I might have exposed the hypocrisy of the Institutional behavior, but I was focused on something else. Just as I'd learned how to fight and win back during my days in the service, I would fight and win in the banking world now. At all costs. I found the money elsewhere.

In a joint statement from London and County Securities and Bank de Paris et des Pays-Bas on February 25, 1971, we stated that London and County had not requested or received any loan facilities from Paribas for the purchase of Leopold Joseph shares. The *Economist* said, "Whatever is next in the City, Mr. Caplan, says that he is in no hurry, and can wait. Can any Institution feel safe from this kind of prowling, and should the Bank of England stand by and approve it?"

I had no friends in this situation, only a large holding of shares in Leopold Joseph, merchant bankers, in the City of London. Here was the problem: I had broken the unwritten rules of the banking community – especially the one that said it was ungentlemanly for anyone to seek to invade established institutions that are under the umbrella of the Bank of England.

The months rolled by. No one was really happy and we were getting uncomfortable, as well. To have over a million pounds tied up in an investment yielding very little wasn't doing us any good either.

Right out of the blue, Elizabeth Rivers-Bulkeley, an old friend of Charles Warburg, and a stockbroker with Capel, Cure, and Carden, invited Charles to lunch at her private apartment in the Barbican, an exclusive apartment building. After the usual exchange of niceties, she asked him, "Charles, you know about Leopold Joseph. What are Joseph's plans?"

Charles was his usual, discreet, unremitting self. "I would have to discuss this with Joseph."

The conversation continued, and they discussed old times, and other matters; they'd known each other for a long time. But the meeting produced no new information for the stock market or the press.

When Charles reported this story to me, having told her in his dignified way that so far as he was aware, I was unlikely to be dissuaded, he appeared quite unperturbed. A man who has seen so much in life, is probably not put out by these minor nuances, particularly since he was shrewd enough to guess the purpose of the lunch.

So the year wore on. One day, through an anonymous source, I was invited to have dinner with two gentlemen, whose names I'd never heard before, to discuss our shareholding in Leopold Joseph Bank. The dinner took place in the discreet environment of the National Liberal Club in Whitehall Place, London. The table was in a corner and our conversation was unlikely to be overheard.

I was curious, very curious. I thought that there was a breakthrough in the offing. Perhaps after six months of wearisome pestering from the press and shareholders (or even the Bank of England) and the mysterious shareholder in Bermuda, they were seeking a solution.

Unfortunately, nothing was to come of this meeting, and the victory I sensed in the offing — my last big step up to the stratosphere of recognition — was still hanging in the balance.

Toward the end of 1971, I let it be known via a City editor that I was a willing seller of Leopold Joseph stock.

No less than seven serious offers came our way.

Finally, on February 2, 1972, London and County announced 11 months after the event that we had placed with a private investor all our shares at £2, ten shillings, which gave us a very large profit. The delight in the Leopold Joseph camp had to be seen to be believed. The shareholders should have sent me a Christmas card for motivating their directors.

No such luck.

*Footnote: On February 6, 2004, Leopold Joseph, the London-based bank with a staff of 120 was sold to the Bermuda Bank of Butterfield for £51 million.

Chapter Twenty

CONTROL

It wasn't that I'd been insincere in my decision to spend more time with Valerie and the children. I wanted to make amends. But it was like I was two people — the man my heart wanted to be and the man my head wanted to be.

There are no excuses for failing to balance my life and make those close to me know and believe their importance. The truth is, something like an adrenalin rush drove me every day, and I loved that rush — that, and I really believed "just one more rung up the ladder" would satisfy.

"I know I said I would be around more," I pleaded with Valerie, "and after this next acquisition I will."

Even as I said those words, however, somewhere in the back of my mind I knew it was not true.

After dealings with the Leopold Joseph group, I poured myself into 1973, impressing on our stockbrokers the need to increase our capital. This was necessary in order for us to expand and have a stronger capital base. I was introduced to someone who was holding a large block of shares in the Inveresk Paper Group. Inveresk was a paper manufacturer in the throes of redeveloping much of their dormant property in different parts of the country. It had considerable financial resources, in spite of having lost £849,000 in the previous year. We studied the Inveresk property holdings, analyzed their uninspiring profit history, determined that their net worth far exceeded their stock market value, and decided to buy their stock.

In anticipation of making a takeover bid for Inveresk, we purchased 20 percent of Inveresk stock from this private shareholder for £1.5 million.

On November 2, 1973, we launched a purchase of approximately £8 million for the whole of Inveresk Paper Group. Inveresk was an old, established company with a reputable and professional board of directors, many of whom had strong City of London connections. They never expected to face a corporate raider. They were in shock.

The press called my offer "derisory," meaning that the price I had offered for the company was far below its true value. That was the whole point. We knew that the company was much more valuable than indicated by the share price on the London Stock Exchange.

We were now the largest shareholder and any other bidder would have to get past us.

On the day our bid was announced, Sir Isaac Wolfson phoned. I loved these calls. Not only was Sir Isaac Wolfson a man of class and distinction and a great businessman, his calls, like my association with Charles Warburg in the banking world, reminded me that I was nearing the very top of the ladder.

"It is a marvelous company you've got there, that Inveresk."

"We haven't got control of it yet," I replied. But I had come to love the word he'd used.

Control. Control of business. Control of capital.

In a way, it was not even about the money anymore. Somehow wanting security for myself and my family had transformed me into wanting greater and greater success… and now it had changed again and become about amassing great power and control of things.

The phone conversation had rolled on, and Sir Isaac was clearly very interested in the company. He knew a great deal about it, whether from past experience or having just examined the statistics, I did not know. It was clear that one way or another I had a deal on my hands. We had clearly opened the door to an exciting deal.

The statistics were interesting. There appeared to be no other shareholder with more than 2 percent of the stock. As far as I could see, there were no institutional stockholders holding any shares at all. The company had stripped itself down to a huge and potentially big-income-producing property, plus its main trading activity, which was paper manufacturing for mail-order companies. We had studied the situation carefully. There was no doubt that as far as the eye could see, their production would allow them very substantial profits, due to the world shortage of paper at the time. In addition to this, the many properties in the group were listed in their balance sheet at cost many years earlier and that's where the hidden profit lay.

Sir Isaac invited me to discuss the company with him. I was only too glad to seek his advice. To my surprise and delight, he offered us a 50-50 partnership in the deal. I pointed out that we needed to increase our capital by acquiring control of the company, unless we were significantly over bid and took a profit on our existing holding in Inveresk.

His attorneys put the deal together quickly.

And so we girded ourselves for a head-on takeover battle for Inveresk. We had taken six and a half weeks to compile the offer documents, after first announcing the bid. During that time, the Inveresk Board of Directors invited me to explain to them what our intentions were for the company.

I went to the meeting with Wolf Perry, our Senior Executive Vice President, expecting a small skirmish. I was wrong.

The board met in a long, foreboding room with a narrow table which seated approximately forty company directors. I was far out-numbered, but not intimidated; not at all. Wolf Perry and I had prepared our presentation. We knew that the most sensitive issue with the press and many of the company directors would be reducing the work force.

Cutting jobs was the normal procedure for a successful asset stripper. We had discovered that their many properties were on the balance sheet at book value only — that is, at the cost at which they had acquired the asset many years earlier. Therefore, the net asset value of the company's shares was far greater than what was reflected in their balance sheet. Sir Isaac obviously knew this, as well.

I looked around the table at their faces; their smart city suits and white-collared shirts, with their ties cradled close to their Adam's apples. I knew that there was unspoken scorn about us, as well as concern about their director's fees disappearing.

If I played this right, however, we would be in control of another great asset very soon and make a great deal more money.

On September 19, *The Guardian* published the following article:

> 'They [Inveresk] recognize that crude asset stripping following a takeover is no longer an occupation for gentlemen. London and County would not have missed that point either. With Mr. Jeremy Thorpe on the Board, and the Liberal Party espousing the calls of worker participation, Mr. Joseph Caplan will no doubt tread softly in the week of the Liberal Party Conference."

The press had me back in politics. What had the Liberal Party Conference have to do with our bid for Inveresk? Nothing. The heading of the article was "Goodies in the Locker." From all sides, hands seemed to be reaching out to stop us from opening the locker.

The other matter I had learned again and again over the years was how important it is to people to have control. Many times, I had persuaded the owners of private companies that giving up control to a larger group would benefit them and their families considerably. Some people like control simply because they don't want someone telling them what to do, but they don't do anything to make their assets grow, they just tick over. They draw their salaries, take vacations, and they don't really care if the stock is up or down. They disregard the fact that people had invested in the stock to make a profit. They want to be important, but they didn't do anything for the shareholders. In addition, this young, unwelcome tycoon — me — was now about to tell the world how badly they had managed their shareholder's assets for the last 20 years.

I felt amused as the phalanx of board members looked me over. I was from the new breed of the young and restless. We had invaded the complacency of the old school, they didn't like it one bit, and I could tell by the looks of disdain they didn't like me personally a whole lot. I had come from nowhere. I was not a traditional banker and I was going around the country upsetting the establishment.

Facing them, knowing their thoughts, I mused, *The fact that they don't like what's about to happen is their problem, not mine.*

At the end of the day, the meeting was inconclusive, because I said very little and they said nothing. They just looked ahead of themselves. I suspected most were mystified and wondering how this threat to take them over had happened.

I left feeling that control of this old company, with so much to offer, was in my grasp – and there was nothing these men could do about it.

Not long after this meeting, the Inveresk board countered by rejecting our offer. The Chairman, the Honorable H.L. Hood, who was also a director of their advisors Schroder Wagg, merchant bankers, indicated clearly that a cash offer, as opposed to a share offer, would be seriously considered, assuming that £8 million in cash was out of our reach. They were not yet aware of our backing from Sir Isaac Wolfson's bank.

I stuck to my guns. Profit or no profit, we needed to increase our capital structure so that we could increase our borrowing power. That was more important than the profit which might result from the intrinsic value of the company itself, or the espousal of its property assets. As often happens in a corporate raid, because the true value of the company had been suppressed for years, the interest of the shareholders, once again, was not being considered.

Nothing would have been more unwelcome in Scotland than to see the company fall into strange hands. We firmly declared that this was not our intention, but undertook to maintain the management and technical continuity of their commercial paper business and study their property assists which had already been isolated.

There was great excitement in the London and County Group's offices. All our directors knew that the Inveresk assets are worth many millions more than their market price. The talk in the office also revolved around the importance of the relationship with Sir Isaac Wolfson's Anglo-Portuguese Bank. Suddenly the bad noises, the clouds and the dust on the street shrank in importance and the prospect of making a huge leap forward was everyone's topic of conversation. Sir Isaac's bank participated by making underwriting funds available so that a cash alternative could be offered to the preference shareholders.

Certainly together with Sir Isaac Wolfson as our partner, we were on the right track. However, the politicians on the Inveresk board, using their influence, pushed us into the "Never Never Land" of the Monopolies Commission and froze the bid.

A transaction of this size could not possibly amount to a monopoly, particularly since the components of our Group, which apart from banking, consisted of diverse industrial interests, and did not in any way infringe upon the trading side of Inveresk Paper Group. We had no paper business at all. It was no monopoly.

Once the bid was referred to the Monopolies Commission, it became an impossible task. We were unable to proceed. Because of the disarray in the financial markets it was clear to me that a larger capital base meant survival, and Inveresk was the perfect answer.

Glasgow Herald March 6, 1974
Sharp increase in earnings for Inveresk

'Even without the reference to the Monopolies Commission, Inveresk Group's defense against the bid from London and County Securities late last year, to say nothing of the paucity of the bid itself, should have assured them of a victory.

Inveresk have how fulfilled the main planks of their defense, duly producing quadrupled pre-tax profits for 1973 of £2.08 million against £511,000 last time.'

Inveresk subsequently made a profit forecast of more than £2,000,000. A year later, their profits reached the staggering figure of £2,566,000 for six months. For 1974, the profit was £4.82 million with a new asset value of 110p, representing at least double our original bid of £8,000,000.

The shareholders should have at least sent me a thank you note.

Although the stock market generally declined during that period, by between 50 percent and 70 percent, their shares were one of the few which remained firm. Even in the worst moments of the bear market, Inveresk stayed steady. The City was unhappy and we were unhappy. In spite of the gilt-edged backing by Sir Isaac Wolfson's group many columnists decided that our attempts to take over Inveresk was unseemly because they were a revered institution and we were nobody. Looking at the profits, however, they were obliged to declare how right we were.

And I felt a deep sense of gratification. My hunches were right. My instinct for scenting-out profits made was accurate.

If I was not yet at the top of the mountain I felt at the top of my game. In control. The thing about being in control is that it's an illusion.

And the thing about being a man near the top is that it's unlikely you will have anyone coming to your rescue when the bottom falls out, as I was about to learn.

Chapter Twenty One

THE COLLAPSE

In the middle of 1973, two prominent attorneys invited me to dinner. There was something in their phone call that sounded a note of warning.

To my dismay, they'd set up the private meeting to subtly warn me that Jeremy Thorpe was about to become a huge embarrassment, one that was highly likely to cause much trouble for my company.

I half-listened to their vague warning, feeling more irritated than grateful. Given my headstrong nature and sense of loyalty to Thorpe – and with an exaggerated sense of my own importance – I dismissed them. Who were these men to warn me about someone on my own board?

Perhaps if I had removed Thorpe from the Board of Directors, things would have gone differently for us. And perhaps not. Second-guessing does no good.

Scandal broke around Jeremy Thorpe and, therefore, around London and County.

In 1973, Norman Scott, a male model in the United States, accused Jeremy Thorpe of having a sexual relationship with him, a criminal offense in England at that time.

Given the fact that Thorpe was one of the Queen's Privy Counselors, this was a *huge* scandal. The newspapers feasted.

Fast on the heels of that, a man named Andrew Newton claimed that Thorpe had hired him to kill Scott. In fact Newton met up with Scott and aimed the pistol at him, but the gun didn't go off. Peter Bessell, a former Liberal member of parliament, was identified as a chief prosecution witness, who claimed to have been present at the discussions with Thorpe about killing Scott.

Thorpe would be arrested and charged together with others of attempted murder.

The press were like sharks in bloody water, of course, and immediately began to link my company with Thorpe. Although they were attacking him with the view of bringing him down, our business was the whipping boy, and all at once his influence on my life and my bank was disastrous.

In the end, Thorpe's jury was split 6-6 and found him not guilty. Mr. Justice Cantley was widely criticized for showing a "nakedly pro-establishment bias" when he summed up for the jury. In other words, because Thorpe was connected to the Royal Family and by reason of his position as head of the Liberal Party the judge chose to diminish the evidence against him and maximize the credits that his attorney placed before the jury.

In the weeks and months that followed, the press slammed London and County, referring to it as "Thorpe's bank." Much damage was done to the company because of its association with Jeremy Thorpe. Especially galling was the fact that it was *not* Thorpe's bank. I had scrambled and put in long, long hours… and years… to build the London and County Group, and now because of the questionable acts of one man it was under siege.

Day after day, the headlines blasted us.

And day after day I paced my office, blaming myself bitterly for choosing someone to be on our board for all the wrong reasons — because of his privileged position and, to my great shame and embarrassment, the thought that perhaps he could one day angle for me a knighthood.

If only the Thorpe scandal had been the only crisis.

The first signs of the oil crisis came in 1973 when the price of oil was quadrupled from $4 to $16 a barrel. The financial markets virtually closed up. Short-term borrowing is a vital ingredient of the banking market, and the price of short term money even for accredited borrowers climbed to over 20 percent.

That year, London and County Securities collapsed, as did numerous other financial institutions and banks. Some of the institutions that normally step in to rescue succumbed to the same problems themselves, because the government did not step in to save them.

A run on a bank occurs when there is fear. A lack of confidence takes place when depositors don't believe anyone is going to step in and help. News being what it is, everyone knew what was going on and the press made it worse.

And when the avalanche starts it cannot be stopped.

I was struggling — in the business and with my emotions. Staring at a sinking ship, unable to do anything about it.

Valerie came close to me in those days. She didn't know all the details, but like everybody else she was reading what the press was saying.

"You've worked so hard all these years and you've done your best. Don't be afraid, you can't be responsible for things that are out of your control."

Out of my control. Yes, that was the truth. But I didn't want to hear that.

"I love you," Valerie said, "and nothing will ever change that. I want you to know that I love you."

I felt a knot in my throat. How had I won the love of such a loyal, compassionate woman? I certainly didn't deserve it.

I would need Valerie's love. Desperately. Very soon so much hatred and venom would be aimed at me.

The London and County Group – the "mountain" of my success — was collapsing daily before my eyes. My company's demise was a symptom of the crash, not the cause of it. The value of our investments dropped considerably. This, quite naturally, aggravated the view that our capital investments needed to be written down in our current financial year. As it did with other banks, including the five major banks in England, this caused worries about the value of our investments and the inherent capital value of the group as a whole.

As a result of this bad publicity, a telephone conversation took place with the Department of Trade and Industry, the equivalent of the Securities and Exchange

Commission (SEC) in the United States. Mr. Skinner, a Labor member of Parliament, had been constantly quoted as referring to the Group as "Mr. Thorpe's Bank." Skinner was the Barney Frank of his day. Since Mr. Thorpe was in an opposing party, London and County became a pawn in the other party's attempt to destroy Jeremy Thorpe's Liberal Party's ascent. Politics is really a sick, slanderous and sometimes ruthless profession.

The Department replied, "There is no reason to investigate the London and County Group in the manner demanded. The questions have been dealt with to the satisfaction of the Department."

Meanwhile, the unclarified situation was broadcast in the press, and it was sapping our strength and the public's confidence. The crisis, the decisions far above our heads, and the surging tide of condemning verbiage caused us to suffer a severe reduction in deposits, and the money market as we were being constantly asked whether or not the matter had been cleared up. Suspicion and uncertainty remained in the air and the whole situation became dangerous, muddled and confusing.

The final straw may have been the association with Thorpe. The hypocritical moral standards of society condemned Thorpe for having a double life. The press continued to have a hey-day with the scandal.

The publicity was pulling us down.

While all this was going on, a door opened which had the potential of taking us a further step forward to becoming an authorized bank and removing the cash flow difficulties. A surge of hope reignited my business.

Here I was, watching my empire crumble, and yet my confidence in myself and my success remained unshaken. It never entered my head that there would be insurmountable obstacles to prevent this from happening. I could have been content with the incredible commercial growth we had experienced and the fact that now we were a rapidly-growing domestic banking company. Personally, the stressful ups and downs of this high level of business were taking a huge toll on me.

Unfortunately, ambition doesn't always have eyes to see or ears to hear.

A year before, in November 1972, we had carefully noted the well devised and monitored launching of Fraser Ansbacher, merchant bankers authorized by the Bank of England to deal in foreign exchange. We bought not a single share, but the planning had begun.

Nearly a year later on September 19, 1973, we made our move toward Fraser Ansbacher, a small well managed bank. Even with stock markets in a bad condition, we were capitalized at approximately £26 million while they were capitalized at something like £10 million.

Their banking expertise and their status in the banking market would give us easier access to professional and money market deposits and the link with Sir Maxwell Joseph and his empire would undoubtedly not only enhance our reputation, but eliminate once and for all the bulk of and the worst of rumors that had been circulating about our Group during the previous six months. This was not the first time I had approached Maxwell Joseph.

I respected him. He was highly regarded in the city and very successful. He was succinct, positive, and immediate in his attitude, which was an essential part of the makeup of his personality.

At my very first meeting with him on the proposed merger, between London and County Securities and Fraser Ansbacher, he said, "I am in favor of the proposition. It would suit me very well at the present time."

The head of our banking division was with me and he was surprised at the immediacy of Maxwell Joseph's response. Nevertheless, there it was. We had a deal on our hands.

A series of meetings followed.

When I met Maxwell Joseph he chuckled and said, "Well, Joseph, you've blotted your copy book in the City. I'm willing to buy your entire shareholding." At the current market value, assuming no more or less, that would have given me and my family holdings something over £5 million; two years earlier it had been over £20 million.

As always I wanted to be in control — of my life, and of more and more capital.

I replied firmly and unhesitatingly, "Sir Maxwell, I don't want to sell out. Banking is my career and that is how I see my future. I have no wish to change it. What I want," I continued, "is to be chairman of the new group."

After a moment's thought, Sir Maxwell nodded in agreement.

Looking back later I would realize many things: I would not regret my unswerving persistence in staying with the job. I had built up my business and I truly, passionately, wanted to see it reach its full potential.

What would never be clear was the moment that pride and ego took over — the moment when my success became inextricably intertwined with what was good for the business. I would later realize that making decisions that are best for the ego is not the same thing as making decisions that are best for one's business.

The meetings with Maxwell Joseph and various directors of his bank progressed from that moment to a very advanced stage. There was a lot to be decided, but the main principles had been agreed. I was happy because, as spelled out in that agreement, the management of all the banking on the Fraser Ansbacher side of the merger would be run by his bankers, while I would continue to manage the Investment Banking and the Industrial Companies in the group.

So far, so good.

A crucial meeting which would have almost certainly resulted in a joint press statement indicating the proposed merger was scheduled to take place on Monday, December 3, 1973.

Unfortunately for me, this was the very day that I was fighting with the Consortium for the survival of the London and County Group, its depositors and shareholders. My negotiations with Sir Maxwell Joseph were to terminate on the day that the Consortium was formed by the Bank of England to take over London and County.

The final ratification of fourteen years of ceaseless effort was therefore denied to me. Banker never-to-be and assets-stripper no more.

It was over.

Chapter Twenty Two

DROP FROM THE TOP

It was over. But I didn't know it was over.

Perhaps more accurately I wouldn't let it be over.

My face remained "set like flint," as the saying goes, to reach the highest rung of the ladder in the financial world. Despite opposition and the fact that the economy was rapidly in decline I would fight through to the end. After all, I'd fought through everything to this point — and had nearly achieved the success I wanted. I was so close to being the man at the pinnacle of the heap. Inside, I was still the young man fighting for the title belt at the university, the barrister-turned businessman fighting for his father's company and financial wellbeing, the wheeler-dealer making a Christmas Club work for struggling working class people. I didn't see myself as a saint, I was no saint; rather I was a man with intensity — one who had become increasingly, intensely over-focused and, therefore, myopic.

Focused on what I now needed and craved – success – I would not look at the bigger picture of what was happening all around me.

Now, in 1973, there was too much buying and selling activity taking place in the company stock, even though there was a general malaise of the stock market as a whole. Its effect was much more damaging since, as stock brokers constantly informed us, "In this market you cannot give away gold bars today." This was a favorite expression by stockbrokers during bad market conditions, meaning that it was difficult or impossible to find buyers.

Unmistakably, we were slipping like everyone else, and the buying and selling of our stocks meant our worth rose and dropped... and kept dropping... like a toy yo-yo running down.

I tried hard not to believe it. I didn't *want* this to happen, and didn't *want* to look at it as a possibility. I tried to convince myself that people were just panicking, and I was tired of people flapping about their sinking stock. For one thing, I had more money invested in the stock than anybody. I was losing more than anyone else.

For another thing, there was too much of me in the business for it to fail. I'd fought and succeeded for 14 years of my life to get this far. I was not going to let myself become a failure. That was simply out of the realm of possibility.

On August 5, 1973, the Sunday *Telegraph* City Column mocked and reviled the front cover of our balance sheet, which depicted a Victorian gentleman with a quill pen designed to portray our founder. Though the company was founded in 1869, The *Telegraph* implied that the vintage character was none other than the Right Honorable Jeremy Thorpe – who had now fallen into utter disgrace.

During August, rumors resulting from the irresponsible articles published by a leading Sunday newspaper prompted one of the directors of the banking division to sell all of his stock in a panic. He wasn't the only one. Some people get comfort in a storm when others share the misery.

This director called me in France. He had been told by the editor of a leading newspaper that they were going to bring London and County down the following Sunday. We would never be the same again, and thus we were a good sale. This prompted me to communicate with Lord Goodman, who explained that in his capacity as Chairman of the Newspaper Publisher's Association, he was unable to act personally on our behalf to retract or apologize for the unwarranted and slanderous attacks.

I could hardly believe it. They wanted to destroy us. And *me*. All because it would be great for newspaper sales.

I dashed back to London. I felt so miserable that I wanted to jump into a whiskey glass. When you have problems like this, you drink a lot – or at any rate I did.

Nothing can more seriously undermine the confidence of a company of the London Stock Exchange, even bad or disappointing results, than the threat of a vicious press attack.

Shortly after this, a popular daily newspaper, The *Daily Mail*, began conducting persistent attacks on our group of companies. The City Editor from the newspaper telephoned Woolf Perry, our Executive Deputy Chairman, on many occasions, cross examining him about a variety of matters affecting the company's affairs. "Are you still getting in deposits?" "Are you planning anymore take-overs?" "Is Jeremy Thorpe active in the company affairs?"

Articles in that newspaper continued up to and beyond the time of the change in management at the London and County Group in December 1973.

Now I felt angry. Grudging.

I had made a lot of people a lot of money. The climb to the top is slow and tedious. Going down is like taking an express elevator.

I had proved to people who, at the beginning, yelled at me for money, that I could make more money than anybody around. Maybe that is what drove me in the direction I went when it all started.

Now I tried to analyze how and why people were beginning to destroy me. I came too far too quickly from the wrong place.

As a result of lawyers informing the editor of the newspaper of the conversation between the director of London and County and his friend, the article which he had stated would appear the following Sunday was never printed.

I needed to rest from all this unfair attention and tension. I had *earned* some rest from it all. I went back to my yacht for another week and tried to get lost at sea. When I was away from the world of telephones and press I could stop reacting and have space to think. Valerie, as always, was by my side. All I wanted to do was look at the water and find some peace.

We set sail from the coast of France, headed to Sardinia. In a short time, a nine-force gale blew in and for a couple of hours life came into proportion as I held tight to the rail, thinking we might drown. When we came through that gale, I took it as symbolic. Maybe our problems would just dissolve the way the wind had suddenly changed.

I checked the ship's compass to see if we were on or off course – and found myself reflecting deeply on my life.

From back home in England, the news continued to penetrate into my getaway that more and more businesses were closing their doors. Each day there was a new headline announcing the demise of another bank or financial institution. The whole of what was known as the secondary banking industry was collapsing. Adding to that, because of my unwise association with Jeremy Thorpe I was receiving an inordinate amount of negative publicity, which only made a bad situation even worse. How quickly I'd gone from being "Midas" — the Money Man — to being a whipping-boy.

Why had I allowed myself to steer my life by the star of making money, grasping for power and control? seeking to have my own ego gratified and imagining myself on top of the heap of success?

I found myself longing for simpler times – wishing I could go back to the days of being with my grandmother and grandfather over a Seder dinner.

What had happened to that young boy who, inspired by a deeply spiritual grandfather, had only wanted to give his life to making the world a better, more just place? It wasn't that my life had gone off-course morally, but this certainly wasn't the course I'd set out on.

For a split-second a realization began to come clear:

Somewhere along the line, I let go of my earliest sense of direction – the values that were all about helping other people. My ambition had only been about personal gratification – about my success. And Valerie and the children – and I – have paid a heavy cost.

In fact, I was also beginning to experience physical ramifications of the stress. Exhaustion. Indigestion. A tightness in my chest I kept ignoring.

And then the thought was gone, swallowed under waves and waves of other thoughts, about the potential loss of my business and my fortune. And strategies I would use to keep fighting.

Too soon, we were back in London and I was in the midst of utter turmoil.

On London and County's last trading day, with the whole stock market plummeting, my stockbroker told me that I could "kill the bears" (by which he meant, other stock market gamblers, who sold shares at higher prices in order to buy them back at a lower price later and make a profit). So I bought 50,000 at 80 pence for £40,000, the lowest price at which our shares had ever traded.

And then, to my helpless horror, the shares were suspended from trading shortly afterwards at 40 pence. I had purchased them at the lowest price ever, and two hours later they were worth nothing.

It really was over. *Still*, I couldn't face it.

After a nightmare, you wake up and the bad memory of it quickly fades. My real nightmare was very different because it went on and on. Few men are able to recognize disaster when it is immanent. You've worked so hard the possibility of it all crashing down and wasted is untenable. The hope it will turn around and begin to come right again stays with us right up to the end. In my case I had many good reasons to hope that things would get better.

In the wake of our financial collapse, the Bank of England swiftly appointed First National Finance Company to manage all the Group's companies.

I went to the office early on the day when my business was taken over, believing that First National would find a way to make us solvent again.

Something was going on inside me, though. I felt dazed, as if I didn't know who I was. Dougherty, the chauffeur was glum and silent, even more so than usual. He must have wondered what on earth I was going to do. The truth is, I didn't know myself. I didn't understand the machinery or the process that I was now a part of. I was anxious about our depositors.

I opened the door that last day and walked in to the banking area of London and County. Customers were lined up in front of the teller windows as always. The staircase to all the offices was to my right. I headed up those familiar stairs.

Two weeks before, I would have been greeting employees as they wished me good morning, my mind busily considering phone calls I had to make and which files on my desk needed attention. Now I dragged myself up the stairs and when I entered my office, my desk was empty and someone had stacked my files in packing boxes. My first inclination was to take all of them out.

I saw strange faces – men from First National, who were nodding at me as if I were superfluous, which, I realized suddenly, I now was. My lips and hands felt numb, as a mild shock set in. I'd known they would be there, but now the world felt hazy and distant. The staff looked at me with extremely worried faces. I tried to smile, but my facial muscles were frozen. This was my office the last time I'd left it, and now I had no idea what I was doing there.

As if someone had not just lost the dream they'd fought so hard for, the men from First National moved about, ignoring me, with big grins on their faces. They were sealing all the filing cabinets and checking anyone who was walking around with a file.

Life surged back into me, and I began to tremble with anger.

"I demand to know what's going on here."

"Your bank is now under our control."

Control. No longer mine. Someone else's.

More waves of numbness and rage went through me. I hadn't agreed to terms of the takeover. In fact, I hadn't even seen them. What was going on here?

The next bombshell hit.

Jeremy Thorpe had illegally signed off on behalf of the corporation without authority or communication with the other directors. In fact, he was not even an executive director and there was no quorum. We were out of money, to be sure. The Bank of England had canceled all our lines of credit. A controlled bankruptcy probably would have made better financial sense. We owed hundreds of millions, but hundreds of millions were also owed to us as accounts receivable from borrowers.

No matter. It was too late to do it differently. As the staff of First National began to seal cabinets containing my personal files I went berserk.

"I demand that you give me my personal files," I nearly shouted at the man in charge.

He hesitated, walked away, then turned around and released my file cabinets to me.

After a couple of days of this turmoil, First National sent me packing. I called our corporate attorney, but he wouldn't take my calls. Later, I was astonished to learn that he was a director of First National, the very company that the Bank of England had appointed to take us over.*

* Less than a year later, First National Finance itself would collapse. The Bank of England who had put them there, did not step in to save them. The nightmare spread. Everyone was going broke. The property market, once a bastion of strength and security, was no longer able to sustain the pressure. It collapsed and took most of the lenders with it.

By now I didn't have the money or the will to continue to fight.

I was lucky that my marriage was not harmed. Valerie did everything as though nothing had changed. We spoke about all the bad things that were going on, if we could ever claim something from the wreckage.

I was unlucky in that, after so many years of fame and fortune, I was suddenly shunned by people and reviled by the press. People love success… and people love failure, so they can stamp on it.

The Times April 28, 1978

'The crash of London & County Securities Group sent waves throughout the whole banking system. Other "fringe" banks followed London & County into collapse, including its rescuer, First National Finance Corporation.

Indeed, at one time it looked like endangering the financial stability of the big four clear banks, National Westminster, Lloyds, Midland and Barclays, and a rescue led by the Bank of England staved off a more general failure. The danger initiated by the Caplan bank crash was of a run on one bank leading to a run on all.'

The first morning after I was ushered out of my own office was not real. The mornings after that were even worse. I had nothing to get up for. I wanted night to go on indefinitely.

People phoned, but not many. Most of the invitations Valerie and I got for dinner or coffee were based on curiosity. How does a man with the "Midas touch" look or speak after losing how many millions?

Valerie didn't say much. She could have said, "I saw this coming, but you wouldn't listen to me." Or she could have said, "Why did you let them do this to you?" In our life together, Valerie had occasionally tried to slow me down, she didn't push. I felt like curling into a ball and tucking myself emotionally inside our marriage.

This impulse was not due to my personal failure alone. Life in relation to the outside world became terrible.

The whole country was in turmoil. Jeremy Thorpe, our infamous director, was being prosecuted for attempted murder and other unsavory charges. Outside the walls of my home there was a search light focused on me as well as him.

My head was spinning. My financial and emotional losses were enormous. We lived in a time when the stock market had collapsed and anybody who was involved in any kind of investment was losing money. As I prepared myself for each session with the Board of Trade enquiry, my attorney, Sir David Napley, looked askance as he saw me take a brandy flask from my pocket and drink from it. He looked away when, at the same time, he saw me swallow a couple of Valium. My head quickly felt like a grocery bag stuffed full of paper.

Looking back I feel shame. You can't close your eyes to imperfection or you fall blindly into an abyss. I always thought of myself as a runner carrying a torch. Sure, I lost my way from time to time and set fire to a few vineyards on my way, but I always left the soil unharmed. This is not how the financial world or the world at large would see me.

Months later, the Board of Trade published a thick volume of opinions which made me look as though I was running a television shop rather than a conglomerate of 84 companies. And so it was. Officialdom called me in over and over and asked me questions. So many questions. They were like parking meter attendants. All they were interested in was issuing tickets. While I was being interrogated, I sometimes felt that I was at my own funeral and the eulogy was terrible.

The London and County Group employed more than 14,000 people in over 30 locations. I suppose it is true that things were sometimes forgotten, overlooked, or even deliberately ignored, but since 1960 we had provided excellent service to many people in industries as wide ranging as banking, pharmaceuticals, property, engineering, construction, and so on.

All in all, however, I felt like a scapegoat for the economic ills of the country.

Prior to the inside information I'd received from the two lawyers, well after installing Thorpe on our Board I'd had no idea of his secret life and just how intense the publicity surrounding him would get. Secrets can remain secret only for so long, and Thorpe's emerged in a particularly ugly way, culminating in his trial for conspiracy to commit the murder of his alleged male lover.

For months it seemed as though everything was falling down around me and now there were no Board Meetings, no stock to support, no financial reports, only one telephone line instead of dozens.

Every morning when I woke up now, all I could hear was the sound of traffic outside my bedroom window. None of those cars were coming to my house.

I have no words to convey the depths of despair when I saw everything I had worked for crumble before me. It is surprising that within myself, I didn't seek to blame other people, but later on, on multiple occasions I tried to analyze how I could have put things right. I realized that the forces against me are much too strong because of my ego and because of my talent and because of my mistakes.

I had gone too far too quickly. I had never stopped to consolidate. I had never stopped to look at the world around me and take advice from decent people who were not out to steal my thunder or encroach upon my ideas. What I had done was develop my own sense of right and wrong. Because of my amazing success, I had taken the view that I was always right. As for me and my house, disaster was around the corner.

And so it was. My capital had evaporated with the stock market. I couldn't see any hope for the future. My path to this point seemed unreal: I began with a wig and gown, got hijacked into a rag factory, pioneered banks in major department stores, went 'round the banking world buffet style and floated to Corsica on a 72-foot yacht. Now I was going back to France with nothing but a telephone that didn't ring.

Valerie and I discussed our next steps incessantly. Frankly, I was in no shape to put two feet on the ground. Who would want to work with someone who had his face in the newspapers with the kind of publicity which would make most people faint? I didn't faint, but I was very unhappy and unsure of my future for a very long time.

We decided to take the children and leave England, park ourselves in France just over the other side of the Mediterranean, and figure it out from there.

I had no clue what I would do next. Or that the worst was not over. Not by a long shot.

Chapter Twenty Three

NO PEACE

Pain drove us from England.

All those thousands of hours of hard work, planning, and stress had left me with nothing to be proud of. Even after spending so much time with so many people, because of the trouble, there were no more friendships. The good memories were eclipsed by the bad.

After months of emigration formalities with the Home Office and immigration formalities with the Consul in France, we arranged to ship our furniture and said good bye to Mum and Dad and the few people who had continued talking to us. My one thought as we flew from London to Nice, where we planned to take refuge in a small house, was that I wanted to be somewhere unfamiliar, where no one would recognize me and there were no London newspapers.

When we arrived in St. Jean Cap Ferrat, a small peninsula jutting out toward the sea, the Mediterranean sprawled open to our right and the cliffs were on our left. We turned into the Boulevard General de Gaulle and came to the Villa Soleillas, where a curving driveway, flanked by plants on either side, swept up and around for about 40 yards to the house.

At the top of the driveway, beside the garage, was a short flight of brick steps which led to a large terra cotta tiled balcony overlooking the sea and the front door of the house. I carried Julia, who was two years old, up the steps. She was fast asleep and I laid her gently down on the living room couch. At least one of us was at peace.

The spacious living room with a sizable fireplace was on the first floor, as well as the kitchen and dining area that looked out over the Mediterranean. The master bedroom also had a view of the sea and doors leading out to a small, oblong swimming pool, and there were several more bedrooms and another large terracotta balcony overlooking the sea on the second floor.

After a brief inspection tour, I stepped outside behind the house, where there were more stone steps, leading to a seating area in the rocks overlooking the water. The first days in our hideaway I would spend many hours there gazing out over the sea.

From my first moment alone here I was sure that one axiom was true: Wherever you go, there you are. Even in this beautiful place my mind was tormented.

In the weeks that followed, we picked up our identity cards and became familiar with the local shops. It was good to look at people and not see them look back.

For a few days, Valerie and I spoke very little. Valerie had a lot of organizing to do. She was busy preparing food, cleaning, and putting the home together. Our furniture from London arrived soon after we did and everything was put in place. This was to be our refuge from the storm that was raging back in London.

I was very restless. Sleep did not come easily. When dawn came, I got up, walked to the window, and stared at the sea. Then came the flood of emotions. The world I knew, that I had built around me, was not there anymore. The phone was not ringing. There was no secretary. No meetings. No clients calling. No directors coming in and out of my office. No propositions to consider. No deals to close. No expensive lawyers. All that: gone. Nothing was happening. Without something to *do*, it felt like there was no reason to *be*.

The house was a few minutes from the sea, and I went down to the beach many times and took long walks. With my shoes in my hand, I would walk along the water's edge, watching as the water came up and covered the sand and then rushed back out again. As it drained away, my toes sank into the sand.

The sand running out beneath my feet…the pull of the tide…it made me think of how quickly everything can come and go. Success. Money. People's admiration for you. Time. Everything. What you believe was solid ground, what you build your life on, can all run out so swiftly.

The water stretched as far as the eye could see, and all I could do was look at its vast emptiness. And that's how I saw my life. Directionless now, without a hill or mountain to climb.

As I walked and stared, the voices inside rose and fell.

Over and over I thought, *It didn't need to happen.* But who exactly was there to blame? A whole set of circumstances and players had brought about the collapse. Back in my boxing days I'd have gone after an opponent. But there was no one to take a swing at.

Somehow, the voice inside wanted to say something, not about the circumstances or all the other people involved, but about *me.*

I hadn't done anything morally wrong, but still…. Something felt amiss in the way I'd been living my life and pursuing my career. But what?

The deep foundation of moral training I'd received from my Jewish faith and heritage came back to have its say – and now it began to speak loudly. It was as if I could see the face of my grandfather Hersh, and hear what he might say to me – lovingly, but firmly, as well:

Yoseleh, you were too ambitious for worldly gain. And so proud. Do you remember how you set out to help other people? You lost your way when you forgot about others in your drive to see yourself at the top. It took control of you and you didn't know when to stop….

It was all there in that recrimination: the truth of how, little by little over time, I had strayed from my original course.

Barrister. Rag Merchant, Banker. Failed Financier.

I had to turn off the recriminations somehow.

I could not.

As I continued my walks along the Mediterranean the sea was sometimes ferocious and sometimes calm, like my moods. I would wade up to my waist in the water. The rise and rush of the waves almost engulfed me, and with every one that broke around me I thought, What now? *What* next?

I felt as if my life, which had once been founded on a sense of community and a mission, had become founded on little more than self-seeking ambition. And now it felt like sand on the beach, running out with every wave.

When I would emerge from the edge of the breakers, my feet and pants were soaked. My body would shiver from the cool weather. There were no tourists in the water or anywhere nearby.

I felt lonely and vulnerable. An inner voice kept coming at me, with each ocean swell. *What has all your ambition gotten for you?*

Looking back, I was aware that I'd been driven by the need for more – more power, more capital, more press, more approbation from clients and stockholders and business moguls. I had loved playing to the crowd. Even when I was abroad, I was in constant contact with the office or with the financial press. Even when I'd travelled, the hotel porters were constantly delivering telephone messages – like the one in Italy who had said to me, "*Signor* Caplan. Telephone, please—your office is give you no peaces."

I almost smiled at that memory. Except it was all gone now. Swept away by economic and political forces beyond my control. Sometimes, along with the memories and the grief and anger, a twinge of pressure would grip me inside my ribcage, as if my heart were doubling into an angry fist.

And so, there we were, isolated in a house by the sea, where I felt like my life, our life, had been swept away.

To compound my own pain, I saw that Valerie and the children had left behind their familiar lives and friends, too. The phone was there, but most of Valerie's friends kept their distance. Her world had changed as much as mine. Somehow – a miracle to me — our love hadn't weakened one bit. In fact, it was even stronger than before.

That was a good thing, considering what lay just ahead.

The depth of our catastrophe was settling deeper into me every day. Not only had I lost my personal fortune, but news from London was bleak and getting bleaker. The media decided that I alone had brought down London's banks. The economy was in a mess, so someone had to be blamed, and I wasn't there to answer back and defend myself.

One politician said, "Caplan has f—-d up the whole stock market."

I felt as if I'd been kicked in the stomach. I had thought, so mistakenly, that one could arrive at some pinnacle of good fortune and that would mean you would be safe, secure, and admired for your hard work. How could I have been so mistaken?

So many people had jumped on board. Many made fortunes over the years as the stock in my companies climbed. In fact, I had kept a private notebook listing about 10 people who had become millionaires by holding my stocks when their companies were bought out. Some had lost money right at the end, just as I had. For the most part, however, they had lived well off my success.

And now – was I to be the scapegoat for the whole economy's collapse? Surely, logical minds would prevail and see that the whole system had weakened and fallen.

As the news from England continued to find us, featuring *me* as an economic villain, it was as if the very energy that keeps you alive was abandoning me.

I lost all hope, and sank into depression.

When I'd set out, so young and eager, to become a barrister I was driven by the sense that I had a destiny, a calling that I would make a difference in the world. But when I'd changed paths and discovered my talent for making money I'd been driven by the excitement of turning rags to riches, and riches to more riches.

Now—did I even *have* a future?

When a man believes he sees the end, he wants to know that there was some meaning to his life. What was the meaning of what I'd accomplished in the business world? Did it mean *anything*? Or was it just *empty* success? Success for the sake of success?

During those days, a strange new thought surfaced — perhaps because the bottom had dropped out and perspective was screaming to be taken into account. A question posed itself, really, more or less out of the blue.

What does God want of me now?

God? — I had not spent much time thinking about God, truthfully, since the days I'd attended synagogue with my grandfather. The fact is I'd never asked God what he wanted for my life. Never. I'd always been so confident with my own strengths and goals.

Now suddenly, I wanted His help. I began to think about the God of my Fathers and what I had done to offend Him by ignoring him all these years. Would He listen to me now? Would He forgive me for all the years of utter indifference?

I wanted Him to let me know He was with me now, and at the same time that felt like far too much to ask.

While these deeper thoughts were going on I occupied myself with routine chores. I had made preparations from London. I went to the local stores. I spoke good French, having been to school in Paris for several months when I was in college. I bought some of the necessities; a broom, cleaning supplies, waste baskets, curtains for some of the windows, English as ever, and all the things we needed to keep house.

Other thoughts crowded in, as well. Less lofty ones.

As the days went by, I told Valerie stories about the people who had let me down, either by turning their backs on me, by deceiving me, or giving me bad advice. People who were shunning me now that I was in trouble.

Why did you put your faith in money and your trust in people. Money comes and goes, as you so well know. And people are as changeable as the wind.

That thought struck me. It seemed to come from somewhere outside me, as if a voice of better reason was starting to make itself heard.

Word continued to reach us that the press was now blaming me, not just for some of the problem, but for all the economic woes. Even though it would have been better if The Bank of England had supported me.

Whereas I thought our escape to France had moved us out of the storm, the storm was growing and would soon find us. By now the entire British financial system had collapsed. Bank after bank failed. Property values tanked. In fact, the balance sheets of the big banks were so depleted that The Bank of England had to change the rules so that the major banks could leave their assets on the balance sheet at the "last valuation" in order to prevent a melt-down of the whole system.

Clearly, this was not all my fault or doing. Yet it was being posited on my shoulders.

Even among my cronies I was the almost the devil himself. Though the fact was none of our bank depositors had lost their money, but there were stock shareholders who, like me, were left with nothing. A failing company is like an illness that you believe will one day get better. So many people hold on. Some of them gave me a piece of their mind – not the best piece — as though I had looked the other way when everything bad was happening. As if I knew.

As H.J. Heinz wrote in his diary, "It was 1877, and I had to go bankrupt. I had no money, so I had no friends."

That was probably the unkindest cut.

Again, the press would pursue me like hounds, declaring that "the money man with the 'Midas touch' made too many mistakes." Of course I saw this as hypocritical. Only a year or so earlier they were scrambling to get the first print of an inside story.

I was like a platoon commander who had led my troops into an enemy trap. Some of those mistakes hurt other people, some hurt me and my family: I didn't stop. I didn't consolidate. I bought companies like a fisherman just filling the nets as fast as I could.

As days passed, I saw something else, though. I'd abandoned one identity - as a legal crusader. I'd traded that for another identity and got caught up in how much I could earn and what I could prove to those who tried blocking my way from becoming a recognized banker. Now that was gone, so was my identity.

At some deep level I was starting to wonder. Stripped of outward resources — stripped of creditability — stripped of my yacht, my mansion, my Rolls Royce, and everything else.

Who was I?

Behind all my thinking were thoughts about God. I wondered if He cared about me and Valerie and our children, or if He would just let me drown. After all, apart from making a lot of money and losing it, it wasn't as though I had done anything worthwhile in my life. Didn't God help deserving people and let the rest of us suffer in our own failures and mistakes?

Emotionally, spiritually, and as a man who'd once known his path in this world, I was lost.

Chapter Twenty Four

A NEW LENS

About a year had gone by since the economic crash. The sting of failure and loss was not lessened by the year, but something was beginning to change, and that was my perspective. I was beginning to see my life through a new lens — that is, through a sense of what's really important and what's left, when external success and achievement is stripped away.

I began by asking myself: If people only care about you and lavish you with attention and praise because you can make them money — is it you they care about? Or is it their money and themselves? Are you just a means to an end, worthless to them apart from that end?

It was becoming clear, too, that my worth to people lay only in what I could do for them – and that I'd absorbed that message. *You are only worthwhile when and if you're making us money.* I would not say I'd gotten that message from my parents, when I'd rescued Dad's business. But I was starting to see that I'd told myself something like, *I will not be a good son if I don't sacrifice my own goals to save my parents financially.*

Maybe that was where I'd begun to lose my own way. In letting someone else's goals replace my own. It *had* been important at the time, to throw myself fully into making money. But then I'd realized I was good at it, and began to bask in the praise that I was good at it. And of course, I'd loved what money could buy for me and my family.

But along the way I'd also lost my sense of worth *apart from* my ability to make money. And I'd become "Midas" – "the Money Man." Now that that identity was stripped away – who was I? Where did my true worth lie? Did I even have any worth apart from this identity?

Trevor Pepperell – he who sought the guidance of "the witch" — came to visit me in France. Interestingly, he was the only one. None of our friends who had any traditional religion sought us out. Trevor, like everyone else, had suffered financially, and we both needed to do something radical and get away from the crumbling, failing world that we knew. So we decided, after discussing it with Valerie, to take a sabbatical in Morocco.

Neither of us had ever been there before. Trevor planned the trip across the mountains of Spain in his jeep and onto a ferry to Morocco. We weren't looking for fun. We were two intellectual guys with nearly empty pockets and we wanted to escape. The world we had known, the empire we had created, had gone. As to what came next, neither of us had any idea.

It is curious how, even when you're not overtly looking for answers to your deepest questions, sometimes they find you anyway.

On our way through Spain, we drove past one or two small villages, then up winding roads leading into the mountains and, suddenly, we reached a narrow overpass, with barely room for two cars to pass each other, we came upon a bloody scene. A young man was sitting on the side of the road beside an overturned vehicle banging his hand on his chest, distraught beyond words. There was glass everywhere. Close to him there was a young woman bleeding to death from a ghastly gash in her throat. Trevor slammed on the brakes and we leapt out of the Jeep.

Quickly we learned that the young couple had just been married and the husband, in a moment of inattention had let their vehicle drift off the broken surface of the roadway, catch a tire, and the vehicle had flipped. Now he was beating on his chest, shaking and staring helplessly at his wife, shouting, "Mea culpo! Mea culpo! "

My knees went weak looking at the young woman. Clearly the girl was about to die. No time for weakness…a life was on the line.

Trevor carefully turned his jeep around, opened the hatch and we gently lifted the woman and placed her on a blanket. The husband was so much in shock that he did not move and Trevor had to shout at him in Italian to get him into the vehicle beside her.

At some terrific speed, we began a wild and unsafe journey back to the next village. I held a white handkerchief out of the window which Trevor said indicated an emergency. This was silly to do because at the speed we were traveling no one could be behind us and in that rugged mountain area, nothing came towards us.

Trevor and I were also in shock and hardly said a word to each other for the whole ten- mile, breakneck journey. I looked back a number of times and the husband was sitting with his hands on his lap just staring at his bride. The blood from her throat and other wounds was seeping onto the blanket. I couldn't imagine how it would be possible to save her life.

When we sped into the village, we quickly learned that there was no hospital and we were directed to the convent. Another wild ride as we pulled up inside a set of wrought iron gates that guarded an old brick building. I jumped out of the vehicle and within a couple of minutes about ten people had come running. I yelled at them in French since I do not speak Spanish to go into the convent and fetch a stretcher.

When it came, everyone stepped back. Trevor — tough a man as he was, with a black belt in karate couldn't bring himself to touch the girl who was by now unconscious and covered in blood. I grabbed one of the onlookers and he and I placed the girl as gently as we could onto the stretcher and carried her into the convent. A nun who spoke with authority came running toward us and said, "We will take over from here."

The husband who was also injured, but not badly, had trailed us inside and was standing against the wall, with his head down and his shoulders drooped, almost lifeless himself.

There was nothing else we could do. We left the injured newlyweds in good prayerful hands and drove back across the mountains, down to Algeciras and took the ferry over to Tangier the port town of Morocco. We then began the long drive along the dirt track south towards Rabat.

Along with the jarring scene we'd come upon, which continued to play over and over in the front of my mind… something deeper was trying speak to me.

The incident had shaken me to the core. Trevor and I talked over and over about the young couple we had left in the convent. Their crisis seemed to overshadow our own. What could be more devastating a few days after getting married than facing a disaster like this?

I thought, *I've only lost money. Possessions. My reputation. I haven't lost what's truly important. My wife and children. My life. That young woman may not have a tomorrow, and I still have one.*

I had the vague sense there was something else still in my possession that I was overlooking. And some deeper voice was trying to speak. I wasn't sure what it was saying.

Arrival in Morocco was something of a shock. As we drive slowly up the ramp onto the pier, boys young and older call out offering, for hardly any money, girls, boys, hashish, and more. I was immediately uncomfortable.

Rabat is the capital city of Morocco, an ancient collection of three towns that have run together into one urban area of over a million people. The site of minarets, and even the scent of exotic spices, greets you almost instantly as you enter its outermost streets.

Situated on the Atlantic coast, the city is exactly what you might expect a port city to be. While it's the seat of foreign embassies, the city's nicer side is surrounded by many shadowy places.

In the past, we would have stayed at a very upscale hotel. Those days were gone.

The hotel we stopped in had mean looking bedrooms but we did get some sleep and something to eat. The food was a lot better than we expected.

Trevor loved going to bars, although he was not a big drinker. At one place we were sitting close to a swing door and it was very easy to see as the door swung open a long line of young people receiving their next "fix".

I thought, Everyone seems to have their own version of the "needle." Something they use to escape simple reality. For these people it's dope. In the world I just fell from it was money, yachts, expensive cars, fancy vacations. Was the madness of these people any worse than the madness I'd left behind in London?

A day or two after our arrival, after a long walk we went into, what we thought, was a nightclub and as we sat at a table waiting for drinks we quickly found out it was a brothel. A young pretty girl danced energetically to the music and ended up in the arms of the patron who must have weighed at least 300 pounds and sat contently in the rear of the dance floor. I wasn't flattered when two awful looking women came over to our table and asked Trevor and I if we wanted to sleep with them.

We finished our brandy and left. This was supposed to be an escape from the stress of the world we'd left behind. A chance to get out of our heads by seeing new sites. I was glad when we were on our way back. Again, the cheapness and meanness of the tawdry side of life here made something inside me turn and twist uncomfortably.

The cheapness of human life here triggered more reflection.

What is the basis of our worth? — to the world? To each other? To ourselves? Is it in our flesh and its ability to bring us pleasure?

Driving north on the dirt track, we crossed the ferry back into Spain. As we drove up into the mountains we were both eager to stop in at the convent and ask after the young couple. Maybe seeing the dark side of life in Rabat had pulled my spirit down, but I was braced for the worst.

At the monastery, they showed us to a room — and there she was swathed in bandages, sitting up in bed. When she saw us her eyes lit up and she thanked us repeatedly in Italian for saving her life. She would have a full recovery. We had a brief word with her husband, who was staying in the next room, and he was grateful to the point of tears. We left that day, amazed that the young woman had made it, and that this couple would have the life together they had dreamed of.

Driving down from the mountains toward the Mediterranean again, we were both beaming. I could tell that Trevor felt as I did: It felt good that we had done something worthwhile for someone.

Which brought me back to my private thoughts. What makes life worthwhile? Surely not things, which can be lost or taken from you at a moment's notice. Surely not in using and letting ourselves be used by other people.

I could not wait to see Valerie and my children again.

One evening, back at home, Valerie and I were sitting around the fireplace in the living room. We'd been marking time in France for months, unable to go anywhere or contact people because of the mounting criticism we kept hearing about towards me, as if we were in exile.

Still not one person from our old life, apart from Trevor, had so much as called or written to see if we and our children were well… or alive or dead.

I was lost in a funk cloud.

"What's wrong?" Valerie asked, trying to drag me out of my gloom.

"Val, there are so many people that have abandoned and hurt us — not just financially but also by failing to reach out to us. Since the trouble started, everyone's recoiled and pulled away. It's like we're poison." My feelings were shot to pieces.

Valerie got up and went to a desk, where she pulled out some paper and a pen. Then she came over and thrust them into my hands, "I want you to write down the names of everyone who has let you down, or let us all down, or behaved badly since things went wrong."

Without saying anything I obeyed her, not sure where this was going. In fact we compiled the list together. Valerie's feelings had been crushed, as well, by the uncaring coldness of former friends and even a few relatives. While my list of injuries grew long by including business cronies who had been "my best friends" only to disappear at the first whiff of trouble.

As our list grew long it was clear: We'd both been tossed aside, like crumpled scrap paper.

Like old rags, came the thought.

Lifting the list of names, Valerie said "And now we are going to pray and ask forgiveness for anything we have done — anything *you* have done — which was harmful to other people."

I stared at her wide-eyed. Was she serious? Anything we had done…*I* had done…to hurt others? Wasn't I the injured party here — the one who was pushed away by everyone after being trampled on by the press?

From somewhere inside of me came a sense of knowing what was wrong. I had never stopped to think what was good for everyone else involved in my business dealings, all I ever thought about was what was "good for the business, or for a few people at the top of the business ladder."

As for me and my goal of being a hugely successful tycoon, the truth was I'd never set out to harm anyone.

But you stopped thinking about other people. You acted in your own best interests.

It was that, in taking the huge risks I'd taken I hadn't *cared* about others. But I had forgotten that taking risks when you have a lot of money, and a cushion to fall back on, is not at all the same as taking risks that can affect people who have less... and no cushion to fall back on.

Was making money – a lot of it – some kind of sin? No, it was not. But I thought of Reggie, my old example from the rag trade days – Reggie who loved, and worked very hard for, and gave everything he could to his family. Now that I and other "tycoons" had rolled the dice and lost because the odds had changed... how were he and his family, and other people like him, faring?

As I saw his face before me, that question drove a nail through my chest.

You used to be all about people. Then you became all about money.

That drove a second nail.

At that moment, in my mind's-eye I also saw the young Italian couple in Spain lying severely injured on the side of the road. That young man's treasure – his wife – was almost taken from him in a split-second. She was everything to him.

It was like being brought back to some kind of ground of sanity. I began to realize several things.

At that very moment, some people had problems far worse than mine. I needed to stop wallowing.

And something else – as if the voice that had been trying to speak to me had finally gotten through my self-centered depression and self-pity.

Community is important, as my grandfather Hersh had said. Every single person is important. Every life is important. Back in the days when I was trying to help my parents and the people who benefited from the Christmas Club, I'd known that. Why did I forget that our true value is not connected to how many fights or competitions we win... or to our money and success and its trappings? It's in how our lives and our work intertwine with and help other people. Even if we make a lot of money, we lose our way when the purpose of making it is separate from the ambition to help people.

Valerie had respected my silence for several minutes, but now she pulled me out of my reverie. "We're not only going to ask forgiveness, we're going to forgive the people that have wronged us. The injuries went both ways, after all."

That was my Valerie. Spiritual but realistic, as well.

Sitting there beside me, she took my hand and began praying. This was going to be difficult for me. My injured ego did not want to remember all this stuff. Besides that I hadn't spoken with God or thought much about God or spiritual things in a very, very long time. I didn't think I even deserved to be heard by God after all the time that had passed and all that had happened. I didn't want to be a hypocrite.

Still, after Valerie finished praying, she squeezed my hand a little, signaling that it was my turn. It was more than helpful for me to listen to her; it was almost as though she opened the door for prayer and enabled me to go through it.

"Dear God, — " I began, awkwardly. My face felt hot and my hands were restless. I, who had met with leaders in government and the financial world, felt like a nervous child before God.

" –please forgive me for…."

…and out came a long list of things I felt I had done and not done, which had resulted in injury to my business contacts, the bank's constituents and stockholders and, also, my family. Then there were the people who I felt had injured me, injured *us* — the government and the Bank of England who could have stepped in to avert our crash but didn't. The press that attacked and ground its heel into everything about my rise and fall…I would never forget my own mistakes. I'd never forget that I'd taken success for granted when everything was going the right way. Nor would I forget how much I'd played to the audience, so to speak: people and the press had made me feel invincible, and I'd let myself perform for their praise and applause. But now the theatre was dark and empty.

When I finished, I wiped the moisture that had risen in my eyes. I felt some relief, but in fact we were not quite done.

"Now," Valerie continued, rising from her chair, "we are going to put this list among the logs on the fire and watch it burn. It's a way of saying, 'I forgive everyone for everything they have done against me and ask forgiveness for myself and my failures, as well.' If we don't let these things go, Joseph, they will fester and we will never have peace."

Walking to the fireplace, she threw the list onto the top logs where they were swiftly engulfed in flames.

As I watched the pages curl and turn brown I had the sense that I'd gotten rid of the past.

I was soon to discover that the past had not finished with me.

And there was still the question of our future. My future. What lay ahead was a trackless landscape, which felt awful, but I, we, had a life to live. What was I to do now?

While I was struggling with thoughts about a career in something, anything, Valerie's sense of faith in God stood there as at least one signpost, pointing me in some direction.

I was still in turmoil about the road ahead… but a small doorway had opened to my interior. One that had not been open in many years.

I had turned away from even thinking about God, much less making God any part of my life, and now that negligence haunted me because I had nothing spiritual to hold on to. I felt ashamed because, when I was a boy my grandparents had tried to immerse me in faith and as soon as I'd become a young man I'd ignored and turned away from any spirituality as though I had never heard of it at all. I'd simply dropped God out of my life entirely, in favor of other "gods" — my abilities as a fighter and an academic, my ambition to be a high-ranked and honored man of the law, and then my drive to be a power in the financial world and a tycoon.

Now that all I had chased after my whole life had been wiped away in a few months as if by a tornado. I found myself going back to roots, to values I'd left behind long ago.

I realized I never wanted to forget where I'd come from. My grandfather in particular had instilled me with a sense of certain things — faith in God, connection with a spiritual community, the value of helping others. These things had made his life worthwhile.

They'd made my life worthwhile, while he was alive and I was a boy riding my bicycle to his house to celebrate Shabbat.

The simple ceremony with Valerie was a turning point of sorts. Or maybe it plugged a drain in the bottom of my soul, down which my soul was plunging into a sewer. I still had no energy, and all I wanted to do was sleep for days and days. My chest felt heavy. I didn't want to die, but in a way I felt dead.

The old Joseph Joseph Caplan is dead, said the inner voice.

I found myself thinking about my funeral. Not in a morose way, but in terms of my legacy. What would I leave behind to show what my life had stood for?

I had nothing to leave behind. I had left behind my early plan to invest myself in helping people. Left off investing the best of myself in my family. There would be no one to step up and say I had changed their life for the better. No one to say I had put them on the road to success. After all that hard work — not one trophy.

What a *shunder*, as my grandmother would have said. What a disgrace.

I was clinging to small homey comforts. Home was my fortress and my wall of defense. I was not ready for the invasion and warfare that was about to take place.

Chapter Twenty Five

TRUE GOLD

After the emptying out of anger and resentment I felt cleansed in a way. Not that those feelings didn't continue to re-emerge from inside me, unbidden, but their force had lost its hold.

I did not want to lose the foothold I'd gained on a healthier way of looking at and approaching life — but it was going to be a tough battle.

For one thing, forces that had been set loose by my past were in vivid motion, like waves from a boulder dropped into a pond.

We had brought one loyal friend with us, Scruffy, our black and white Welsh Collie. Sadly, some days he felt like my only friend in the world.

One day, we returned home from shopping… and there was Scruffy motionless at the top of the driveway. Valerie and I jumped from the car, panicked, thinking Scruffy was dead. But when I lifted his head, he opened one eye, barely, and then it rolled back in his sleep, like he was on the verge of a coma.

What on earth…?

Seeing we'd returned, the housekeeper rushed outside to tell us that French and English reporters had come up the drive and given him something to eat. After which Scruffy more or less fell over.

I was furious. "Reporters *drugged* my dog?"

Valerie was still cradling Scruffy's head in her hands, speaking gently to him. "Don't leave us…. Oh Joseph, this is terrible. Poor Scruffy. What's happening? Why are reporters stalking you?"

The housekeeper explained, in a teary agitated way, how these men had accosted her, banging on the door and, when she opened it, demanding to know how much I'd paid for this house and how many cars there were in the garage.

She had replied in French, "One hundred."

They had asked her to let them into the house, but she had refused.

I rushed back over to Valerie and Scruffy, and cradled his head on my lap. "Come on, boy. Come back to us…."

Thankfully, the dog recovered. But didn't, exactly. Suddenly, we were on high-alert. What did the press want with us? What would they stop, at to get to me? At Valerie and the children? Would they try again to get inside our home – our private sanctuary?

I didn't have the strength to deal with this. I felt weak much of the time. I assumed the stress had drained me, because if I exerted myself I'd feel tired and out of breath.

Because of this incident, we decided to move into an apartment building called Les Gemeaux ("The Twins"), so called because one half of the building was in France and the other half was in Monaco. I thought if we lived there we'd get away from the press, since our home would be much less conspicuous.

It didn't work out that way.

Even though we were now reduced to living in an apartment, reporters somehow found us and kept calling. I refused to speak to them, and simply hung up after saying, "*Vous vous etes trompez de numero.*"

Now, Valerie was afraid to answer the phone, and when we left home and stepped into the street I found myself looking in all directions, to see if men with cameras and tape recorders might be about.

What had I brought upon my family?

In time, the phone calls subsided, and I thought perhaps we could start living a normal life again. The building in which we lived was flanked by a narrow street lined with little bars and food shops. No one knew or recognized me.

But in the greater sense I knew this was no life for us. The apartment was only one room and miserable to look at. We weren't going to make friends with any of the people around us. And then there were the children to consider: Julia was growing up and needed to be in pre-schools, and Justin had to see his parents in the setting of a stable home life.

There is only one narrow main street in Monte Carlo and, at the end of it, is the Europa Residence; a tall apartment building. We leased a small two-bedroom apartment at the top of the building. No one could go past the concierge without being announced. I felt safe there. I told myself that I was ready to start a new life — though it wasn't at all clear to me what that would be.

Monte Carlo is tax free to foreigners who obtain residency. There, a few very wealthy people from England save millions of pounds sterling in tax by dying in Monte Carlo. If I needed a reminder of what life among the wealthy was like, I would get it there.

Truthfully, during this time, the questions that had surfaced after Morocco and after Valerie's work to help me let go of the past and take a new course… well, they began to sink back in my thinking again. Way back. Telling myself money and power and fame were not as important as people was one thing. But wealth and its trappings still had an incredible draw.

Occasionally, only briefly, I felt like I was involved in an inner war – a war for my soul, if you will – and most certainly for my time and energy. What could I do now, to gain back power and status… and wealth… I had come to crave?

While this struggle was going on, it was as if lessons were still being placed right in my path.

One day I was asked to go to a meeting, where a distraught lady was seeking friendly advice from accountants and lawyers like myself. I was stunned when she said that her husband who had taken ill and didn't speak a word of French, didn't trust the French doctors anyway, had flown to London for treatment, and there he had died.

Something disturbed me deeply about this woman. After over 50 years of marriage, there were no tears. She didn't say a word about loving or missing her now-deceased husband. All she could focus on was how to save her millions. I left the meeting and found out later that a private plane was chartered from an airport in London to transport the man's body to Nice, in France, and then driven to Monte Carlo. If she claimed the man was a resident of, and had died here, she would save money. After decades of marriage, even at the moment of his death, this man's only worth was a number on a bank ledger. Nothing more.

Had he ever been the object of her affection? All around me, it seemed, both back in London and here in Monte Carlo, people seemed far more attached to other objects – villas, yachts, furs and jewelry, cash....

Driving home that day, I felt a chasm of cold emptiness open inside me. I wanted to forget this woman and the unpleasantness of what I had witnessed and felt.

Juxtaposed with this incident, two other incidents – one involving Julia and involving Justin—*really* got my attention.

Not far away, across the border in Italy, was the town of Ventimiglia that had one narrow main street with a large department store and shops of all kinds. One wintry afternoon, Valerie wanted to shop for shoes, and I went with her to keep an eye on Julia, who was not five, while Valerie shopped. I had nothing else to do.

As I wandered around the store, Julia sat playing quietly with her doll near the bench where Valerie was slipping on various shoes, while the clerk went back and forth bringing her different pairs. It was necessary to change our French francs into Italian lire to pay for our purchases, so I told Valerie I would nip down to the *Bureau de Change* and get some currency for her shoes.

Leaving Valerie and Julia behind I walked down the corridor from the shoe department, then down a very large winding staircase and out of the main entrance.

The currency exchange was a five-minute walk down the street, where I got some Italian currency and then went back. Valerie was still in the shoe department when I arrived.

She looked up at me and asked, "Joseph, where's Julia? When you left I saw she'd gone too. I thought you'd taken her."

For the whole of my life I will never forget the panic that seized Valerie and me in that instant. In horror we dashed around the store, pleading with complete strangers.

"Have you seen a little girl in a pale blue coat? *Please*…. Has anyone seen her?"
No one had.

The manager of the store ran over to us, looking almost as devastated as we felt. While he and Valerie raced through the store calling for Julia I plunged down the stairs and back out into the street again

Looking up and down the sidewalk, through the throngs of people, no little girl in a blue coat was to be seen.

Where is Julia? my thoughts raced.

I began to run madly up and down the street, shouting for her. A dozen kids were gathered at one of the street corners on their mopeds. I offered them a huge reward if they found her, and off they went in all directions.

But a half-hour passed. An hour. Two hours. The sun was sinking quickly behind the Italian alps, and the cold and dark night was coming on, and the kids on mopeds had not returned.

My little girl had vanished.

With my heart in my throat I ran back to the store, where Valerie was still pacing around and around, her face a mask of anguish and despair.

At that moment, the manager walked into the lobby… with Julia in his arms.

I grabbed my child and squeezed her to my heart. Her little hands were like ice.

Valerie threw her arms around the two of us, and we said over and over through tears to the store manager, "Thank you, Thank you…."

He told us that Julia had crossed the main road and walked about a 100 yards to an open market, where, after charging around the streets himself for hours, he had finally found her. The look of relief on his face mirrored our own.

As the details of her travels sank in, I felt a chill.

My tiny little girl had crossed a busy street. I asked her, "How did you get across the street, sweetheart?"

"Daddy, a strange man picked me up."

A strange man had picked up my little daughter. What if… ? A shudder went through me.

Driving home that evening, Valerie and Julia asleep with exhaustion from the day's harrowing events, I was alone with my thoughts. The Mini's headlights cut through the darkness engulfing the mountain roads, and some sort of inner light dawned. *My family was indeed everything to me. Nothing mattered as much as these three people. Perhaps I wasn't as completely lost a soul as I thought.*

I looked over at Valerie, dozing beside me. She, I knew, forgave me completely for my years of distraction and inattention. Glancing in the mirror I could see Julia, with her small chin resting on her blue coat. I still had plenty of time with her, to be a good father.

If , the inner voice said, *you remember what you've learned and don't start chasing the wrong things again.*

Could I do that? Could I hold the focus, that what was truly important were these three people in my life?

The incident with Justin was fast on the heels of nearly losing Julia.

Justin's school was minutes away by air in Geneva, Switzerland. One day Justin, who was just 16 years old, called and told me that he had a girlfriend and surprised me with this, "I want to bring her home to live with us permanently."

A huge request. I swallowed my first answer and asked, "Why?"

Justin told me that the girl had been treated very badly by her father and would like to be an *au pair* for our family until she found a better job.

After I hung up I discussed this with Valerie. We decided that we needed to learn more about this girl and meet her, because Justin sounded quite serious about this — and surely there was something more to the story. My barrister training told me there had to be.

Off I went to Geneva, planning meet them at the Beau Rivage Hotel.

When Justin came into the lounge with the girl – my heart went out to him. Perhaps it was to look as if he belonged in the atmosphere of this fine hotel, and perhaps he'd done it in order to look older than his age and, therefore, mature enough to make grown-up decisions: Justin had borrowed a jacket from a friend and it reached almost down to his knees. On one hand, of course, he'd shown good instincts about the need for a jacket in a place like this. On the other... well, the truth was, he needed an older male – like his oft-absent father – to guide him through the subtleties of how to impress the ladies with "sophistication."

I didn't spoil his efforts or the moment by mentioning the jacket. We sat down and ordered lunch for the three of us. And there the story spilled out. The girl, who was very pretty, was from Germany, and although she was only a year older than Justin she seemed very worldly.

"I just need a good job. With a good family." Her eyes told me she was telling the truth. But perhaps not everything.

I told them that I would think about their plan.

Later I made inquiries about her at the school. I discovered that she was a ward of the court. Anyone who took her away from the school or Switzerland would be subject to major legal problems. About a week later, I went back to Geneva to meet with Justin.

How would he take the news? Would it come across to him as another time when he'd wanted or needed something from me and I'd let him down again?

It was winter and the beautiful Alps were covered with snow. Justin and I went for a very long walk. I explained to him that his girlfriend had had family problems in the past and that it would be illegal for us to take her out of Switzerland.

He looked very disappointed, as I would have at that age with such a beautiful girl wanting to come home with me. Most important to me, he indicated that he understood and accepted my reasoning.

Did he know, despite my turning down the request, how much I deeply cared about him, though?

He seemed to know that I did care, deeply, about his life and all things affecting or involving him. That meant all the world to me. Maybe we could redeem something of what I'd given up.

When we parted company that day I watched my son heading back to school — and beyond that I imagined the life that was just opening up for him. He was a thoughtful, gracious young man. I felt something I wished my own father had said of me. *Pride*. I felt so deeply proud of my son.

And so, as I wrestled with inner focus on what was important in life, lessons and warnings emerged. Through the incidents with Julia and Justin, that deeper, more grounding, and now urgent voice continued to sound.

I was connecting with my son in a way I had seldom done before. While it felt great it felt awful, as well. Every time we did connect about an important issue now I was reminded of the many, many times I was not there for him.

Did my presence now begin to make up for the absence? He was an adolescent, pressing for his independence. And very soon he'd be going out into the world on his own. He would be prepared to stand on his own two feet – and would he want a relationship with his father after that? I could only hope.

Julia was now in school and making friends and wanting to spend longer bits of time away from us, too. Where had the time gone, and what had I been doing, while she and Justin were growing up? — I would say "before my eyes" but to my horror and shame I had seen them and not seen them.

Did I know anything about my own children really? Or what they really needed from their own father… besides money and things?

Justin, Valerie and Julia really were my true gold. Not my cars, or houses, or yachts, or collections… or my connections to men of power and wealth. Those were all gone now. How had I let objects and goals become so important to me? And what had I missed, by being caught up chasing my own dream of success and not investing time and interest in the people I said I loved?

Those questions would cut sharper than a scalpel, agonizingly deep, for a long time to come.

Months went by, and Valerie and I continued to do quiet things – shopping or taking walks down by the sea. Life started to feel more normal. The reporters had not returned and, after the storms of London, I was content. Happy to be doing almost nothing.

Best of all, Valerie and I learned how to hold onto each other again. How to listen to each other. Understand each other. Look into each other's eyes and know we were looking into the eyes of someone who was the friend of our soul. From the day we met, we'd held onto each other, but this was different. We had somehow made it through very thin and trying times, and we were starting over. Together. And that's what mattered.

Valerie's unqualified belief in me was a healing force. Whereas I'd come from London bruised and beaten and blamed, she made me feel as if I still had something in me to give to the business world. That both I and my talents were valuable. What a treasure.

And what a necessary boost. Because we had been in a foreign environment with limited options and I'd lost myself. Night after night now, we began to talk about where we might go and what I might do. I called people I knew in the United States, but the bad news about me was known everywhere. So far, no one wanted to get involved with me or recommend me to anyone.

With Valerie at my side, though, I felt as if I might be able make my way back into the financial world again. Somehow. I'd lost my confidence; she was helping to build me back up. And I knew I had to keep trying. *How?* was the question.

Sometimes the unexpected event emerges, like a stepping stone, to help you along the way.

Chapter Twenty Six

INTO THE PIT

Still the inner battles raged, because I could not quite let go of the past and my former lifestyle. Images of all I had lost – the elite business contacts, the friends, the houses, the cars, the vacations – tortured me. I kept telling myself, *Career-wise you have no future.*

In the past I'd had an image: I was the man with a golden touch for making money. Now I was a *nobody*, and felt terrible emptiness inside from which I could not escape.

I would wake up in the morning, often trying to understand what happened, how it happened. How much was I to blame? How much was Jeremy Thorpe to blame? How much was the economy to blame? My mind kept dragging me into these maelstroms, when what I really wanted was peace and a way forward. In searching for someone, something to blame I did not see what I was doing to myself. The endless stressing was taking a toll on my body, often giving me indigestion and chest pains.

How was I to heal from these bitter losses, let alone move on to a new life?

Struggling to rebuild myself and our life I teamed up with a wealthy Englishman, who lived in Monte Carlo, and a French accountant. We formed a new company with the intention of becoming consultants to small businesses. My colleagues leaned on my corporate experience and organizational skills. It was a big step down from where I'd been, but it was a start.

If only I could have been left alone.

One afternoon the three of us were in a café on the hills behind Monte Carlo. We were sitting at a small table by a window discussing plans for our new consulting business. I looked up and a man came in with a camera. He knelt down from about ten feet away and was about to photograph me together with my associates.

I stood up and moved quickly towards him. He got up on his feet as I approached, the camera dangling from his hand. Two of the waiters joined me and we escorted him to the exit. The film was removed from his camera, which was returned to him on his way out.

A pressure gripped my chest, and I felt slightly nauseous – attributing it to my distaste and reaction to the media hounds. Hadn't they done enough to contribute to everyone's downfall by capitalizing on molehills of news, blowing them up into mountains?

That Sunday, without a photograph, the *Daily Mail* ran the following headline, "Caplan Sips Champagne with Prince Rainier."

Of course, I was not sitting with Prince Rainier. I didn't know him and he certainly didn't know me. And in fact, I had been drinking orange juice, not champagne.

My two partners were a little taken aback, but they appeared to quickly forget the incident.

For me, the whole past came rushing back, the meteoric rise, the fall from success and grace. I felt another surge of those terrible feelings that collect inside, when you've been wrongly vilified. I'd been aggressive, that was true. Nothing wrong with that in business. But when your dreams and promises to others collapse — either because of an errant call or circumstances far beyond your control, it doesn't matter which — *you* are at fault.

It became clear to me: Touch someone's money and you are the Devil. Truly I could see, as spiritual texts proclaim, that money is the god of this world.

And then, suddenly, my hopes for a new beginning were shattered.

My new associates called me and said that I must come to meet them immediately.

"The British Board of Trade has published a report in London. It lists many alleged improprieties on your part, Joseph, which they claim occurred during the development of your London and County Group in England."

What improprieties? In looking for a scapegoat, why was the Board of Trade trying to pin the whole disaster on me? The people who hated me seemed to be out for blood.

I opened my mouth to speak, but it was futile.

"There is no way for us to succeed together, with the press bandying this report about."

The partnership ended then and there.

My former secretary flew over from London and brought me a copy of the report. It was like reading a police report of some raging alcoholic's drunkenness and excess and resultant crimes—as though, in all my business years I had never been sober.

My mind began to spin again. *Do I call a press conference? Will it go away if I ignore it?*

I found myself back to wandering the empty beaches again, unable to grasp what was going on. Why were they still coming after me? I looked out at the endless ocean and the boundaries I thought I'd set between myself and the past disappeared. It seemed like everyone was against me.

Valerie took me by the shoulders. "You *have* to move on, regardless of what they say. *We* have to move on. Start thinking about your wife, your children, and our future."

I was angry, though, that powerful people in London had put together a deranged story of my life based in one period of failure, like someone focusing on a single bad apple in a whole bushel and ignoring the rest of the harvest.

It was clear to both Valerie and me now that whatever personal healing I'd hoped to find in secluded Monte Carlo was not going to come about. And there was the family to consider.

One evening, walking by the ocean, Valerie and I were holding hands and talking as we did most evenings. "Joseph, there is nothing for us here, and we're too young to carry on like this. You have more to do with your life than shuffle along the beach."

She was right. Enough time had gone by. In all our married years, Valerie had never seen me drifting without purpose. And there were no prospects for me in Europe.

We decided, with the children in mind, that America was the direction that we should go. The United States had many more opportunities for someone like me. I was

45 years old and I wanted to get back to work. I wouldn't be the only man who had lost a fortune and needed to start up again.

And with a few friends in America and a fresh business landscape, surely the past would just curl up and fall away behind me. I felt a small surge of hope — hope, at least, of finding my career path again.

I wondered, however, if the gaping emptiness and anxiety would ever go away. Maybe, now that we were moving away from all the blame and anger aimed at me, it would.

We emigrated once again, renting a small house in West Los Angeles, where we had a few friends. The schools in this area were highly rated and we wanted the children to have a good start.

L.A. was so different from France. Everyone was busy doing something. I felt like a castaway. Because of my background in finance and real estate I set up a consulting firm. Since I had a lot of knowledge and had met people at all levels this would make a great new beginning.

Unfortunately, the past would find me even here.

One evening there was a knock at door of our house on Carmelita Avenue. I opened the door and saw two tall men standing before me on the porch. If life was like the movies, there would have been ominous music to let the audience know that bad things were coming. I was oblivious.

One of the men said, "We're sorry to bother you, sir, but we've locked our keys in the car. Could you lend us a coat hanger?"

I turned to the foyer closet to get one, and when I turned around both men seemed to be staring at me intently, as if studying my face. I shook it off, wished them luck, and closed the door.

They had found me, however — *they* being the press.

An article appeared in the Daily Express:

Daily Express, January 1978
California here he comes....

Jeremy Thorpes's old chum Joseph Caplan, the man credited with bringing Britain's secondary banking system to its knees, has turned up in California.

Caplan left us before he had time to read a Department of Trade report which castigated him over the 50-million pound crash of London and Counties Securities, of which the former Liberal leader was a director.

Now he is dealing in land, looking very tired and quite uninterested in talking about the past.

With so many of our former City brains residing overseas these days — Judah Binstock and Lord Moynihan, and so forth — it is a wonder that we are getting on so well, isn't it.

Getting on so well? I was scrambling to survive. And somehow the article made it sound as if I had absconded and was in hiding.

The morning I read this article I developed chest pains. These were sharp pains that took over my arms and my shoulders, leaving me with a feeling of helplessness.

Valerie immediately drove me to a cardiologist. When I came off the treadmill, two physicians told us that I had significant blockages in my arteries. The angina was evidence of his, and they recommended immediate hospitalization.

When I hesitated they said, "Mr. Caplan, listen. You are at great risk."

So much for a new start. The press was still biting at my heels — and now this.

In spite of the warnings of the doctors and Valerie's objections I obstinately went back to the office. It had been hard enough for me to get back to work. The idea of stopping yet again after establishing a small consulting firm with a few clients was so distressing. I couldn't afford to advertise, so I'd called as many people as I could to drum up any business at all, and I was at the very beginning of a long, long road to rebuild our lives. The last thing I needed was illness.

And at a deeper level, my self-esteem had gone into no-man's land. Maybe the press and the detractors were correct, and I was just not a good man. Not worth helping or saving. Even so I kept telling myself, *The bad dream of the past is over. We're in a new place and I've made a new start. I have to keep moving.*

And then the bottom fell out.

Four months later, in April 1978, I was sitting in my office waiting for the phone to ring so that I could do some business. The same two tall men who had asked me for a coat hanger at home walked into my office. They asked, "Are you Joseph Caplan?"

With some surprise I said, "I am."

One of them stepped forward and began handcuffing me, while the other announced, "We are with the FBI, and we are here to arrest you on behalf of the British government."

My eyes clouded over. My heart was pounding, and my chest hurt. I couldn't think clearly.

As we descended in the elevator to the parking garage, a woman entered from a floor below. She stared at my handcuffed wrists as though they were on fire. I wanted to say to her, "It is a terrible mistake," but I said nothing. The elevator took forever.

Downtown, at the Los Angeles County Jail the FBI agents signed me over to the jail staff, and I was fingerprinted.

The old bad dream had become my new nightmare.

There are no words to describe the gaping emptiness that comes over you when you realize you are not a person anymore but a prisoner. A number. And then there was the bitter, painful irony. I had been in and out of jail cells before as a barrister at law, but this time it was a one-way trip.

I made my one phone call to my lawyer, who would phone Valerie. Then I sat in the holding tank, with about forty other men who were being processed. There was a stinking toilet sitting out in the open. Many of the men were young and looked lost and scared, while others were older and looked bored, as if they knew what was going on or bemused like this was just a joke.

My lips began to tingle and my arms and legs felt weak.

During the interminable wait, as more men were shoved into the tank, everybody was interested in how everyone got there. This guy was accused of raping a girl in an alley outside a nightclub, but, of course, he didn't do it. Another had been in a street fight and someone died, but he didn't start it. Yet another was accused of sexually assaulting a girl, but of course, she wanted it more than he did.

"So… you look like a business dude," said one guy, turning to me. "What did you do?"

"Well I didn't do what they say I did," I protested, hearing the same tinny-sounding protestation coming out of my own lips. "This is a huge mistake…. It's all political…."

I got blank stares. No one understood me and, for sure, no one believed me.

Night was horrible, and the following day, while I was still in a daze, I was "processed" by the prison staff, which meant losing the last vestige of dignity and normalcy.

About thirty of us lined up in front of a row of prison guards.

"Strip off all your clothes," one of them ordered.

As we complied, another looked down the line with a smirk on his face.

We were then led to the showers to get deloused.

By the time I put my prison uniform on I was emotionally, mentally, and physically depleted.

That night, I shared a cell with three other men. I had a bunk with a pillow and a blanket which stank. They murmured constantly, and I was too scared to sleep.

Now all I could do was wait for the authorities to allow anyone to see me. I, who had once been able to pick up the phone and reach the wealthy and powerful, could contact no one. I had not spoken to Valerie or the children — which was an agony to me — or to my lawyer.

Meantime I was in hell.

So many terrible things were going on in jail. Gangs from different racial backgrounds were constantly bartering. Sex was rampant. Drugs available to anyone with money. And there was great bitterness among the races. It was a time in Los Angeles when civil rights were disregarded and the LAPD were, at that time, notorious for targeting the black minority.

It took about a week before Valerie was allowed to see me. She was accompanied by attorneys Douglas Dalton and George Buehler.

They sat across the table from me and I told them the story. I didn't really know what I was talking about, because my mind had all but shut down as I tried to assess this new crisis in my life. I had assumed that I would be released on bail. People who commit serious crimes like murder get bail.

"Unfortunately," said one of the lawyers, "the British government doesn't want you to be out on the street because they say you're a flight risk."

"Of course," the other interjected, "the real reason is that keeping you in prison is an attempt to break your spirit and restrict you from helping to prepare a defense."

How indeed was I going to be able to communicate complicated financial dealings to men who were not financiers and who, nonetheless, would have to mount my defense?

When they left Valerie looked at me with a mixture of pain and love in her face. I looked at her and put my hand on my forehead. She and the children did not deserve to go through this chaos. By now I felt that I did, but they did not.

Even as I sank deeper into despair, all I could think about was that I needed to fight very hard to get out of jail for their sake if nothing else.

More endless days went by. A week. Another week. A month.

The Los Angeles County Jail has long corridors with hundreds of prisoners and guards moving rapidly up and down all day long. And it was unbearably hot. I found myself gasping for air, felt my chest pounding, and wondered when it would just quit and I would die.

The tormenting thought circled endlessly in my head. *You are going to die in prison.*

How had this happened.

Every night, under the stinking blanket and with the sounds of men groaning or quietly cursing I did something I had not done on my own in years. I prayed.

Where are you? Will you help me? I don't ask for myself, but for Valerie and the children. I don't know how they will get on in this world without me. Please....

Very shortly thereafter, and to my surprise, I was ordered to visit the prison doctor. To this point, no one had so much as blinked an eye when I told them I had serious heart condition. I'm sure they'd heard it all before. When I finally got to see the doctor I told him what my physicians had told me just two weeks earlier about my blocked arteries. He made notes. He didn't look at me or examine me.

On the way back to my cell, I got lost among scores of inmates in the myriad of corridors. My head was pounding. I had no idea what direction to go in, so I stopped one of prison guards to ask him to help me. The look of seething contempt on his face startled me. "You gonna jump me?"

When he saw my fear, he laughed, and led me back to where I belonged.

That night I prayed again. *Please help me. Help us....*

As I prayed I listened again to the way the inmates communicated with each other at night. Because they couldn't speak all at once, there was a central figure and everyone spoke through him. He was like a pastor, so to speak, passing out fragments of wisdom and advice to the dozens of men who called his name.

I imagined God to be something like that, only infinite — listening to the cries of all humankind – and wondered, *Is he listening to mine?*

The day of my court hearing I was transported in a van along with six other men all shackled together. The FBI agents provided their evidence of arrest to the judge. They relayed what I had said to them: that the arrest was a mistake because they must be looking for another Joseph Caplan. They interpreted my shocked, disbelieving response as an attempt to conceal my identity.

Back at the LA County jail, I focused on my case as best I could. I had to think about what I needed to do to get out. And I was sick about Valerie and the children. What had she told them about why their father was in jail? What about my parents, who were reading about me in the London newspapers every day?

Meantime, my heart seemed to be slowly crushing itself inside my chest. My left arm ached and my lips and fingertips sometimes went numb. No one seemed to care.

After a couple of weeks, I had another court hearing, in which the judge was presented with the charges filed against me by the British government – *66 charges in all* — accusing me of a wide variety of corporate misdeeds.

My knees went weak. *Sixty-six charges?* The British government clearly wanted to be sure I would never see the light of day again.

The judge said to the U.S. Attorney, "What is your position on bail?"

"The British government says that, if Mr. Caplan is released he and his family will flee the U.S. and hide somewhere."

My own attorney argued our position, giving the judge plenty of good reasons why I couldn't be a flight risk.

I watched anxiously as the judge considered, then raised his gavel. "Bail denied."

When the gavel struck, it was a blow to my heart. To my spirit.

Riding back to lock-up, I felt as if in piling on charge after charge, the British government was wrapping coils around me and I was being pulled down into a pit from which I would never rise.

Things got worse than I imagined possible.

One day, the correction officers came for me. I thought something good had happened. Maybe at last bail had been granted. My spirit rose a little.

And was crushed. The British government had asked the American authorities to put me in solitary confinement. I suppose isolation can break your spirit.

In solitary I was bored and frightened, so I asked for all kinds of files and papers. Eventually, to my surprise, a thick wad of legal papers was handed to me.

Now my son, Justin, was allowed to visit. It was beyond wonderful to see him. He was growing into such a fine young man – all without a dad to contribute anything to his life. I had to force that thought from my head.

When he left I would hand him yellow pads, containing pages and pages of notes with information for the attorneys. Despite all those charges against me, this was the only way we could communicate

And the charges were grim and complicated. The British government's documents described all the things which I had allegedly done wrong. The main charge was using company money to buy company shares, the sort of things that usually get picked up by auditors once a year. In addition, I was provided with hundreds of witness statements and exhibits of my wrongdoing.

Overall, I was amazed at how trivial most of the charges were. My head was crammed with anxiety, ideas, and determination. Day after day, I made pages of notes for my attorney, providing my answers to the charges.

Then there was another court hearing. The judge said to the U.S Attorney, after hearing presentation, "What do I have to do?"

The U.S. Attorney replied, "You have to be extradite him."

And that was the ruling: I was to be extradited.

When I heard the word "extradite" an avalanche of emotions slid down on me. Fear. Anxiety. When extradition is involved it becomes a battle of semantics and law. I felt like I was at the end, the bottom. And it was just beginning. *This will go on for months. Maybe years.* My stomach turned and my heart surged.

I will never live through this.

Valerie was distraught and desolate. She could be left alone with the children for a long time. She had nowhere to go.

I sank into despair. Our life together was over.

Where Valerie's deep faith came from, I did not know, but — as she had done in the past — she looked me in the face and said, "This is bad, Joseph. Very bad. But God has not abandoned us."

In spite of the morass of legal and financial stuff that was tormenting Valerie, nothing would convince her that God had turned his back on us.

I was not at all convinced.

The story of my fall from grace was splashed across the U.K.

Daily Telegraph, April 27, 1978
FBI Hold London Bank Chief

'Joseph Caplan, former chairman of collapsed banking group London and County Securities, has been arrested by the FBI in Los Angeles.

He was arrested on charges claiming he stole 2,400,000 pounds from the group, London and County crashed in December 1973.

The 45-year-old banker was detained on a warrant issued to Scotland Yard Fraud and officers who flew to California last week.

Papers for his arrest and extradition were issued at Bow Street 10 days ago.'

Now, it seemed, rather than "misusing" the bank's money I had "stolen" it. I was furious and mortified at the charge.

In spite of the morass of legal and financial stuff that was tormenting us, nothing would convince Valerie that God had turned his back on us.

Second and third applications for bail were made to the court without success.

While this was going on, my Mum and Dad back in London were fully aware of my serious medical condition and the trouble I was in. It was a huge effort for them to go and see their Member of Parliament and explain the dilemma. It took weeks and weeks when they finally received a letter, which they forwarded to me. The letter advised nothing could be done. In spite of my health problems, the British government wanted me back in England.

Then the crisis deepened, I developed chest pains, just as the cardiologist who had examined me before the charges were filed had predicted.

Every day I did nothing but lie on the floor of my cell, which had no windows, with my head facing the bottom of the door so I could get every bit of air through the gap. I could not breathe properly. I didn't have much time left. My clogged arteries were shutting me down.

I don't know what it took, but permission was given for me to visit an outside cardiologist under armed guard. After all the tests were performed, the physician issued a written opinion saying that I needed immediate by-pass surgery due to the severity of the coronary artery disease.

That fell on deaf ears.

After another two weeks, with my whole body aching and going numb, the guards came for me. My mind seemed totally detached from everything that was going on. I was put in the back of a prison van. My feet were secured with leg irons and I was handcuffed. They took me to Cedars Sinai Medical Center in Los Angeles, in order to have an angiogram.

The scene was worthy of a Franz Kafka novel. I was taken to the top floor of one of the hospital's wings. The room was at the very end of a dark corridor. At the insistence of the guards, I was chained to the bed. Valerie came to see me, but was not allowed to touch me or hand me anything.

"Please," she begged, "I just want to be near him for a moment."

"Sorry. Those are our orders."

Still, Valerie looked at me and, with tears in her eyes, said in a quiet voice, "You are going to be all right."

I think I was the only "patient" on the top floor of the hospital at that time. The following day, when I was wheeled toward the surgical department, my feet were chained together and my hands were cuffed.

When I finally got to see the surgeon, I could feel my heart thumping in protest. I didn't know if I would die, faint, or cry out in pain. Though he must have had many different experiences during his career, I could see that he was troubled.

I did not know till later that Valerie was walking the halls, praying for a miracle and asking God to heal me.

All I could think about was the end of it all. What will Valerie's life be like without me? How will she survive? How will my children remember me? They don't deserve this....

Far beyond the walls of this hospital, the story of my private pain and horror was continuing to hit the news.

Manchester Evening News, May 4, 1978
Joseph Caplan in Leg Irons for Heart Tests

'Arrested British banker Joseph Caplan, who faces extradition from America, was put in leg irons during painful heart tests on a California hospital's operating table, his lawyer claimed.

Gary Fleischman said he would go to court next Monday to protest about Caplan's treatment and would try to get bail for the 46 year old financier taken into custody last month at the request of Scotland Yard's Fraud Squad.

Mr. Fleischman said the leg irons were removed at a Santa Monica hospital after Caplan's doctors complained that they did not want to perform tests — which involved putting needles in his chest — with the patient chained to the bed.'

Days later, when it was time for my surgery, I was taken to Cedars Sinai Hospital in a haze of pain, with everything in my body going numb.

If I thought I'd been at a low point back in Monte Carlo that was nothing compared to this moment. I felt like a sailor who had fallen overboard and I was going down into an ocean of blackness.

They put me in a room with armed guards at the door and my feet were again chained to the bed. I wondered if I would make it through the night.

Early in the morning, the orderlies came to take me to surgery after the nurse administered sedation.

As I was wheeled down the corridor, just before I lost consciousness, I tried to whisper the most heartfelt prayer I had ever uttered, but my jaws and lips would not move... and so I shouted, from somewhere inside:

God, I have worked so hard. Why is this happening to me?

This wasn't even a real prayer; it was a dying man's reaction to circumstances.

If God had replied, he might have said, *Joseph, listen, you are 46 years old. For most of your life, I have hardly heard from you. You've enjoyed beautiful homes, you've traveled, met people, made millions. When did you ever even thank me? You believed you did it all on your own, that's why. And when did you ever pray for direction or guidance? Never. Because you took hold of the reins of your life and believed you didn't need me. Your ego got in the way. Now look at you.*

Then I felt the hallway start to swirl around me. Felt myself sinking into a dark pit. Felt as if I was a candle being snuffed out. Not only was I now a nobody in everyone's eyes, I was a nobody who was probably dying. Did I even want to return?

Chapter Twenty Seven

ANSWERED PRAYER

The surgery lasted for 8 hours and 40 minutes. My heart required six by-passes — the largest number of bypasses carried out at that time at Cedars Sinai Hospital. Dr. Jack Matloff, the surgeon, wrote in his report, "This man has reached the lowest ebb a human being can reach and still survive."

He was unaware how true those words were, not just in the physical sense but in the spiritual sense, as well.

There is a scripture from Psalms, one I did not now at the time; if I had I might have prayed it, as I swam up from unconsciousness in the recovery room.

From the depths I cry out to Thee…!

Confused, my head spinning and body aching, I found myself in a room with white walls, white curtains and people dressed in white.

Valerie and Justin were standing beside my bed in the ICU; that was the only way I knew I'd survived. I wanted to say something, but I could barely even open my eyelids let alone speak. Justin looked shocked. Undoubtedly, he was horrified to see me with all the tubes and I-Vs sticking in me.

He was holding something in his hand.

"Show your father your diploma."

If my spirit could have sunk any lower it would have. Through my haze I recalled that this was his graduation day. *Once again* I had missed an important part of his life.

"There's no way he even knows I'm here," Justin said, with a forlorn look.

"Yes, he does," Valerie insisted. "Show him."

My eyes were barely open, but I saw him lean toward me, close to my face. "Daddy, I graduated from high school today."

I remained motionless for what seemed like the longest period of time. He was so full of promise. And I felt useless to him and Julia and Valerie. All I had to offer them was nothing but my passel of struggles, whether with legal issues, finances, or health. And yet....

The will to live is an imprecise factor, and yet physicians know that a man's will is an indefinable component when it comes to recovery. Some people who come very close to death just give it up and say, "I haven't got the strength to fight this anymore." Nonetheless, something happened for me at that particular moment. It was as if it was meant to be — that my son would be standing at my bedside the moment I opened my eyes from a bypass surgery that had saved me in the physical sense. His presence, his diploma — a gateway to his future — was like a rope saving me from the emotional depths into which I'd sunk.

I wanted to live. That's all. Just live. No matter what. Not just for me and my future. For my family.

Something surged inside me, and finally, a single tear flowed.

The raw truth is, that was the beginning of my recovery. Not just physically, but of my life.

And it was a very good thing I'd had this shift in my spirit, because the prognosis was bad. I'd gone through an intense procedure and there was much uncertainty about its success and whether I could make much of a recovery — my body had been that battered by psychological and physical stresses.

Again, if I'd truly been a praying man, rather than a man crying out for help in a crisis, I might have prayed. *God, give me a new heart. Not just a repaired physical heart, but a new sense of life at the core of my being.*

In fact that's what I needed, though I did not know that then. The one that had beat for "the deal" and for making money had only gotten me so far. Now what I needed was a whole new beginning. If nothing else, I had the vaguest sense that maybe a way through of all this mess *could* open up for me and my family, though I didn't at all see *how*.

While I was in recovery, Valerie and Julia, who was then six years old, came to see me. Julia put her hand on her hips and looked me in the eye.

"Daddy, when are you going to come home?"

Again, I felt a small surge inside — the way I'd felt it when Justin had showed me his diploma. I realized how much my family wanted me back. How much I wanted them back. How much I valued them. They were better than gold to me. I'd never lost sight of this, not totally. But I'd let *so much else* cloud my vision. First, my career in the financial world, then my own angst and self-pity when that world came down around my head, then my self-loathing that I had "failed" everyone who needed me to be their Money Man.

It was time to get beyond all that, if only I could make it physically.

Suddenly—I don't know how exactly—some small part of the old Joseph Caplan was back. The one from my days in university and the military. The guy with the will to fight. Yes, I needed some of his strength and determination again – but this time not just for me. For other people.

About a week later, two orderlies came in and told me that it was time to take out the staples. They were large staples in a neat row all the way down the center of my chest. One orderly firmly held me down while the other pulled and they were all taken out.

The pain had no effect on me. I was alive.

When I was ready to be released from the hospital, my attorney was finally able to convince the judge that in my condition I couldn't get very far.

And this time we won our argument.

Bail was set at $500,000, of which $50,000 had to be in cash and the rest was in the form of a lien on our home. We did not have that kind of cash. Valerie turned to an old friend from London who had relocated to Los Angeles.

Don Arden had been a banking client of mine in England for many years. He managed rock bands, including Black Sabbath, Ozzie Osbourne, and The Electric

Light Orchestra. Don was living in Beverly Hills, in what was formerly Howard Hughes' mansion behind the Beverly Hills Hotel. He had money and influence. But would he help us? He certainly *could* — if he hadn't bought into all the bad press about me.

I had assisted Don many times by financing concerts and even meeting his payroll. Valerie gave him all the information he needed…and we waited.

In just a few hours, Don sent his chauffeur around to our house with a bail bond for $50,000.

I was out of jail.

The details of all the legal wrangling over my fate felt interminable. But in fact, my case was finally decided on July 6, 1981, over three years after I had been arrested.

That morning my lawyer went to court on my behalf to receive the verdict.

I was at home seated on a sofa, looking out at the open, blue sky. My heart was pounding, and I felt the old weakness wanting to come back. Fear tried to grip me, but I fought it. *I could be back in prison in hours.…*

Later, my lawyer repeated the verdict to me:

"The United States 9th Circuit Court of Appeals, after hearing arguments from the U.S. Attorney on behalf of the United Kingdom and Mr. Caplan's attorney, have determined unanimously that *nothing* in the record shows that Caplan's alleged acts constitute crimes in England, nor that they constitute corresponding offenses in the United States under the duel criminality requirement. Furthermore, the British government failed to meet its burden of proving that Mr. Caplan ever concealed himself with intent to avoid arrest or prosecution."

When the phone rang, and it was my lawyer, I was standing up, looking out of the window at the sky. He spoke, and I pressed the phone tighter to my ear. The words did not sink in. I'd had so many legal ropes wrapped around me, pulling me to the bottom — *What had he said?*

"They found unanimously *in your favor*," he repeated.

" Please, say that *again*. I have to be sure."

"*They found* you *not guilty*. They cleared you of all charges of wrongdoing. You're *free*."

I'm free.

I couldn't think clearly.

I went outside. The front of our home had a low wall surrounding the driveway. I sat on it. The sun was searching for an opening in the clouds. I smiled. I knew that the sun would break through again.

As soon as Valerie came home I rushed over to her car. She stepped out, staring at me, eyes wide with anticipation.

"It's over, Valerie. I've been cleared. We're free again."

She seized my hand, tears rushing to her eyes. "We should thank God! And now we can start a new life together."

New life.

Yes. That's what I wanted, more than anything I'd ever wanted before. A life not only free from my attackers and from prison, but from my old self. Had I been *that* self-consumed? Apparently I had. It suddenly occurred to me, then and there, how much Valerie had prayed in the three years which had gone by — and long before that even. Had she been praying for me, for all of us, throughout all the years I had virtually absented myself by preoccupations?

She began to pray now, and I listened, mesmerized. The words of her prayer suddenly seemed beautiful. Not perfunctory, but deeply sincere. And — what was it? — *genuine.* As if she was standing and talking in a dimension of reality I had never stepped into before.

"God, we want to thank you…." Her words and her spirit were extraordinarily peaceful. I could feel peace coming from her. Who was this woman? — someone who had become deeply believing during the last three years.

I suspected that she and her praying friends had spoken to God on our behalf many, many times. Beyond a few inarticulate gropings and wishings for some sort of divine help I had not.

It took time for the fact of my freedom, our freedom, to sink in. Years of our lives had gone by. Having just escaped from a no-man's land I now saw how my whole existence — from the outermost level of my life, which was my career, to the innermost level of my spirit — had been stopped in a wasteland.

I felt like a man coming up out of the ocean, where there had been nothing to stand on. I was so eager for life to begin again. If only I knew how to make that happen.

I didn't.

In terms of a career I'd lost all my prestige. In terms of my soul, dignity was a word that I could not even spell. Nothing was left to me.

Valerie gently led the way, "Pray Joseph. You'll see. Something will open up."

For the first time ever, together with Valerie, I began to ask God what I could do to put things right.

I was now 50 years old, but I began to feel a little hope that life was not over after all. For years, we had been too scared to even contemplate the future. I didn't know how to speak to God, but at least my repaired heart was trying. I had been humbled. I was no longer strong physically, but I was alive and making the first tiny steps toward a future. Tentative steps. As if my spirit had been lost, lost, lost for a long time and was seeking its way.

Dimly, I became aware that many years before I had lost my spiritual compass. Through my grandfather I had encountered the great question, posed by Maimonides, "If I am not for me, then who is for me? And if I am *only* for me, then what am I?" He had tried to pass onto me, among other things, the spiritual value of connecting with other people at the deep level of compassion and caring. People are always to be in our focus.

After my grandfather's passing, however, spiritual values had fallen away. When I'd set out to become a Barrister—yes, in some measure it was to bring justice for others, but in equal if not greater measure it was to win a name for myself. Then I'd bailed into the rag business and then started the Christmas Club—yes, to help my dad and the others, but also to prove I could make money. When I'd seen a way to make lots of it, more and more and more, my focus had shifted – from people, to money. I had become The Money Man. yes, it was to collect or then to make money for others, but even more I'd been driven to climb to the top of the financial world so I could say, "Look what *I* have done." My focus shifted again, and whatever turns it had taken, everything had been about *me*.

I now had my own answer to Maimonides' question, "…if I am only for me, then what am I?" The answer is this: You become a person who is adrift in the changing ocean of people and things that come and go so quickly. You become a person who is all about "me" and what I can own, what I can achieve, what power

I can amass. You become like a mini-god in your own eyes, believing you are and should be the center of everything.

Little wonder my world had spun out of control. By ignoring spiritual wisdom, I allowed my world to spin around a very small axis named Joseph Caplan. No wonder at all that, by focusing entirely on personal ambition, my values had become confused.

And so the question loomed: Without a spiritual center, how would I ever find my way again?

Chapter Twenty Eight

SOMEONE NEW AT THE HELM

The case was over, and with it a very long, dark night. I now freely acknowledged it was only by the grace of God that I'd survived a disaster that was equal to the disaster that began years before, when the entire English economy had crashed and my banking business with it.

Life of some sort lay ahead of me, unbegun. If only it would dawn on me what that was to be. I was leery of my ambition now, and so as to direction — I was clueless.

And then by chance or some other agency....

Valerie and I were walking down Rodeo Drive in Beverly Hills one spring evening. Jaguars, Bentleys, and Mercedes were purring by, filled with beautiful people. I felt anything but like a beautiful person. My days of needing a flashy car were over.

We passed in front of a stock broker's office. Pausing, I turned to Valerie. "Let's go inside for a moment."

She looked at me, puzzled. "Whatever for?" We had no stocks now.

I wasn't sure, really. "I don't know. Just to see what's going on in the financial world these days maybe." I felt lightyears from the financial world in spirit, but a mild curiosity remained.

We walked into the office, which was standing room only. Men and women were crowded together, riveted on the television screens all around, which were showing the latest financial news. From the varied sounds of thrill and disgust I could tell we were surrounded by a mix of winners and losers.

How had I ever been so caught up in this world? Yes, as I looked at the streaming stock positions I could feel the old excitement…but now it was as if I was also looking at it from some great distance, from a different perspective. How had I allowed my life to ride the choppy and surging waves of something as unpredictable as the world of money? Why had I pinned my sense of wellbeing to the amount of cash and numbers and kind of possessions I had?

I felt a tug on my right sleeve.

I turned to Valerie, but she was not the one tugging at me. Next to me stood an elderly lady with her husband.

"We are Mr. and Mrs. Cohen," said the older gentleman.

"Hello," I responded, feeling some uncertainty. Were they looking for investment advice? Did they think I was a broker?

Mrs. Cohen was looking me straight in the face, smiling enigmatically, "The Lord has sent me to save you."

Valerie had turned by this time and was looking at the Cohens with great curiosity.

Normally, I would have been polite and said, "Thank you very much" — and swiftly moved on. Instead, I opened my mouth and heard myself say, "We don't live very far from here. Will you come and have tea with us?"

Valerie stared at me. I wondered at myself and the words that had just leapt from my lips.

Without batting an eye, Mrs. Cohen said, "We attend a Bible study, where there are both Jews and Gentiles. It takes place every Tuesday night."

Mr. Cohen smiled. "Would you like to go?"

I turned to Valerie and — again to my surprise — said, "I want to go."

"So do I," she beamed.

In a short time, the Cohen's were seated around our table sipping English Breakfast tea and having biscuits with us. I had no idea why I made a decision to invite two strangers to our home or why Valerie and I both wanted to go to a Bible study. It just…happened.

As the Cohens spoke, with great animation and joy, about their faith I felt a deep, calm stillness in my heart. They spoke about "coming to know the Lord," and it was clear they really did know, if not God, then at least something I didn't. There was a vibrancy, a radiance, a deeply relaxed and relaxing spirit about them. So different than people I knew from the financial world, who were always so tightly wound.

I was aware that I was listening—for the first time in decades *listening*—to two people talk about something other than building an empire or making money or traveling to exotic places or buying expensive artworks.

I didn't understand what was happening to us.

The following Tuesday, we met the Cohens at the house where the Bible study was taking place.

As it happened, Valerie and I got separated during introductions. When it was time for the study to begin I couldn't see Valerie, because she was seated in the other room. For some reason, the house had been divided in such a way that two rooms opened into a third room. It was an unusual set up. Neither side was able to see the people in the other room, but the people in each room could see the speaker. I didn't know any of the people I was sitting with and didn't know what to expect. I hoped Valerie would be alright.

Everyone was talking about "the Lord" and about "Jesus." But Valerie and I were Jewish. Had we done a good thing by coming here?

A man stood in the open area in front of us and gave a lesson from the Bible. I listened carefully. I wondered what this information had to do with me.

But it wasn't just information. I could not escape the fact that throughout this house there was a distinct sense of *presence*.

God seemed to be here. In this house, these rooms.

All around me, people were listening to the speaker and I was listening, as well. Or at least half-listening to him. More, I was listening to a voice speaking without words inside me.

Joseph.

I felt as if someone was not looking at me but into me. Joseph Caplan. Examining me. Wanting me to see myself just as I was, without the false or surface identity of the Money Man.

Who was I? Who had I been? Who was I at this moment? Who would I be from this moment forward?

I had done so much. I had been to so many places and was drained from all that had gone before. With all my worldly knowledge and skill, what good had I done with my life?

When the speaker finished, people shifted in their seats and most got up to have coffee and a chat. Perhaps Valerie was among them. I imagined Mrs. Cohen introducing her to her friends. But I sat there, stock-still. Inwardly, a voice was now speaking very clearly:

You have been your own master. And because of all your success you believed that God could be left in the background until you were ready for Him.

With that realization I felt ashamed. My grandfather had showed me that God is to be revered and served, not ignored and pressed into service whenever I had a twinge of discomfort or worry or needed him to support my ambitions. I saw what a huge mistake I had made, how I'd gotten it backwards and upside-down. Beyond my desire to be a good husband and father, was there anything of my life worth salvaging?

I began to cry.

The crying led to sobbing. It was uncontrollable. Yes, I'd cried before in my life, but these tears came from some very deep well within my soul. This was a cry of anguish. My heart ached, but in a good, relieving way.

Forgive me. I have wronged you and I have not worshiped you as God…

An elderly woman put her hand gently on my shoulder, and I looked up. She had alert, intelligent eyes.

"My name is Miriam. Joseph," she said "the Hebrew name of Jesus is *Yeshua.* He is the son of God. God will forgive you for your sins and remember them no more. That's what He promises. Are you ready to receive him as Lord and Savior?"

There was no discussion, no further explanation. Somehow I understood her and let her take my hands in her hands.

"All that I know to say is that I have made terrible mistakes in my life and gone far off the path I knew as a boy. And I want to be involved with God for the first time since I was a child. I don't know how else to say it."

And then I dropped my head and prayed:

"Jesus... *Yeshua*... save me. I surrender. My life is yours."

It was a moment out of time. Without a doubt, the most important moment of my life. Gone was the pride. A sense of hope sprang up in me — and at the same instant, a sense that a Person far greater and more vast than me or any of the important people I'd ever known was breathing into my being something that I had not known before... something I had been thirsting for.

New life.

If electricity had rushed through my whole being, it would not have been more palpable than the energy of the presence of Someone greater, filling me.

I felt clean. Whole. Forgiven.

And as if maybe, now that Joseph Joseph Caplan was out of the way, there might be a new start.

Miriam blessed me and walked away.

I sat there stunned. Overjoyed. Something was missing. Guilt and shame. Was this possible—had I really been released from the past?

At that moment my heart understood what had taken place was a gift from God. Later, I would read a scripture that says, "I... am He who blots out your transgressions, for my own sake, and remembers your sins no more," (Isaiah 43:25).

I did not understand till that moment what was meant by "redemption," but what came clear to me was that God had done just that in a moment of time: He had taken a man whose life was a wreck and showed him that Jesus is the Messiah who came down from the heaven as the Son of God to save the world and give people like me a door to go through so we could be forgiven for our sins and start a new life. What I had experienced was the power of grace, the life-giving power of the living God.

Miriam had vanished into the crowd of people, and I was still sitting dumbstruck.

Valerie came in from the other room. Without thinking I blurted out to her what I had just done. "I have turned my life over to God. I've accepted Jesus as my savior."

She put her hands on my face and with her thumbs wiped the tears from my eyes. She said, with joy bursting in her words, "Joseph! I have also accepted Jesus, because I know in my heart he is the Messiah."

I got up then, and we wandered through the small crowd, not saying much to anyone. People began to leave and we did the same. When we were a few minutes away from the house and before we got into our car to drive home, Valerie turned to me.

"Joseph, what have we done?"

I knew, of course, what she was thinking. Here I was, a Jew from an Orthodox family, believing in the life and meaning of Christ. Nonetheless, I said, "I believe that Jesus is the Messiah."

Valerie relaxed. "God has opened our eyes at the same time. Isn't that amazing?"

What happened at that Bible study was not what I had expected. I'm not sure what I expected. It reached my inner being and changed my life. I had felt emotion before, but this was quite different. I knew that what I had done touched every part of me that was important; my heart, my feelings, and it was the same with Valerie. It was tempting to think that, after all we'd been through, we were just desperate to clutch at something. I rather think that, maybe for a man like me, what we'd gone through was exactly what it took to make me take notice and think about something outside my own ego – to allow someone else to stand at the helm of my life and give me direction, apart from seeking what I thought was best for *me*.

In the days that followed I seemed to gain more perspective. On myself and my life choices. On people all around me, striving to be *someone* and achieve *something*. And not only people of my ilk, who prize the idea of being self-made *whatevers*, all of us as human beings. We all make mistakes. We don't like to admit to them because we are pretty sure that we are right about most of our actions. Many of us confuse radical independence from God and everyone else as individualism, and when things don't go our way and we keep pushing we confuse stubbornness with strength.

Now God had entered my life, not merely to save me from defeat, but to show me that he is far bigger than anything I had encountered. To show me my life in the rear-view mirror, as it were. It was like looking back over the trail of my life, with some kind of wisdom and understanding I can promise you I'd never had before. I was both chagrined and set free at the same time by what I saw.

What had I wanted out of life? —success, power, recognition. At some point I had all of that, but it hadn't made me happy for very long. I'd experienced what can be called a "predatory joy" that is, I only experienced the joy that a predator feels during the hunting of its prey. The minute the prey is apprehended and consumed, a dissatisfaction sets in and the hunt must begin again. Why had I gotten caught in this ceaseless grind? The answer was: because I had been driven by pride, selfishness, hedonism, narcissism. No prize had been big enough. Little wonder my original drive — to do something good for others and myself—had turned into anxiety. Little wonder it had ground my soul to almost nothing.

Thanks to the Cohens and Miriam I had begun to learn about hope, faith, and forgiveness. When I was finally emptied of pride, they had found me and put me on the right road. It was only later that the unusual first words Mrs. Cohen had said to me in the stockbrokers officer fully registered:

"God has sent me to save you."

Valerie and I attended both synagogues and churches in the weeks that followed. Rabbis came to see us to explain why our understanding of the Bible was wrong. One rabbi was with us for four hours at our home. At the end of it all, I told him that I believed in Yeshua. I thanked him warmly for his insight, but I assured him that I knew I was right. The 132 prophecies in the Hebrew scriptures were already fulfilled in Jesus. He is the Messiah. He came for His people. He will come again. He will come back for everyone. That's what he said. I believed it.

I earnestly studied the Bible, excited by the way the *Old Testament* foreshadowed the *New Testament*, "just as if" it had been orchestrated. The Bible predicts where Jesus would be born, the manner of his death, the reason why God sent him, that he will return to this earth and judge the living and the dead, what will happen to those who believe that Jesus is the Son of God, and what will happen to those who do not.

While I had great respect for my Jewish heritage I now knew that I had the Spirit of God living within to guide me. This was not the same spirit which had driven me to search for success. Why? Because in my heart I was now asking God to forgive me for losing my integrity and be willing to manipulate people and situations for the sake of making money. Yes, if throwing every bit of energy and devotion into a pursuit can be construed as a form of worship, ambition and money had been my gods.

They were no longer.

And still there was work to be done. At some level I needed to know that this change was real. Would it actually make a difference, not just in what I believed but how I lived? After all the years of self-centeredness, I wanted someone else to direct the course of my life. And I wondered how such a thing would take place.

Chapter Twenty Nine

FINDING MY WAY...
GOD'S WAY

It is one thing to turn to God at a low and aimless time in your life. I had been seeking help to get out of a problem, and now my outer troubles had largely resolved, and given enough time, I would likely have landed in a good position in a business. The thing was, however, something had changed dramatically in me.

I could clearly see that a person sets the course of their life in the direction of what they value most. I had valued strength, making a name for myself, then making a fortune for myself. After surrendering myself to the will of God, I valued whatever it was the Lord wanted for me.

Which is why, as time went by, I went to seminary and studied for a Master of Divinity degree, with an eye toward pursuing a doctorate later. Studying the Bible and even receiving degrees in Divinity are not the same as allowing the Spirit of God to continue to lead and guide you, though. Lots of men and women pursue seminary degrees, who haven't really conquered ego. Having lived so long without God I knew

I needed to be careful not to let my own drives take over again or I would just wind up building my own little kingdom all over again, in a church or ministry.

More than anything I wanted to remain as close to God as possible, no matter what that took.

It was going to take more "surgery," so to speak, on my soul.

One day, as part of the admissions process when I enrolled at Talbot Theological Seminary in California, I was asked to work through a long questionnaire. I sat down to fill it out, sure I was an excellent candidate.

One of the questions was: "What is your relationship with your mother and your father."

I shocked myself by answering: "I love my mother and I hate my father."

Good candidate? Oh yes, I was sure I had a mind sharp enough to earn a degree. But I would be a spiritual fraud with a shingle on my wall if I did not address this critical issue. It could remain hidden in my heart and no one would know about the weak condition of my soul in this regard.

God knew the truth, though. And now, I felt, he was revealing it to me.

I still had not forgiven my father for the events that happened just as I was about to begin my legal career, when my father became very ill. Obviously it was not his fault that he became ill — but he had never once thanked me or even acknowledged that I had set my dream aside to help him. Yes, in old world families it's *expected* that family members will do what's necessary to help and support one another. But still…not one word of thanks. And never once in my whole life had he said, "I love you, son" or "I'm proud of you."

My hand gripped the pen, and my gut twisted in knots. The stabs of pain and anger were that strong. Like old dregs from the bottom of a cup, the application had stirred something that needed to be dealt with.

Embarrassed as I felt that such personal feelings had come to light I also felt grateful. It seemed that God had not just reached out to me once, to save me, he was staying close and continuing to push me to grow in spirit, which is what I'd asked.

Valerie had taught me about forgiveness. The difference between forgiveness and unforgiveness is one of the main issues in how we live our lives on earth and the qualifications we have when it is time to move on. Forgiveness is one of those traits which measures the kind of person that you are. It had taken me a long time, but now I understood why God says in the Bible, "If you forgive others, then I will forgive you for all that you have done wrong."

In the end I placed the soul of my father, along with my own soul, in God's hands. I transferred to God the sovereign right over everything that had ever happened to me in my life — all its circumstances that lay beyond my control. By placing both Dad and me into God's hands I was able to forgive my Dad, releasing both him and me from the past, and an even greater sense of freedom and peace filled me.

This experience taught me more about spiritual values and their importance. In this world, it's all about setting the balances right, struggling to get back what was taken from you. It had once been my job to doggedly pursue people for money and wring the last penny out of them. That had introduced me to men like Raymond Nash, whose values were, like mine at that time, how much money you can make. The only difference between us was that he had no conscience about making money from gambling, drugs…and God knew what else. I'd *thought* of myself as better than him; at least I wasn't doing questionable things. But the fact was we were both serving money. My little standard of difference was my own illusion, preventing me from seeing that we were much alike, grubbing after a buck.

I now knew that God valued a heart that was open to him and clean of destructive resentment, anger, and bitterness.

And he was far from finished with me.

A lot of time had now passed, and Justin graduated from The University of Southern California. In a while we began to visit businesses for sale, we talked about his future, he wasn't sure where to start so we looked at a variety of options.

I wanted so much to be the good father I felt I had not been to him during all my earlier years.

Since Justin wanted to own a small business, my business acumen began to kick in again. We ended up in Norco, California, looking at a feed store. After months of negotiations, tax returns, bargaining and studying the flow of customers, Justin decided that he would like to be a seller of hay, dog and cat feed, saddles, and so on. Valerie's parents advanced the money and we purchased the business for him.

Because the owners had been there for so many years and we were paying a chunk of money for goodwill, I insisted on a restrictive covenant — something quite usual, which simply meant that the sellers could not compete against the business they had sold us for a period of five years and a radius of five miles.

Only two weeks after we signed the deal, however, the former manager of the feed store opened her own feed store less than two hundred yards down the street. Clearly, the man who sold us the business, Bob Delorme, was behind her financially, because he was seen frequently going in and out of the feed store.

More than a little irritated I went over to talk to him, to appeal to him.

He looked at me and laughed. "I'm just here as a friend, I just drop in now and then."

In my spirit I knew this was completely untrue.

Meanwhile our customer base was rapidly evaporating and the sales had already dropped 30 percent in less than four weeks. My fear was it would go beyond that and we would lose everything we had put into it.

I went to see Delorme again. We had evidence that he was, in fact, working full-time in a competing business right under our noses. This time he shrugged his shoulders, looked me straight in the eyes and said, "If you want to sue me, *sue* me."

Justin and I discussed the dire situation. We were both very worried, and the old fighter in me was beginning to steam. I sent Justin over to chat with him, but as before, it brought no result.

I made an appointment with Myron James, a local attorney. He listened, then shrugged. "There's nothing else to do but to file a lawsuit against the man."

I felt angry and aggrieved, and was about to say, "Let's do it." But a strong inner nudge, like an elbow in the soul, got my attention. Suing the man, though it had to be done, was not the *only* thing we could do.

I decided we should pray. It wasn't easy. I didn't exactly feel comfortable praying with someone in a business setting, but if I valued being a good father to Justin, as I claimed, then I would have to lead the way spiritually and model faith for him. Not just mouth it, but show it in action.

Again and again the old, aggressive nature kept showing up. Especially when, after the first day of a three-day hearing, Myron shocked us by saying, "The judge has confided in me that he will look at all the evidence, but that he is going to rule in favor of the defendants."

I was greatly disturbed. "How can he do that, when we have a contract proving he signed a restrictive covenant? *And* we have proof he is working full time with his former manager in the business. And we have figures that show our sales have now dropped by 50 percent. We are about to lose the money we put into this business."

Myron James was a good man, I had no doubt of that. But he could only shake his head. "Right or wrong, the judge is going to rule for the other side. They are local people, and the judge has known them for many years, and you guys are outsiders."

This wasn't law, this was small-town madness… much like the big city and big government madness that had been perpetrated upon me years before. It was so tempting to lose my spiritual stance, to stop trusting in God and want to fire back with everything in me.

That evening I drove the 55 miles back home to Valerie, feeling angry, helpless… and finally reaching out for help.

There is nothing we can do here, Lord, I prayed. *We are powerless. If you don't defend us we will lose everything.*

No, not everything, came the reminder.

In God, and in terms of my family, I had much. I could not lose my focus again, and trust in riches and worldly strengths.

I am so sorry, Lord. I nearly forgot. Thank you for your kindness and patience with me.

And so, however shaky my faith felt at the moment — and even though I wanted the best outcome for us business-wise I *would* be the best example I could be for my son and continue to trust in the Lord and not in power or wealth.

After the second day of the hearing, an unusual thing happened. I was not there, but Justin reported back to me.

A man came into the store toward the end of the afternoon. He chatted with Justin and then asked if he could go into the office and pray. The man had a Bible in hand and, as highly unusual as that request was, Justin agreed.

After about 10 minutes he looked into the office: The man was kneeling on the floor and he was praying. Justin didn't disturb him.

Eventually, the man finished praying and, without saying a word, he left.

The following morning was the last day of the trial. Justin opened the feed store as usual just before 8 a.m., and immediately received a phone call from a woman named Mary, the bookkeeper for the competing feed business. "Please," she said, "I have to see you before court opens at 10 a.m."

Justin called me excitedly. "Dad, there's something going on. You have to get over here right away."

When the three of us sat down in the office together the woman poured out a confession. At the request of the former owners, she admitted, she had falsified the tax returns at the time of the sale to us. This was done, of course, to boost the purchase price way up. The truth was, the feed store we had purchased was barely making any money at all.

"I know I committed perjury by giving evidence for the other side. But I don't care what happens to me. You're good, honest people, and last night I could not sleep. I cannot live the rest of my life knowing that I helped to cheat you."

With a quick phone call, I passed all the information onto our attorney, and we agreed to keep this woman in a room in the courthouse where she would not be seen until he sent for her to give evidence again.

I will always remember when the former owners turned around to see who was coming into the court — only to see me walking down the aisle with their own bookkeeper, their heads dropped.

The woman's evidence was clear. She was not cross-examined by the defendant's attorney. When the very unhappy judge dropped his gavel it was to rule in our favor. The defendants were ordered to pay us back all the money we had given him.

Unfortunately for the sellers, they had spent much of the money on their new feed store. Therefore, the judge ordered it to be closed down immediately.

In the end, we acquired the buildings from them at a good price, partly in exchange for the money they owed us.

But that was just the outward outcome.

What we had witnessed was the importance of not relying on our own strength alone and the value of relying on the Lord. Why had the man shown up out of the blue to pray in Justin's office? Why had I been reminded that more than a building and business was at stake here? Obviously, the Lord had wanted us to keep our eyes on him and our priorities and values clear.

I had learned a great lesson in faith: that when I kept my values straight, trusting God no matter what the outcome, *I was a different person*. And that is what God wants most of all – evidence in human form that he is real and that his peace within us is the victory over any outward circumstance.

Years later, after Justin worked very hard to build the business, we sold the buildings and the feed store together with the business at a handsome profit. Justin decided to move to Virginia and marry the love of his life, a lovely young woman named Michelle.

And later, still, when my son and I discussed what happened, he said, "The man who came to the feed store — no one ever saw him before or after that. He was either an angel or a godly man. Whichever it was, his prayers obviously helped us to win."

For me, there were more lessons to come — even tougher ones.

To say I didn't get along very well with my father-in-law, Simon Morris, is an understatement. He didn't believe in anything. He read pornographic books. He would hear us speaking about our faith and butt in to say, "When we die, we go to dust."

Every time he said that I gritted my teeth. I felt he was doing it to challenge me, and I still didn't like to be challenged. Nonetheless, Valerie and I spoke to him and her mother frequently and gently about the need for God.

"Simon, listen to my radio program, which is on every day at the same time," I said, "I talk about the Bible and who wrote the Bible. I discuss what it means to us today."

"Joseph," he'd say dismissively. "It's all nonsense. These people who wrote the Bible, none of them knew what they were talking about. It was all hearsay and I don't believe any of it is true."

Betty, Valerie's mother, was disillusioned anyway. Simon had never loved her that much and their life together had been very difficult.

In a way I felt as though I was up against possibly the greatest challenge of my life. It was one thing to fight for something in business, and to trust God to win those battles. I was only just learning how to do that. Now there was something greater at stake, and more difficult to win:

Someone's soul.

How would God work this out, given the fact that these two people were so entirely closed to any thought of him?

In time, Simon and Betty came to live nearby us in Los Angeles.

Very shortly thereafter, Simon had several strokes, and he ended up in a hospital in Woodland Hills, California. He and I hardly ever spoke. We had nothing in common except that I was married to his daughter. We just visited them once in a while, as children do. At a certain level I saw Valerie's parents as case-hardened — a more or less "lost cause" where faith was concerned.

It was up to God to crack those two completely disinterested hearts, I thought. I had no interest in verbally jousting with them. Or for that matter, hearing my faith attacked and ridiculed.

One day I was in my office, however, I had the strongest feeling that I needed to go and see Simon. I didn't hear an audible voice, I didn't see a vision, I just got up from my desk, told my receptionist that I needed to leave, and left.

I drove toward the hospital, and suddenly found myself in tears. The thing was, I didn't know *why*. People were driving past and could see me, and I felt ridiculous. In my spirit I knew there had to be some special reason for this unusual behavior on my part, but I still felt foolish.

When I reached Simon's bedside, he was unable to speak to me, but I knew that I needed to speak to him.

Leaning down close to his ear I said, "Simon, would you like to receive Jesus Christ as your Messiah?"

He looked at me, and it was the only time I could ever remember that he had a kind look in his eyes. He blinked. That was our code for "Yes."

I said, "If you are *sure* about this, Simon, please squeeze my hand."

He did.

Bowing my head, I prayed with him. I asked God to forgive him for his sins and to show him the way, the truth, and the life. On the way back to my office I felt somewhat amazed at the divine appointment I'd been prompted to keep.

Less than four hours later, Simon died.

When I saw Valerie that evening at home, I told her what had happened at the hospital earlier in the day.

She put her arms around my neck and kissed me on both cheeks. "Joseph, I love you. My Daddy is safe with God now."

After a few months went by, we sold Betty's house for her. She moved into a small assisted living facility in Santa Monica. One day, *apropos* of nothing, Betty said to me in a sharp voice, "Give me a Bible."

I gladly took a Bible to her on my next visit.

A few months later, we were visiting her and she looked me straight in the eyes and said, "Joseph, I've read the Bible from beginning to end. It's clear to me that Jesus is the Messiah."

I blinked at her. This is the woman who, years earlier, had told Valerie and Justin to leave me because I had joined a "cult" called "Jews for Jesus."

A few weeks later, one of Betty's friends prayed her into the kingdom of God.

I think I got it that time — perhaps the most important learning experience of all:

What does God value? Every single one of us. Who does God give up on? Absolutely no one.

I had been ready to back away from these two hard cases; he had not.

As time continued to pass, I was more and more profoundly grateful that God had worked in an old heart like mine— one that once had no interest in things of the spirit at all.

By now I was the senior pastor of a small church in Los Angeles. One day my Mum, after hearing the sermon and the call to salvation, stood up and began to walk forward. My dad immediately jumped up and pulled her back.

A few months later the same thing happened. This time dad sat still and Mum received the Lord.

Later that year, my dad walked forward and received Jesus… *Yeshua*… as his Messiah.

My heart nearly burst … this time with unutterable joy and happiness.

Jesus said, "Do not store up for yourselves treasures on earth, where moth and rust destroy and thieves break in and steal.

Easy for me to say, someone might respond, given the fact that I'd lost my earthly wealth. Not so. I could have spent the rest of my life grieving my losses, struggling to make my way back to "the top" again. But in fact, when you see through the veil of material wealth and possessions and position, and finally recognize how much more valuable are people and things spiritual, there is no going back. *Things* lose their taste, when you realize how unsatisfying they really are in the ultimate sense. You know that no amount of money or things or power are ever enough.

Today, as an old Gospel song goes, I can tell you "I'd rather have Jesus than silver or gold…." Yes, of course, I and my family have earthly needs and there are still bills to pay. But I have no words to explain what it meant for my father, my mother and me to experience the incredible peace of mind that comes in knowing the Messiah, Jesus Christ. And no way to tell you about the wealth of contentment I know, now that they have gone on to heaven.

My wish for you is that, whatever you are holding onto as your earthly treasure, you will place it in the hands of God and let him do with it whatever he will, to bring you close to himself. May he bring you to Jesus, his son, so that you, too, will experience the richness of knowing him.

May it be so.

EPILOGUE

Valerie was a person who, like my grandpa never lived apart from God, even though for years of her life she was gravely ill with cancer. There was chemotherapy, radiation and surgery. She took pain for granted, but there was never a solution. Valerie fought many battles to maintain a normal existence. The doctors had given her a few months to live, because the cancer had metastasized. One day she had to stop fighting.

That was the day I had been dreading. I was in the office, and the housekeeper called me, distraught. I rushed home and ran up the stairs. Valerie's eyes flickered. I kissed her. She held on until I got home and then she drew her last breath. She had waited for me.

On January 11, 1993, Valerie – my beloved – went to be with the Lord she had spoken to so many times. The minister prayed. The earth was shoveled on. The children were there. We cried and cried and then I was alone.

My heart was broken and it took me a long time to come to terms with what had happened. It was very hard to go into an empty room night after night. Familiar things stared at me everywhere in the house but they couldn't speak to me because they were things, not Valerie. I wrestled with my feelings. I was bewildered and I was lonely. I went to places, many people invited me, but the worst kind of loneliness is feeling lonely with people all around you.

Valerie loved me with a love that made me secure by day and by night throughout my career. Even if I had been an unknown barrister or a rag merchant, she would have been the same. I'd become famous, and then infamous, and through all of it she had loved me.

After Valerie was gone, everything changed. Once again I wanted to lay down and quit – but my soul refused to die. Somewhere in the wreckage an ember flickered, almost went out, and gradually came back.

Years have passed… God has let me live, and I am still looking to the future.

My son, Justin and his wife Michelle, have four beautiful daughters. My daughter, Julia, is married to Allen, and it means so much to me that my children are building careers and living happily.

As for me personally you never know when God is going to do something special in your life.

A few months after Valerie died, the phone rang at home. "Joseph do you remember me? It's Elaine Lane. I was a friend of Valerie's, and you baptized me in your swimming pool a long time ago. I just heard that Valerie is with the Lord. I am so sorry for your loss. She was a wonderful friend."

I listened quietly to her English voice. Elaine had visited Los Angeles every summer with her children, where she had been introduced to Valerie who became her mentor. Two Jewish girls, who learned from the Bible that Jesus is the Messiah.

"Thank you for calling, Elaine. I feel like I am walking around in circles. Without Valerie I don't have any direction."

"I understand how you feel," Elaine replied. "My life has also reached a point where I don't know what to do next."

Elaine's husband had left her and she had just finalized her divorce.

I began to call Elaine again and again. And one day I said to her, "I would like to meet you."

A couple of months later, she arrived in Los Angeles and stayed in a nearby hotel. I saw her every day for a week....

.... And we fell in love!

I proposed to Elaine like a traditional Englishman and we planned to get married. It was hard for both of us to say goodbye at the airport, something special had happened to us and we needed each other.

On October 31, 1993, we were married in the garden of a hotel near where I was living. There was a canopy covered with flowers. A small lake, called Swan Lake, ran alongside and the swans were floating by and gave the area a feeling of grace and peace. The guests were waiting expectantly and the children were gathered under the canopy.

As the music started Jamie, Elaine's son, walked her down the aisle. The hotel balconies were full of on-lookers. Justin stood by my side and our daughters, Chantal and Julia, completed the wedding group, together with Chelsea my granddaughter, then age 4, the adorable flower girl.

A new life and a new hope had begun for both of us.

Today, so much of my help and strength comes from Elaine. She is the most, loving person. She has endured her own adversity like so many others and she has shed more tears than there are blades of grass in the fields. Many times in her life she wondered, "Where is God?" But that is her own story of turning to trust in God.

Without Elaine, this book would not have been written. She is an inspiration to me and to many of those who meet her. I have been blessed with two wonderful women in one lifetime. I don't feel I deserve it.

A few weeks after Elaine and I were married, I was rummaging through a small antique desk in the garage when I came across a letter in a sealed envelope addressed to me. It was in Valerie's handwriting.

I ran into the house and called out to Elaine. As I read the letter out loud, the tears fell down my cheeks and Elaine gripped my hand and we cried together – the letter had been written by Valerie, just a short time before her death.

My Darling Gerald Joseph,

Being married to you has been the most wonderful thing in my life, through all the good times and the bad times.

It is my prayer and desire that you marry again as fast as possible. I pray God will give you a woman to be your mate. You will not have to look, the women will descend on you and you will have plenty of choices. Pray hard for the right one. Keep close to God at all times and never let your faith waiver.

I would like my mother's jewelry to go to Julia.... Feel free to do anything with any of our worldly goods. I leave complete discretion as to the children and grandchildren to you. I would like them all the have a keepsake....

Love never dies,

Valerie

EPILOGUE CONTINUED
LAST CALL

There is only one authority in this world and that is God. God's love is constant, our love varies as we confront adversity or experience problems in our life which cause our level of tolerance to drop as well as our level of faith.

God has given us freewill, but we have to surrender it back to Him. Does this mean giving up our right to make decisions? Absolutely not. It means we do well to trust God with our hope and our future.

There's the world as it is, and the world as we'd like it to be. It can be very depressing to wake up in the morning and hear about terrorism, drug addiction, persecution, murder, etc. We have seen the displacement of millions of people in countries with social and economic consequences far beyond our imagination. No one can stop it. And everywhere you look in the world, there is fear.

We have no power whatsoever unless we reach for God, His blessings, promises, and forgiveness.

Then we can understand what Jesus meant when he said: "In the world you will have trouble, but be of good cheer, I have overcome the world". (John chapter 16 verse 33).

Further, God Himself buried Moses. (Deuteronomy chapter 4 verses 6,7).The reason I mention this extraordinary event is to demonstrate how involved God chooses to be in the lives of His people.

I didn't trust God, I trusted myself. I didn't pray. I turned to valium and brandy. I wasn't listening to God, I didn't know Him I was too busy and hadn't made the effort.

We need something much stronger than ourselves to hold onto or we will drown in our anger and sorrow and unleash the bitterness and fear that will follow. When we do this, we hurt ourselves and those who are close to us.

I went on to the path to find God and Jesus. I searched for the depth and meaning of existence on this earth where human and divine come together. Like anything worthwhile it takes time and effort. I tell you no matter who you are this is the only road to travel, and the only road to find peace in this world and the next.

The arrival of Jesus the Messiah was foretold over a 100 times in the Old Testament— when He would be born, and where. How He would live and then be crucified, raised from the dead, and why.

It is the Holy Spirit of God who leads us to understand that Jesus is the bread of life, who explains the truth about God. He was here among us. He came down from heaven, not to do His own will, but the will of God who sent Him. He will return to judge everyone, those who believe in God, and those who do not.

If we turn to God in Jesus' name it is life changing. He will guide us and protect us. Our sins are forgiven and forgotten. Redemption will come upon us now in this world and when we reach the finish line we will know that our names are written in the book of life. We will meet up with Him when He returns to this earth. We will give thanks and pay homage to God the Father of all. And we shall see His face.

ACKNOWLEDGEMENTS

I would like to acknowledge and thank the following professional individuals and friends for their support, without which this publication would not have been possible.

The whole team at Morgan James Publishing, and Aubrey Kosa for her communication, valuable advice, and encouragement.

My wife Elaine, whose faith, wisdom, and love never faltered.

David Hazzard, Senior editor, whose experience and patience over a period of two years showed me how to develop the story.

Gary and Kim Terashita, my prayerful, true friends who corrected the grammar.

Leslie Stobbe, Literary agent wise and worldly.

Annie Bremer for her technical support.

Nettie Fischer for organizational skills and friendship.

Cole Fraser for technical support.

Peter Fraser, a pillar of strength.

Wendy Giancoli for her love and friendship.

Traci Klass for technical support.

Joyce Moran for love and friendship.

Victoria Phillips for her tireless friendship.

Donna Steele for technical support.

Liza Tarling in London for faith in the dark seasons.

Tom Noon, a wise friend in all seasons.

Autumn Watson who took me to the finish line.

ABOUT THE AUTHOR

Joseph began his career as a Barrister at Law at the Old Bailey criminal law courts in London England. He is a member of the Honorable Society of Lincoln's Inn.

Due to his father's illness, he became a rag merchant in his father's business on the East side of London in a railway arch. The area was known for drugs and deprivation.

Later he formed a Christmas Club collecting small amounts of money door to door. This developed into a finance company. Ten years later Joseph formed a bank which grew to 22 branches and 80 companies. The group was listed on the London stock exchange and Joseph became very successful and wealthy.

He was awarded the Freedom of the city of London for work in the business community, and is a member of the Guild of Freemen of the city. He was appointed Hon. Citizen of Houston, Texas (Mayor Louis Welch).

When the recession took place in the 70s, the economy collapsed. He lost everything and eventually emigrated to France with his wife and two children, and then to the United States.

Joseph survived open heart surgery in the Cedars Sinai medical Center in 1978 with 6 by-passes.

Joseph and Valerie turned their lives over to God and received Jesus Christ as their Messiah. He was ordained at the Church of the Open Door in downtown Los Angeles.

Valerie, who suffered for much of her life from cancer, died on January 11th. 1993.

A year later, Joseph married Elaine and for 15 years they had an interior design company in Virginia. Today Joseph is a Taekwondo Master and has 4 black belts. In The Money Man he shares his experiences, the people he met, and the lessons he learned.

Morgan James
Speakers Group

➤ www.TheMorganJamesSpeakersGroup.com

We connect Morgan James published
authors with live and online events
and audiences who will benefit
from their expertise.

Printed in the USA
CPSIA information can be obtained
at www.ICGtesting.com
JSHW082229140824
68134JS00017B/798

9 781683 507673